AF540603

ENVIRONMENTAL HEALTH AND PROBLEMS

ENVIRONMENTAL HEALTH AND PROBLEMS

Edited by

Dr. Pawan Kumar 'Bharti'

M.Sc., Ph.D., FASEA

Centre for Agro-Rural Technologies,

RIIT Campus, Barwala, Panchkula, (Haryana)

&

Dr. Khwairakpam Gajananda

M.Sc., M.Tech., Ph.D.

Associate Professor

Deptt. of Environmental Science

Faculty of Science, Addis Ababa University

Addis Ababa, Ethiopia

DISCOVERY PUBLISHING HOUSE PVT. LTD.

NEW DELHI-110 002

Published by:
Tilak Wasan

DISCOVERY PUBLISHING HOUSE PVT. LTD.
4383/4B, Ansari Road, Darya Ganj
New Delhi-110 002 (India)
Phone : +91-11-23279245, 43596064-65
Fax : +91-11-23253475
E-mail : parul.wasan@gmail.com
discoverypublishinghouse@gmail.com
web : www.discoverypublishinggroup.com

***First Edition:* 2013**

ISBN: 978-93-5056-263-5

Environmental Health and Problems

Printed at:
Aditi Fine Art Press
Delhi

Preface

Pollution is the introduction of contaminants into a natural environment that causes instability, disorder, harm or discomfort to the ecosystem i.e. physical systems or living organisms. Pollution can take the form of chemical substances or energy, such as noise, heat or light. Pollutants, the elements of pollution, can be either foreign substances/energies or naturally occurring contaminants. Pollution is often classed as point source or non point source pollution.

Pollution is the beginning of a waste into the atmosphere making it impossible to make life on earth possible to sustain. Pollution harms the Earth's environment and its people in many ways.

Pollution effects are indeed many and wide-ranging. There is no doubt that excessive levels of pollution are causing a lot of damage to human & animal health, tropical rainforests, as well as the wider environment. All types of pollution – air, water and soil pollution – have an impact on the living environment. The effects in living organisms may range from mild discomfort to serious diseases such as cancer to physical deformities; ex., extra or missing limbs in frogs. Experts admit that pollution effects are quite often underestimated and that more research is needed to understand the connections between pollution and its effects on all life forms.

Air pollution can affect our health in many ways with both short-term and long-term effects. Different groups of individuals are affected by air pollution in different ways. Some individuals are much more sensitive to pollutants than are others. Young children and elderly people often suffer more from the effects of air pollution. People with health problems such as asthma, heart and lung disease may also suffer more when the air is polluted. The extent to which an individual is harmed by air pollution usually depends on the total exposure to the damaging chemicals, i.e., the duration of exposure and the concentration of the chemicals must be taken into account.

Air pollution is a major environmental health problem affecting the developing and the developed countries alike. The effects of air pollution on health are very complex as there are many different sources and their individual effects vary from one to the other. It is not only the ambient air quality in the cities but also the indoor air quality in the rural and the urban areas that are causing concern. In fact in the developing world the highest air pollution exposures occur in the indoor environment. Air pollutants that are inhaled have serious impact on human health affecting the lungs and the respiratory system; they are also taken up by the blood and pumped all round the body. These pollutants are also deposited on soil, plants, and in the water, further contributing to human exposure.

Water-borne diseases are infectious diseases spread primarily through contaminated water. Though these diseases are spread either directly or through flies or filth, water is the chief medium for spread of these diseases and hence they are termed as water-borne diseases.

Exposure to polluted water can cause diarrhoea, skin irritation, respiratory problems, and other diseases, depending on the pollutant that is in the water body. Stagnant water and other untreated water provide a habitat for the mosquito and a host of other parasites and insects that cause a large number of diseases especially in the tropical regions. Among these, malaria is undoubtedly the most widely distributed and causes most damage to human health.

Tonnes and tonnes of domestic wastes are dumped every day. Since people do not follow proper methods for the disposal of such wastes, it leaves the places look dirty and makes them unhealthy. Land pollution indirectly affects the respiratory system of human beings. Breathing in polluted dust or particle can result in a number of health problems related to the respiratory system. Skin problems are often diagnosed due to land pollution.

This book provides comprehensive coverage of the fundamental principles and current practices and trends in the field of Environmental health, pollution and problems. This book updates the subject matter, illustrations and problems to incorporate new concepts and issues related to Environmental health and various problems.

Particularly thanks are due to all contributors from China, Ethiopia and various parts of India; and publisher also for their contribution and assistance.

I hope this book will be of benefit to both present and future colleagues, who teach, study and working in the field of environmental health, ecology, environmental pollution, safety and various environmental issues and problems.

Dr. Pawan Kumar 'Bharti'

Contents

List of Contributors

Archana Tyagi, Department of Geography, Kurukshetra University Kurukshetra (HR)-136119, India

Avadhesh Kumar Koshal*, Research Associate (GIS), NICRA Project, P.D.F.S.R., Modipuram, Meerut, (UP)-250110, India

D.K. Singh, Lanco House, Plot 270, Udyog Vihar, Phase II, Gurgaon – 122016, (New Delhi Region), India

G.C. Kisku*, Environmental Monitoring Section, Indian Institute of Toxicology Research, (Council of Scientific and Industrial Research), Lucknow-226 001, U.P., India

Khwairakpam Gajananda, Department of Environmental Science, Faculty of Science, Addis Ababa University, Addis Ababa, Ethiopia

Kumar Satish Chandra*, Lanco House, Plot 270, Udyog Vihar, Phase II, Gurgaon – 122016, (New Delhi Region), India

Li Peiyue*, School of Environmental Science and Engineering, Chang'an University, No. 126 Yanta Road, Xi'an, 710054, China

Meenu Srivastava*, Department of Textiles and Apparel Designing, College of Home Science, MPUAT, Udaipur-313001 (Rajasthan)-India

Pawan Kumar Bharti, 1. 30th Indian Antarctica expedition member, Bharti Island, Larsemann Hills, East Antarctica, 2. Centre for Agro-Rural Technologies (CART), Panchkula, India, 3. Shriram Institute for Industrial Research, Delhi, India

Pawan Kumar*, Department of Zoology and Environmental Science, Gurukula Kangri University, Haridwar (Uttarakhand)-249404, India

Pragnesh N Dave*, Department of Chemistry, Kachchh University, Mundra Road, Bhuj, Kachchh- 370001 (Gujarat), India

Pankaj Tyagi*, Department of Biotechnology, M.I.E.T. Meerut (U.P.)-250005, India

Qian Hui, School of Environmental Science and Engineering, Chang'an University, No. 126 Yanta Road, Xi'an, 710054, China

Rais Ahmad*, Environmental Research Laboratory, Department of Applied Chemistry, Aligarh Muslim University, Aligarh 202002, UP, India

Saroj Palawat, Department of Textiles and Apparel Designing, College of Home Science, MPUAT, Udaipur-313001 (Rajasthan), India

S.P. Kaushik, Department of Geography, Kurukshetra University Kurukshetra (HR)-136119, India

Shreerup Goswami*, P.G. Department of Geology, Ravenshaw University, Cuttack-753003, Orissa, India

Swati Pattanayak, Rural Development Center, Indian Institute of Technology Khargpur, Kharagpur-721302, West Bengal, India

Uma Maheshwar K., Lanco House, Plot 270, Udyog Vihar, Phase II, Gurgaon – 122016, (New Delhi Region), India

Vijender Singh, Haryana Test House, 50C, Sec-25, Part-II, HUDA, Panipat (HR)-132104, India

1

Environmental Pollution and Human Health

—*Pragnesh N. Dave, India*

ABSTRACT

Environmental pollution is a wide-reaching problem and it is likely to influence the health of human populations is great. This chapter provides the insight view about the effects of environment pollution in the perspective of air pollution, water and land/ soil waste pollution on human by diseases.

Key words: *Pollution; Human health, Air pollution; Land pollution and Soil pollution*

Introduction

The biological and physical environment of the planet is changing at an unprecedented rate as a result of human activity, and these changes may have an enormous impact on human health. One of the goals of human development is to protect health in the face of rapid environmental change, but we often fail to do this.

Pollution is the introduction of contaminants into a natural environment that causes instability, disorder, harm or discomfort to the ecosystem i.e. physical systems or living organisms [1]. Pollution can take the form of chemical substances or energy, such as noise, heat or light. Pollutants, the elements of pollution, can be either foreign substances/energies or naturally occurring contaminants. Pollution is often classed as point source or non point source pollution. The Blacksmith Institute issues an annual list of the world's worst polluted places. In the 2007 issues the ten top nominees are located in Azerbaijan, China, India, Peru, Russia, Ukraine and Zambia.

Over the last three decades there has been increasing global concern over the public health impacts attributed to environmental pollution, in particular, the global burden of disease. The World Health Organization (WHO) estimates that about a quarter of the diseases facing mankind today occur due to prolonged exposure to environmental pollution. Most of these environment-related diseases are however not easily detected and may be acquired during childhood and manifested later in adulthood [1, 2]. Improper management of solid waste is one of the main causes of environmental pollution and degradation in many cities, especially in developing countries. Many of these cities lack solid waste regulations and proper disposal facilities, including for harmful waste. Such waste may be infectious, toxic or radioactive. Municipal waste dumping sites are designated places set aside for waste disposal. Depending on a city's level of waste management, such waste may be dumped in an uncontrolled manner, segregated for recycling purposes, or simply burnt. Poor waste management poses a great challenge to the well-being of city residents, particularly those living adjacent the dumpsites due to the potential of the waste to pollute water, food sources, land, air and vegetation. The poor disposal and handling of waste thus leads to environmental degradation, destruction of the ecosystem and poses great risks to public health.

To emphasize the link between environmental pollution and public health in an urban setting, United Nations Environment Programme (UNEP) commissioned a pilot study of the Dandora municipal waste dumping site in Nairobi, Kenya. Environmental samples (soil and water) were analyzed to determine the content and concentrations of various pollutants (heavy metals, polychlorinated biphenyls and pesticides) that are known to affect human health. Soil samples from the dumpsite were compared to samples taken from another site - Waithaka, which is a peri-urban residential area on the outskirts of Nairobi.

A medical camp was set up at the St. John Informal School that is located next to the dumpsite. A total of 328 children and adolescents living and schooling adjacent the dumpsite were examined and treated for various ailments. Of these, 40 were referred for further laboratory tests that entailed blood and urine sampling to assess the impact of exposure to environmental pollutants from the dumpsite on human health.

Effect of Pollution on Human Health

Pollution is the beginning of a waste into the atmosphere making it impossible to make life on earth possible to sustain. Pollution harms the Earth's environment and its people in many ways.

Pollution effects are indeed many and wide-ranging. There is no doubt that excessive levels of pollution are causing a lot of damage to human & animal health, tropical rainforests, as well as the wider environment.

All types of pollution – air, water and soil pollution – have an impact on the living environment. The effects in living organisms may range from mild discomfort to serious diseases such as cancer to physical deformities; ex., extra or missing limbs in frogs. Experts admit that pollution effects are quite often underestimated and that more research is needed to understand the connections between pollution and its effects on all life forms.

Land pollution is pollution of the Earth's natural land surface by industrial, commercial, domestic and agricultural activities. Some of the main contributions to land pollution are deforestation, construction debris, industrial factories etc. Air pollution is the accumulation of harmful substances into the atmosphere that danger human life and other living matter on the earth. The number one way to prevent air pollution is to walk or bike more and drive less. This will prevent fossil fuels from further polluting the air. Water pollution is the introduction of chemical, biological and physical matter into large bodies of water that corrupt the quality of life that lives in it and consumes it. Oil spills, household chemicals, pesticides and fertilizers are the major sources of water pollution. The best way to prevent water pollution is to not throw trash and other harmful chemicals into our water supplies because it causes harm to the rivers and lakes.

Land Pollution

Land pollution is characterized by the contamination of Earth's surface, where humans and other creatures live. One of the major causes of land pollution is human activities. The Industrial Revolution set a series of events into motion which destroyed natural habitats and polluted the environment, causing diseases in both humans and other species of animals.

Causes of Land Pollution

Increase in urbanization is one of the major causes of land pollution. Construction uses up forestland. This leads to the exploitation and destruction of forests. There is more demand for water. Reservoirs are built resulting in the loss of land. The disposal of non-biodegradable wastes, including containers, bottles and cans made of plastic, used cars and electronic goods, leads to the pollution of land. Agricultural wastes including the waste matters produced by crop, animal manure and residues of the farm land are one of the major causes of land pollution. The pesticides and fertilizers used by farmers to increase the crop yield, leach into the nearby land areas and pollutes them [1, 4].

The process of mining leads to the formation of piles of coal and slag. When these wastes are not disposed through proper channel, they are accumulated and contaminate the land. Industrial wastes are major contributors of land pollution. Dumping of toxic materials such as chemicals and paints makes the areas surrounding the industries, look very filthy. Improper treatment of sewage leads to the accumulation of solids, such as biomass sludge. These solid wastes overflow through the sewage, making the entire area look dirty. Burning of solid fuels leads to the formation of ashes, which is yet another cause of land pollution. Although domestic and industrial wastes are collected and recycled or burnt in incinerators, a large amount of rubbish is left untreated [4-6]. These are then dumped into grounds, leading to land pollution. Garbage dumped by people makes the streets unhealthy, unfit and dirty to reside in. The waste matter usually consists of leftover food, fruit and vegetable peels and other non decomposable solid materials such as glass, cloth, plastic, wood, paper etc.

Harmful Effects of Land Pollution

Land pollution impacts human health predominantly by contaminating drinking water supplies, such as reservoirs, groundwater and wells. Contaminants include metals like aluminum, lead and cadmium, as well as pesticides and microorganisms. Effects on human health will vary depending on the contaminant and its concentration in the water. For example, low concentrations of nitrate, a chemical used in fertilizer, can cause shortness of breath. On the other hand, aluminum can cause severe damage to the central nervous system. Nearly all toxins are naturally occurring in the environment. However, human activities have polluted and disrupted the soil, thereby increasing the transport of pollutants to drinking water sources [6]. In 2009, over 5,000 water supplies reported contaminants above the regulated amount for various chemicals; over 19 million people were served by these water systems, according to the U. S. Environmental Protection Agency.

Tonnes and tonnes of domestic wastes are dumped every day. Since people do not follow proper methods for the disposal of such wastes, it leaves the places look dirty and makes them unhealthy. Land pollution indirectly affects the respiratory system of human beings. Breathing in polluted dust or particle can result in a number of health problems related to the respiratory system. Skin problems are often diagnosed due to land pollution. It is said that the improper disposal of household wastes leads to allergic reactions on the skin. Land pollution has been found as one of the leading causes for birth defects. Pregnant women living in unhealthy and dirty environment can incur breathing problems and a number of diseases, which may affect the health of the baby as well.Land pollution has serious effect on wildlife. Flora, which provides food and shelter to wildlife, are destroyed. Land pollution often disrupts the balance of Nature, causing human fatalities [6-8].

The major concern is that there are many sensitive land uses where people are in direct contact with soils such as residences, parks, schools and playgrounds. Other contact mechanisms include contamination of drinking water or inhalation of soil contaminants which have vaporized. There is a very large set of health consequences from exposure to soil contamination depending on pollutant type, pathway of attack and vulnerability of the exposed population. Chromium and obsolete pesticide formulations are carcinogenic to populations. Lead is especially hazardous to young children, in which group there is a high risk of developmental damage to the brain, while to all populations kidney damage is a risk. Chronic exposure to at sufficient concentrations is known to be associated with higher incidence of leukemia. Obsolete pesticides such as mercury and cyclodienes are known to induce higher incidences of kidney damage, some irreversible; cyclodienes are linked to liver toxicity. Organophosphates and carbamates can induce a chain of responses leading to neuromuscular blockage. Many chlorinated solvents induce liver changes, kidney changes and depression of the central nervous system. There is an entire spectrum of further health effects such as headache, nausea, fatigue (physical), eye irritation and skin rash for the above cited and other chemicals [7, 9, 10] .

Water Pollution

It is a well-known fact that clean water is absolutely essential for healthy living. Adequate supply of fresh and clean drinking water is a basic need for all human beings on the earth, yet it has been observed that millions of people worldwide are deprived of this.

Freshwater resources all over the world are threatened not only by over exploitation and poor management but also by ecological degradation. The main source of freshwater pollution can be attributed to discharge of untreated waste, dumping of industrial effluent, and run-off from agricultural fields. Industrial growth, urbanization and the increasing use of synthetic organic substances have serious and adverse impacts on freshwater bodies. It is a generally accepted fact that the developed countries suffer from problems of chemical discharge into the water sources mainly groundwater, while developing countries face problems of agricultural run-off in water sources. Polluted water like chemicals in drinking water causes problem to health and leads to water-borne diseases which can be prevented by taking measures can be taken even at the household level [11].

Groundwater and its Contamination

Many areas of groundwater and surface water are now contaminated with heavy metals, POPs (persistent organic pollutants), and nutrients that have an adverse affect on health. Water-borne diseases and water-caused health problems are mostly due to inadequate and incompetent management of water resources. Safe water for all can only be assured when access, sustainability, and equity can be guaranteed. Access can be defined as the number of people who are guaranteed safe drinking water and sufficient quantities of it. There has to be an effort to sustain it, and there has to be a fair and equal distribution of water to all segments of the society. Urban areas generally have a higher coverage of safe water than the rural areas. Even within an area there is variation: areas that can pay for the services have access to safe water whereas areas that cannot pay for the services have to make do with water from hand pumps and other sources [12].

In the urban areas water gets contaminated in many different ways, some of the most common reasons being leaky water pipe joints in areas where the water pipe and sewage line pass close together. Sometimes the water gets polluted at source due to various reasons and mainly due to inflow of sewage into the source.

Cause of Water Pollution

Ground water can be contaminated through various sources and some of these are mentioned below [13].

Pesticides: Run-off from farms, backyards, and golf courses contain pesticides such as DDT that in turn contaminate the water. Leechate from landfill sites is another major contaminating source. Its effects on the ecosystems and health are endocrine and reproductive damage in wildlife. Groundwater is susceptible to contamination, as pesticides are mobile in the soil. It is a matter of concern as these chemicals are persistent in the soil and water.

Sewage: Untreated or inadequately treated municipal sewage is a major source of groundwater and surface water pollution in the developing countries. The organic material that is discharged with municipal waste into the watercourses uses substantial oxygen for biological degradation thereby upsetting the ecological balance of rivers and lakes. Sewage also carries microbial pathogens that are the cause of the spread of disease.

Nutrients: Domestic waste water, agricultural run-off, and industrial effluents contain phosphorus and nitrogen, fertilizer run-off, manure from livestock operations, which increase the level of nutrients in water bodies and can cause eutrophication in the lakes and rivers and continue on to the coastal areas. The nitrates come mainly from the fertilizer that is added to the fields. Excessive use of fertilizers cause nitrate contamination of groundwater, with the result that nitrate levels in drinking water is far above the safety levels recommended. Good agricultural practices can help in reducing the amount of nitrates in the soil and thereby lower its content in the water.

Synthetic organics: Many of the 100 000 synthetic compounds in use today are found in the aquatic environment and accumulate in the food chain. POPs or Persistent organic pollutants, represent the most harmful element for the ecosystem and for human health, for example, industrial chemicals and agricultural pesticides. These chemicals can accumulate in fish and cause serious damage to human health. Where pesticides are used on a large-scale, groundwater gets contaminated and this leads to the chemical contamination of drinking water.

Acidification: Acidification of surface water, mainly lakes and reservoirs, is one of the major environmental impacts of transport over long distance of air pollutants such as sulfur dioxide from power plants, other heavy industry such as steel plants, and motor vehicles. This problem is more severe in the US and in parts of Europe.

Chemicals: Chemicals in water can be both naturally occurring or introduced by human interference and can have serious health effects.

Fluoride in the water is essential for protection against dental caries and weakening of the bones, but higher levels can have an adverse effect on health. In India, high fluoride content is found naturally in the waters in Rajasthan.

Arsenic occurs naturally or is possibly aggrevated by over powering aquifers and by phosphorus from fertilizers. High concentrations of arsenic in water can have an adverse effect on health [14 - 16]. A few years back, high concentrations of this element was found in drinking water in six districts in West Bengal. A majority of people in the area was found suffering from arsenic skin lesions. It was felt that arsenic contamination in the groundwater was due to natural causes. The government is trying to provide an alternative drinking water source and a method through which the arsenic content from water can be removed [17].

Pipes, fittings, solder, and the service connections of some household plumbing systems contain lead that contaminates the drinking water source.

Recreational use of water: Untreated sewage, industrial effluents, and agricultural waste are often discharged into the water bodies such as the lakes, coastal areas and rivers endangering their use for recreational purposes such as swimming and canoeing.

Petrochemicals contaminate the groundwater from underground petroleum storage tanks.

Other heavy metals: These contaminants come from mining waste and tailings, landfills, or hazardous waste dumps.

Chlorinated solvents Metal and plastic effluents, fabric cleaning, electronic and aircraft manufacturing are often discharged and contaminate groundwater

Harmful Impact of Water Pollution

Virtually all types of water pollution are harmful to the health of humans and animals. Water pollution may not damage our health immediately but can be harmful after long term exposure. Different forms of pollutants affect the health of animals in different ways:

- Heavy metals from industrial processes can accumulate in nearby lakes and rivers. These are toxic to marine life such as fish and shellfish, and subsequently to the humans who eat them. Heavy metals can slow development; result in birth defects and some are carcinogenic [18].

- Industrial waste often contains many toxic compounds that damage the health of aquatic animals and those who eat them. Some of the toxins in industrial waste may only have a mild effect whereas other can be fatal. They can cause immune suppression, reproductive failure or acute poisoning.
- Microbial pollutants from sewage often result in infectious diseases that infect aquatic life and terrestrial life through drinking water. Microbial water pollution is a major problem in the developing world, with diseases such as cholera and typhoid fever being the primary cause of infant mortality.
- Organic matter and nutrients causes an increase in aerobic algae and depletes oxygen from the water column. This causes the suffocation of fish and other aquatic organisms.
- Sulfate particles from acid rain can cause harm the health of marine life in the rivers and lakes it contaminates, and can result in mortality.
- Suspended particles in freshwater reduces the quality of drinking water for humans and the aquatic environment for marine life. Suspended particles can often reduce the amount of sunlight penetrating the water, disrupting the growth of photosynthetic plants and micro-organisms.

Water-borne diseases are infectious diseases spread primarily through contaminated water. Though these diseases are spread either directly or through flies or filth, water is the chief medium for spread of these diseases and hence they are termed as water-borne diseases.

Most intestinal (enteric) diseases are infectious and are transmitted through faecal waste. Pathogens – which include virus, bacteria, protozoa, and parasitic worms – are disease-producing agents found in the faeces of infected persons. These diseases are more prevalent in areas with poor sanitary conditions. These pathogens travel through water sources and interfuses directly through persons handling food and water. Since these diseases are highly infectious, extreme care and hygiene should be maintained by people looking after an infected patient. Hepatitis, cholera, dysentery, and typhoid are the more common water-borne diseases that affect large populations in the tropical regions.

A large number of chemicals that either exist naturally in the land or are added due to human activity dissolve in the water, thereby contaminating it and leading to various diseases.

The organophosphates and the carbonates present in pesticides affect and damage the nervous system and can cause cancer. Some of the pesticides contain carcinogens that exceed recommended levels. They contain chlorides that cause reproductive and endocrinal damage.

Lead is hazardous to health as it accumulates in the body and affects the central nervous system. Children and pregnant women are most at risk. Excess fluorides can cause yellowing of the teeth and damage to the spinal cord and other crippling diseases.

Drinking water that gets contaminated with nitrates can prove fatal especially to infants that drink formula milk as it restricts the amount of oxygen that reaches the brain causing the 'blue baby' syndrome. It is also linked to digestive tract cancers. It causes algae to bloom resulting in eutrophication in surface water.

Benzene and other petrochemicals can cause cancer even at low exposure levels. Chlorinated solvents are linked to reproduction disorders and to some cancers. Arsenic poisoning through water can cause liver and nervous system damage, vascular diseases and also skin cancer. Heavy metals cause damage to the nervous system and the kidney, and other metabolic disruptions. While Salts makes the fresh water unusable for drinking and irrigation purposes.

Exposure to polluted water can cause diarrhoea, skin irritation, respiratory problems, and other diseases, depending on the pollutant that is in the water body. Stagnant water and other untreated water provide a habitat for the mosquito and a host of other parasites and insects that cause a large number of diseases especially in the tropical regions. Among these, malaria is undoubtedly the most widely distributed and causes most damage to human health.

Minamata: Environmental Contamination with Methyl Mercury

In Minamata, Japan, inorganic mercury was used in the industrial production of acetaldehyde. It was discharged into the nearby bay as waste water and was ingested by organisms in the bottom sediments. Fish and other creatures in the sea were soon contaminated and eventually residents of this area who consumed the fish suffered from MeHg (methyl mercury) intoxication, later known as the Minamata disease. The disease was first detected in 1956 but the mercury emissions continued until 1968. But even after the emission of mercury stopped, the bottom sediment of the polluted water contained high levels of this mercury [18].

Various measures were taken to deal with this disease. Environmental pollution control, which included cessation of the mercury process; industrial effluent control, environmental restoration of the bay; and restrictions on the intake of fish from the bay. This apart research and investigative activities were promoted assiduously, and compensation and help was offered by the Japanese Government to all those affected by the disease.

The Minamata disease proved a turning point, towards progress in environment protection measures. This experience clearly showed that health and environment considerations must be integrated into the process of economic and industrial development from an early stage.

Air Pollution

Air pollution is the introduction of chemicals, particulate matter, or biological materials that cause harm or discomfort to humans or other living organisms, or cause damage to the natural environment or built environment, into the atmosphere.

The atmosphere is a complex dynamic natural gaseous system that is essential to support life on planet Earth. Stratospheric ozone depletiondue to air pollution has long been recognized as a threat to human health as well as to the Earth's ecosystems.

Indoor air pollution and urban air quality are listed as two of the world's worst pollution problems in the 2008 Blacksmith Institute World's Worst Polluted Places report [19].

Cause of Air Pollution

Air pollutants are main source of air pollution. They are mainly consist of gaseous pollutants, odours, and SPM, (suspended particulate matter) such as dust, fumes, mist, and smoke. The concentration of these in and near the urban areas causes severe pollution to the surroundings. The largest sources of human-created air pollution are energy generation, transportation, and industries that use a great deal of energy sources. Depending on their source and interactions with other components of the air, they can have different chemical compositions and health impacts. Since these pollutants are generally concentrated in and around urban areas [21], the outdoor urban pollution levels [22] are far higher than in the rural areas.

Fires are another major source of air pollution and can lead to severe problems if the smoke is inhaled for a period of time. These fires can either be forest fires, oil well fires, burning of leaves in the backyard or as in the case of rural areas, large-scale burning of agricultural waste. Other sources include industries and power plants located in these areas.

Harmful Impact of Air Pollution

Air pollution can affect our health in many ways with both short-term and long-term effects. Different groups of individuals are affected by air pollution in different ways. Some individuals are much more sensitive to pollutants than are others. Young children and elderly people often suffer more from the effects of air pollution. People with health problems such as asthma, heart and lung disease may also suffer more when the air is polluted. The extent to which an individual is harmed by air pollution usually depends on the total exposure to the damaging chemicals, i.e., the duration of exposure and the concentration of the chemicals must be taken into account.

Examples of short-term effects include irritation to the eyes, nose and throat, and upper respiratory infections such as bronchitis and pneumonia. Other symptoms can include headaches, nausea, and allergic reactions. Short-term air pollution can aggravate the medical conditions of individuals with asthma and emphysema. In the great "Smog Disaster" in London in 1952, four thousand people died in a few days due to the high concentrations of pollution.

Long-term health effects can include chronic respiratory disease, lung cancer, heart disease, and even damage to the brain, nerves, liver, or kidneys. Continual exposure to air pollution affects the lungs of growing children and may aggravate or complicate medical conditions in the elderly. It is estimated that half a million people die prematurely every year in the United States as a result of smoking cigarettes.

Research into the health effects of air pollution is ongoing. Medical conditions arising from air pollution can be very expensive. Healthcare costs, lost productivity in the workplace, and human welfare impacts cost billions of dollars each year.

Since the onset of the industrial revolution, there has been a steady change in the composition of the atmosphere mainly due to the combustion of fossil fuels used for the generation of energy and transportation. Air pollution is a major environmental health problem affecting the developing and the developed countries alike. The effects of air pollution on health are very complex as there are many different sources and their individual effects vary from one to the other. It is not only the ambient air quality in the cities but also the indoor air quality in the rural and the urban areas that are causing concern. In fact in the developing world the highest air pollution exposures occur in the indoor environment. Air pollutants that are inhaled have serious impact on human health affecting the lungs and the respiratory system; they are also taken up by the blood and pumped all round the body. These pollutants are also deposited on soil, plants, and in the water, further contributing to human exposure.

The magnitude of the London fog of 1952, which affected such a large number of people, was the first incident that made people aware of the damage done to the atmosphere due to industrialization. The SPM levels increased manifold and resulted in over 4000 deaths.

Indoor air pollution can be particularly hazardous to health as it is released in close proximity to people. It is stated that a pollutant released indoors is many times more likely to reach the lung than that released outdoors. In the developing countries a fairly large portion of the population is dependent on biomass for their energy requirements. These include wood, charcoal, agricultural residue, and animal waste. Open fires used for cooking and heating are commonly found in the household both in the rural and the urban areas. The stove is often at floor level, adding to the risk of accident and the hygiene factor. In addition, they are often not fitted with a chimney to remove the pollutants. In such households the children and women are most likely to be affected, as they are the group that spends more time indoors. The main pollutant in this environment is the SPM. In fact, death due to indoor air pollution, mainly particulate matters, in the rural areas of India are one of the highest in the world. Many of the deaths are due to acute respiratory infections in children; others are due to cardiovascular diseases, lung cancer, and chronic respiratory diseases in adults. If emissions are high and ventilation is poor, household use of coal and biomass can severely affect the indoor air quality [20].

Pollutant emissions per meal are also very high compared to those of other fuels. Household use of fossil fuel is also fairly common in the developing countries, particularly coal—both bituminous and lignite. These are particularly damaging as they burn inefficiently and emit considerable quantities of air pollutants. If emissions are high and ventilation poor, then the exposure levels to the gases emitted are far higher. The most harmful of the gases and agents that are emitted are particulate matter, carbon dioxide, polycyclic organic matter, and formaldehyde. The indoor concentrations of these are far higher than the acceptable levels and is cause for concern in rural areas.

Health Impact of Specific Air Pollutants

Some of these gases can seriously and adversely affect the health of the population and should be given due attention by the concerned authority. The gases mentioned below are mainly outdoor air pollutants but some of them can and do occur indoor depending on the source and the circumstances [22].

Tobacco smoke. Tobacco smoke generates a wide range of harmful chemicals and is a major cause of ill health, as it is known to cause cancer, not only to the smoker but affecting passive smokers too. It is well-known that smoking affects the passive smoker (the person who is in the vicinity of a smoker and is not himself/herself a smoker) ranging from burning sensation in the eyes or nose, and throat irritation, to cancer, bronchitis, severe asthma, and a decrease in lung function.

Biological pollutants. These are mostly allergens that can cause asthma, hay fever, and other allergic diseases.

Volatile organic compounds. Volatile compounds can cause irritation of the eye, nose and throat. In severe cases there may be headaches, nausea, and loss of coordination. In the longer run, some of them are suspected to cause damage to the liver and other parts of the body.

Formaldehyde. Exposure causes irritation to the eyes, nose and may cause allergies in some people.

Lead. Prolonged exposure can cause damage to the nervous system, digestive problems, and in some cases cause cancer. It is especially hazardous to small children.

Radon. A radioactive gas that can accumulate inside the house, it originates from the rocks and soil under the house and its level is dominated by the outdoor air and also to some extent the other gases being emitted indoors. Exposure to this gas increases the risk of lung cancer.

Ozone. Exposure to this gas makes our eyes itch, burn, and water and it has also been associated with increase in respiratory disorders such as asthma. It lowers our resistance to colds and pneumonia.

Oxides of nitrogen. This gas can make children susceptible to respiratory diseases in the winters.

Carbon monoxide. CO (carbon monoxide) combines with haemoglobin to lessen the amount of oxygen that enters our blood through our lungs. The binding with other haeme proteins causes changes in the function of the affected organs such as the brain and the cardiovascular system, and also the developing foetus. It can impair our concentration, slow our reflexes, and make us confused and sleepy.

Sulphur dioxide. SO2 (sulphur dioxide) in the air is caused due to the rise in combustion of fossil fuels. It can oxidize and form sulphuric acid mist. SO2 in the air leads to diseases of the lung and other lung disorders such as wheezing and shortness of breath. Long-term effects are more difficult to ascertain as SO2 exposure is often combined with that of SPM.

SPM (suspended particulate matter). Suspended matter consists of dust, fumes, mist and smoke. The main chemical component of SPM that is of major concern is lead, others being nickel, arsenic, and those present in diesel exhaust. These particles when breathed in, lodge in our lung tissues and cause lung damage and respiratory problems. The importance of SPM as a major pollutant needs special emphasis as

(*a*) It affects more people globally than any other pollutant on a continuing basis.

(*b*) There is more monitoring data available on this than any other pollutant.

(*c*) More epidemiological evidence has been collected on the exposure to this than to any other pollutant.

Noise Pollution

Noise pollution is excessive, displeasing human, animal or machine-created environmental noise that disrupts the activity or balance of human or animal life. The word noise comes from the Latin word nauseas, meaning seasickness.

The source of most outdoor noise worldwide is mainly construction and transportation systems, including motor vehicle noise, aircraft noiseand rail noise [23, 24]. Poor urban planning may give rise to noise pollution, since side-by-side industrial and residential buildings can result in noise pollution in the residential area.

Noise may be the root cause of around three deaths in every hundred traditionally blamed on heart disease according to a study that suggests many thousands of people in Britain may be dying because of a lack of peace and quiet.

More people than ever are now complaining about unwanted noise pollution - from rowdy neighbours and loud traffic to late-night pubs and clubs.

Now ground-breaking research from the World Health Organisation has provided estimates of the impact of noise on the European population, reports New Scientist today, revealing a striking contribution of noise to premature deaths from accidents and disease.

Though preliminary, the WHO's findings suggest that long-term exposure to traffic noise may account for three per cent of deaths from ischaemic heart disease typically strokes and heart attacks.

Impact of Noise Pollution

The WHO has documented seven categories of adverse health effects of noise pollution on humans. Much of the following comes from the WHO Guideline on Community Noise and follows its format.The guideline provides an excellent, reasonably up-to-date, and comprehensive overview of noise-related issues, as do the other recent reviews on this subject.

Noise health effects are the health consequences of elevated sound levels. Elevated workplace or other noise can cause hearing impairment, hypertension, ischemic heart disease, annoyance and sleep disturbance. Changes in the immune systemand birth defects have been attributed to noise exposure [25]. Although some presbycusis may occur naturally with age [26]. in many developed nations the cumulative impact of noise is sufficient to impair the hearing of a large fraction of the population over the course of a lifetime [27, 28] Noise exposure has also been known to induce tinnitus, hypertension, vasoconstriction and other cardiovascular impacts [29] Beyond these effects, elevated noise levels can create stress, increase workplace accident rates, and stimulate aggression and other anti-social behaviors [31]. The most significant causes are vehicle and aircraft noise, prolonged exposure to loud music, and industrial noise. Road traffic causes almost 80% of the noise annoyances in Norway[31].

There may be psychological definitions of noise as well. Firecrackers may upset some animals or noise-traumatized individuals. The most common noise traumatized persons are those exposed to military conflicts, but often loud groups of people can trigger complaints and other behaviors about noise.

The social costs of traffic noise in EU22 are over •40 billion per year, and passenger cars and lorries (trucks) are responsible for bulk of costs. Traffic noise alone is harming the health of almost every third person in the WHO European Region. One in five Europeans is regularly exposed to sound levels at night that could significantly damage health. Noise is also a threat to marine and terrestrial ecosystems [32].

Hearing loss

The mechanism of hearing loss arises from trauma to stereocilia of the cochlea, the principal fluid filled structure of the inner ear. The pinna combined with the middle ear amplifies sound pressure levels by a factor of twenty, so that extremely high sound pressure levels arrive in the cochlea, even from moderate atmospheric sound stimuli. Underlying pathology to the cochlea are reactive oxygen species, which play a significant role in noise-induced necrosis and apoptosis of the stereocilia [33]. Exposure to high levels of noise have differing effects within a given population, and the involvement of reactive oxygen species suggests possible avenues to treat or prevent damage to hearing and related cellular structures [34].

The elevated sound levels cause trauma to cochlear structure in the inner ear, which gives rise to irreversible hearing loss. A very loud sound in a particular frequency range can damage the cochlea's hair cells that respond to that range thereby reducing the ear's ability to hear those frequencies in the future. However, loud noise in any frequency range has deleterious effects across the entire range of human hearing [35]. The outer ear (visible portion of the human ear) combined with the middle ear amplifies sound levels by a factor of 20 when sound reaches the inner ear [36].

Presbycusis

Hearing loss is somewhat inevitable with age. Though older males exposed to significant occupational noise demonstrate significantly reduced hearing sensitivity than their non-exposed peers, differences in hearing sensitivity decrease with time and the two groups are indistinguishable by age 79 [25]. Women exposed to occupational noise do not differ from their peers in hearing sensitivity, though they do hear better than their non-exposed male counterparts. Due to loud music and a generally noisy environment, young people in the United States have a rate of impaired hearing 2.5 times greater than their parents and grandparents, with an estimated 50 million individuals with impaired hearing estimated in 2050 [26].

In Rosen's work on health effects and hearing loss, one of his findings derived from tracking Maaban tribesmen, who were insignificantly exposed to transportation or industrial noise. This population was systematically compared by cohort group to a typical U.S. population. The findings proved that aging is an almost insignificant cause of hearing loss, which instead is associated with chronic exposure to moderately high levels of environmental noise [28].

Cardiovascular Effects

Noise has been associated with important cardiovascular health problems [37]. In 1999, the World Health Organization concluded that the available evidence showed suggested a weak association between long-term noise exposure above 67-70 dB(A) and hypertension [38]. More recent studies have suggested that noise levels of 50 dB(A) at night may also increase the risk of myocardial infarction by chronically elevating cortisol production [40].

Fairly typical roadway noise levels are sufficient to constrict arterial blood flow and lead to elevated blood pressure; in this case, it appears that a certain fraction of the population is more susceptible to vasoconstriction. This may result because annoyance from the sound causes elevated adrenaline levels trigger a narrowing of the blood vessels (vasoconstriction), or independently through medical stress reactions. Other effects of high noise levels are increased frequency of headaches, fatigue, stomach ulcers and vertigo [41].

The U.S. Environmental Protection Agency authored a pamphlet in 1978 that suggested a correlation between low-birthweight babies (using the World Health Organization definition of less than 2,500 g (~5.5 lb) and high sound levels, and also correlations in abnormally high rates of birth defects, where expectant mothers are exposed to elevated sound levels, such as typical airport environs. Specific birth abnormalities included harelip, cleft palate, and defects in the spine. According to Lester W. Sontag of The Fels Research Institute (as presented in the same EPA study): "There is ample evidence that environment has a role in shaping the physique, behavior and function of animals, including man, from conception and not merely from birth. The fetus is capable of perceiving sounds and responding to them by motor activity and cardiac rate change." Noise exposure is deemed to be particularly pernicious when it occurs between 15 and 60 days after conception, when major internal organs and the central nervous system are formed. Later developmental effects occur as vasoconstriction in the mother reduces blood flow and hence oxygen and nutrition to the fetus. Low birth weights and noise were also associated with lower levels of certain hormones in the mother, these hormones being thought to affect fetal growth and to be a good indicator of protein production. The difference between the hormone levels of pregnant mothers in noisy versus quiet areas increased as birth approached. In a more recent publication, Passchier-Vermeer and Passchier (2000) while reviewing recent studies on birth weight and noise exposure note that while some older studies suggest that when women are exposed to >65 dB aircraft noise a small decrease in birthweight occurs, in a more recent study of 200 Taiwanese women including noise dosimetry measurements of individual noise exposure the authors found no significant association between noise exposure and birth weight after adjusting for relevant confounders, e.g. social class, maternal weight gain during pregnancy, etc.

Stress

Research commissioned by Rockwool, a UK insulation manufacturer, reveals in the UK one third (33%) of victims of domestic disturbances claim loud parties have left them unable to sleep or made them stressed in the last two years. Almost one in ten (9%) of those affected by domestic disturbances claims it has left them continually disturbed and stressed. Over 1.8 million people claim noisy neighbours have made their life a misery and they cannot enjoy their own homes. The impact of noise on health is potentially a significant problem across the UK given over 17.5 million Britons (38%) have been disturbed by the inhabitants of neighbouring properties in the last two years. For almost one in ten (7%) Britons this is a regular occurrence [39].

Annoyance

Because some stressful effects depend on qualities of the sound other than its absolute decibel value, the annoyance associated with sound may need to be considered in regard to health effects. For example, noise from airports is typically perceived as more bothersome than noise from traffic of equal volume. Annoyance effects of noise are minimally affected by demographics, but fear of the noise source and sensitivity to noise both strongly affect the 'annoyance' of a noise [40]. Even sound levels as low as 40 dB(A) (about as loud as a refrigerator or library) can generate noise complaints [41] and the lower threshold for noise producing sleep disturbance is 45 dB(A) or lower [41].

Other factors that affect the 'annoyance level' of sound include beliefs about noise prevention and the importance of the noise source, and annoyance at the cause (i.e. non-noise related factors) of the noise [44]. For instance, in an office setting, audible telephone conversations and discussions between co-workers were considered to be irritating, depending upon the contents of the conversations. Many of the interpretations of the level of annoyance and the relationship between noise levels and resulting health symptoms could be influenced by the quality of interpersonal relationships at the workplace, as well as the stress level generated by the work itself [45]. Evidence regarding the impact of long-term noise versus recent changes in ongoing noise is equivocal on its impact on annoyance [40].

When young children are exposed to speech interference levels of noise on a regular basis (the actual volume of which varies depending on distance and loudness of the speaker), they may develop speech or reading difficulties, because auditory processing functions are compromised. Children continue to develop their speech perception abilities until they reach their teenage years. Evidence has shown that when children learn in noisier classrooms, they have a more difficult time understanding speech than those who learn in quieter settings. In a study conducted by Cornell University in 1993, children exposed to noise in learning environments experienced trouble with word discrimination as well as various cognitive developmental delays. In particular the writing learning impairment known as dysgraphia is commonly associated with environmental stressors in the classroom. The effect of high noise levels on small children has been known to cause physical health damages as well. Children from noisy residences often possess a heart rate that is significantly higher (by 2 beats/min on average) than in children from quieter residences [41].

Furthermore, studies have shown that neighborhood noise (consisting of noise from neighboring apartments, as well as noise within one's own apartment or home) can cause significant irritation and noise stress within people, due to the great deal of time people spend within their residences. This can result in an increased risk of depression and psychological disorders, migraines, and even emotional stress [42].

In the workplace, noise pollution is generally a problem once the noise level is greater than 55 dB(A). Selected studies show that approximately 35 to 40% of workers in office settings find noise levels from 55 to 60 dB(A) to be extremely irritating. In fact, the noise standard in Germany for mentally stressful tasks is set at 55 dB(A). However, if the noise is source is continuous, the threshold level for tolerable noise levels amongst office workers actually becomes lower than 55 dB(A).

One important effect of noise is to make a person's speech less easy to hear. The human brain automatically compensates the production of speech for background noise in a process called the Lombard effect in which it becomes louder with more distinct syllables. But this cannot fully remove the problems of communication intelligibility made in noise.

Thermal Pollution

In a very general way, thermal pollution can be defined as the phenomenon by which the normal temperature of ambient sources of water faces an increase in temperature. It can be contributed to the high temperature discharges from industries, power stations etcetera, into the adjoining water body whereby the heated or warm water increases the water temperature

Effect of Thermal Pollution in Water

Other than man-made sources of aquatic thermal pollution, changes in vegetation cover along the banks of the water body or increase in turbidity has been reported to cause increasing in temperature.

Sources of Thermal Pollution

- Removal of trees along the shore line increases solar incidence and hence warms up the water along with deforestation
- In power plants both nuclear and coal use thousands of gallons of water for their reactor but return water is much hotter.
- Dumping of waste warm water by nuclear plants.

Effects of Thermal Pollution

- There are several effects of thermal pollution.
- Sudden and periodic increase in temperature producing a thermal effect.
- Changed dissolved oxygen.
- Distribution of organisms among major and minor communities.
- Changes to reproductive powers and increased susceptibility to disease.
- Production of heat shock proteins for thermo tolerance.
- Changes in migration time and pattern may be affected.
- Bio indicators are the first to show the effects.
- Decrease in productivity of the water body.
- Economic and environmental damage.

Control of Thermal Pollution

- Construction of cooling ponds —artificial water bodies for cooling due to radiation, convection and radiation.
- Construction of cooling towers for radiation.
- Use cogeneration where the heat is recycled.

REFERENCES

1. Spengler, John D. and Sexton, Ken (1983) Indoor Air Pollution: A Public Health Perspective. Science (New Series) 221(4605): pp. 9-17.
2. Robert Mendelsohn; Enviormental Health Persepectives, Vol. 110, 2002.
3. Environmental Pollution and Impacts on Public Health; Report of UNEP.
4. Lepers, Erika. et al; "A Synthesis of Information on Rapid Land-cover Change for the Period 1980-2000"; Bioscience. Washington: Feb 2005.Vol.55, Iss. 2; pg. 115.
5. Affects of environmental pollution; e: Business Recorder (7/11/2005).
6. New World Encyclopedia: Land Pollution
7. Earth — A Graphic Look at the State of the World: Toxic Pollution
8. U. S. E.P.A. Office of Pollution, Prevention and Toxics: Occupational Exposures and Environmental Releases of Lead Wheel-Balancing Weights
9. Ecology Center: Ecolink — May 2009 — Washington Becomes First State to Ban Lead Wheel Weights
10. Oregon Department of Environmental Quality: Fact Sheet: Sources of Polychlorinated Biphenyls.
11. Edward A. Laws; Aquatic pollution: An introductory Text; 3 rd edition; 2000; John Wiely & sons.
12. United States Geological Survey (USGS). Denver, CO. "Ground Water and Surface Water: A Single Resource." USGS Circular 1139. 1998.
13. Richard Helmer, Ivanildo Hespanhol; Water Pollution Control: A guide to the use of water quality management principles; 1997, 526 pages; ISBN 0419229108; published on behalf of WHO.

14. Ahmad, S. A, M. H. Sayed, S. Barua, M. H. Khan, M. H. Faruquee, A. Jalil et al (2001), 'Arsenic in drinking water and pregnancy outcomes' , Environmental Health Perspective 109(6):29-31.

15. Astolfi, E., A. Maccagno, J. C. G. Fernandez, R. Vaccara and R. Stimola (1981), 'Relation between arsenic in drinking water and skin cancer', Biological Trace Element Research 3:133-143.

16. Buchet, J. P., A. Geubel, S. Pauwels, P. Mahieu and R. Lauwerys (1984), ' The influence of liver disease on the methylation of arsenite in humans', Archives of Toxicology 55:151-154.

17. Chakraborty, D., M. K. Sengupta, M. M. Rahman, S. Ahmad, U. K. Chowdhury, S. C. Mukherjee et al. (2004), 'Groundwater arsenic contamination and its health effects in Ganga-Meghna-Brahmaputra plain', Journal of Environmental Monitoring 6:74-83.

18. 14. Fewtrell, L. and J. M. Colford Jr. (2004), 'Water, sanitation and hygiene: interventions and diarrhoea –A systematic review and meta-analysis', Water supply and sanitation board, The World Bank.

19. Blacksmith Institute World's Worst Polluted Places report; 2008; WorstPolluted.org. Retrieved 2010-08-29.

20. B. Berglund1, B. Brunekreef2, H. Knöppe3, T. Lindvall4, M. Maroni*, L. Mølhave5, P. Skov; "Effects of Indoor Air Pollution on Human Health; " Indoor Air Volume 2, Issue 1, pages 2–25, March 1992.

21. Schwela D.; Air pollution and health in urban areas; Rev Environ Health. 2000 Jan-Jun;15(1-2):13-42.

22. L. J. Folinsbee; Human health effects of air pollution; Environ Health Perspect. 1993 April; 100: 45–56.

23. Senate Public Works Committee, Noise Pollution and Abatement Act of 1972, S. Rep. No. 1160, 92nd Cong. 2nd session.

24. C. Michael Hogan and Gary L. Latshaw, The relationship between highway planning and urision specialty conference, May 21-23, 1973, Chicago, Illinois. by American Society of Civil Engineers. Urban Transportation Division.

25. Passchier-Vermeer W, Passchier WF (2000). "Noise exposure and public health". Environ. Health Perspect. 108 Suppl 1: 123-31. doi:10.2307/3454637. JSTOR 3454637.PMC 1637786. PMID 10698728.

26. Rosenhall U, Pedersen K, Svanborg A (1990). "Presbycusis and noise-induced hearing loss". Ear Hear 11 (4): 257–63. doi:10.1097/00003446-199008000-00002. PMID 2210099.

27. Schmid, RE (2007-02-18). "Aging nation faces growing hearing loss". CBS News. Retrieved 2007-02-18.

28. Senate Public Works Committee, Noise Pollution and Abatement Act of 1972, S. Rep. No. 1160, 92nd Cong. 2nd session.

29. Kryter, Karl D. (1994). The handbook of hearing and the effects of noise: physiology, psychology, and public health. Boston: Academic Press. ISBN 0-12-427455-2.

30. Henderson D, Bielefeld EC, Harris KC, Hu BH (2006). "The role of oxidative stress in noise-induced hearing loss". Ear Hear 27 (1): 1–19. doi:10.1097/01.aud.0000191942.36672.f3.PMID 16446561.

31. Rosen and P. Olin, Hearing Loss and Coronary Heart Disease, Archives of Otolaryngology, 82:236 (1965).

32. Ising H, Babisch W, Kruppa B (1999). "Noise-Induced Endocrine Effects and Cardiovascular Risk". Noise Health 1 (4): 37–48. PMID 12689488.

33. Berglund, B; Lindvall T, Schwela D, Goh KT (1999). "World Health Organization: Guidelines for Community Noise". World Health Organization.

34. Maschke C (2003). "Stress Hormone Changes in Persons exposed to Simulated Night Noise". Noise Health 5 (17): 35–45. PMID 12537833. Retrieved 2007-12-22.

35. Franssen EA, van Wiechen CM, Nagelkerke NJ, Lebret E (2004). "Aircraft noise around a large international airport and its impact on general health and medication use". Occup Environ Med 61 (5): 405–13. doi:10.1136/oem.2002.005488. PMC 1740783. PMID 15090660.

36. Lercher P, Hörtnagl J, Kofler WW (1993). "Work noise annoyance and blood pressure: combined effects with stressful working conditions". Int Arch Occup Environ Health 65 (1): 23–8.doi:10.1007/BF00586054. PMID 8354571.

37. Miedema HME, Vos H (1999). "Demographic and attitudinal factors that modify annoyance from transportation noise". Journal of the Acoustical Society of America 105 (6): 3336–44.doi:10.1121/1.424662.

38. Gelfand, Stanley A (2001). Essentials of Audiology. New York: Thieme Medical Publishers. ISBN 1-58890-017-7.

39. Walker, JR; Fahy, Frank (1998). Fundamentals of noise and vibration. London: E & FN Spon. ISBN 0419227008.

40. Field, JM (1993). "Effect of personal and situational variables upon noise annoyance in residential areas". Journal of the Acoustical Society of America 93 (5): 2753–63.doi:10.1121/1.405851.

41. Marilena Kampa, Elias Castanas; Human health effects of air pollution; Environmental Pollution; Volume 151, Issue 2, January 2008, Pages 362-367.

42. Lesley Rushton; Health hazards and waste management; Br Med Buil (2003) 68 (1): 183-197.

2

Environmental Standards and Human Health

—Pawan Kumar 'Bharti', India
—Vijender Singh, India

ABSTRACT

Standards and limits are the important variables to control the quality of environmental components like air, water, soil and noise. Many pollutants present in environment may change its quality characteristics and cause harms and diseases to human community. So, the standards and limits were set by various authorities, boards, etc. to regulate classified the category and quality of environment. The water quality standards and limits show the potability and suitability of water. Polluted water may create problems to human beings after consumption. Even standards were set up for the wastewater discharged from different type of industries. In the present chapter, a brief was made to elaborate the air quality standards, water quality standards, pollutants in soil, Noise level, and heavy metal in drinking water, which cause problems to human health.

Key words: *Environmental standards, Water quality, air quality, permissible limits, heavy metal, pollutants, Human health.*

Introduction

In the last three decades, the rapid growth of industrialization and urbanization has created negative impacts on the environment. The industrial, municipal and agricultural wastes containing pesticides, insecticides, fertilizers residues, organic pollutants and heavy metals in their effluents have been polluted surface and ground water. In India, the industrial emissions and effluents have contributed a major source of environmental pollution. In the modern industrial era, rapidly growing of industrialization and urbanization has posed adverse impacts on the environment and its all components. Air, soil and water everything on earth surface may changed its quality due to the increasing pollution (Bharti, 2012a).

Air Quality

A substance in the air that can cause harm to humans and the environment is known as an air pollutant. Pollutants can be in the form of solid particles, liquid droplets, or gases. In addition, they may be natural or man-made. Pollutants can be classified as primary or secondary. Usually, primary pollutants are directly emitted from a process, such as ash from a volcanic eruption, the carbon monoxide gas from a motor vehicle exhaust or sulfur dioxide released from factories. Secondary pollutants are not emitted directly. Rather, they form in the air when primary pollutants react or interact.

Table 2.1: National Ambient Air Quality Standard (CPCB, 2009)

Sl. No.	Pollutant	Time Weighted Average	Concentration in Ambient Air		
			Industrial, Residential, Rural & Other Areas	Ecological Sensitive Area	Method of measurement
1	2	3	4	5	6
1.	Sulphur Dioxide (SO_2)	Annual Average* 24 hours**	50 μg/m³ 80 μg/m³	20 μg/m³ 80 μg/m³	- Improved west & Gaeke method - Ultraviolet fluorescence
2.	Nitrogen Dioxides (NO_2)	Annual Average* 24 hours**	40 μg/m³ 80 μg/m³	30 μg/m³ 80 μg/m³	- Modified Jacob & Hochheiser (Na-Arsenite) method - Chemiluminescence
3.	Particulate Matter less than 10 μm or PM_{10}	Annual Average* 24 hours**	60 μg/m³ 100 μg/m³	60 μg/m³ 100 μg/m³	- Gravimetric - TOEM - Beta attenuation
4.	Particulate Matter less than 2.5 μm or $PM_{2.5}$	Annual Average* 24 hours**	40 μg/m³ 60 μg/m³	40 μg/m³ 60 μg/m³	- Gravimetric - TOEM - Beta attenuation
5.	Ozone (O_3)	8 hours** 1 hour**	100 μg/m³ 180 μg/m³	100 μg/m³ 180 μg/m³	- UV photometric - Chemiluminescence - Chemical method
6.	Lead (Pb)	Annual Average* 24 hours**	0.5 μg/m³ 1.0 μg/m³	0.5 μg/m³ 1.0 μg/m³	- AAS/ICP Method after sampling using EPM 2000 or equivalent filter paper - ED-XRF using Teflon filter
7.	Carbon Monoxide (CO)	8 hours** 1 hour**	2.0 mg/m³ 4.0 mg/m³	2.0 mg/m³ 4.0 mg/m³	- Non dispersive infrared (NDIR) spectroscopy

1	2	3	4	5	6
8.	Ammonia (NH_3)	Annual Average* 24 hours**	100 µg/m^3 400 µg/m^3	100 µg/m^3 400 µg/m^3	- Chemiluminescence - Indophenol blue method
9.	Benzene (C_6H_6)	Annual Average*	5 µg/m^3	5 µg/m^3	- Gas chromatography based continuous analyser - Adsorption & desorption followed by GC analysis
10.	Benzo (O) Pyrene (BaP)- particulate phase only	Annual Average*	01 ng/m^3	01 ng/m^3	- Gas chromatography based continuous analyser - Adsorption & desorption followed by GC analysis
11.	Arsenic (As)	Annual Average*	06 ng/m^3	06 ng/m^3	- AAS/ICP Method after sampling using EPM 2000 or equivalent filter paper
12.	Nickel (Ni)	Annual Average*	20 ng/m^3	20 ng/m^3	- AAS/ICP Method after sampling using EPM 2000 or equivalent filter paper

Water Pollution

Water is the most Essential commodity for all living creatures. Man needs it for his physiological existence water is the elixir of life. It is the source of energy and govern the evaluation and function of the universe on the earth 97.3% of the worlds water i.e. 1.4 billion cubic kilometer ocean salty water cannot be used for agriculture domestic and industries purposes. Out of it 2.7% fresh water i.e. 73 x 10^6 cubic in the form of streams, lakes, wells and tube wells i.e. 0.6% 8.5 x $10^{15}m^3$ is ground water which oceans at the depth of 80 meter below the ground surface (Kataria et al., 1995).

The origin of water on earth is not clear so far. However, the current presumption is that the primordial earth had no oceans and perhaps very little atmosphere. It is believed that the volatile constituents bound in the earth crust, oozing to the surface through volcanoes, rock movements and hot springs, condensed to form the ocean, atmosphere and mountains. This way perhaps this remarkable combination of hydrogen and oxygen called water come into being and eventually became an indispensable component of earth's environments.

In Vedic Literature water is called as Apha. We all know that water is the elixir of life. All living organisms, plants and animals are structurally 30-98% water (Bharti, 2004). Besides being a structural component of body water is essential environmentally too. Water is the medium through which nutrients of soil underneath and above on the surface move horizontally as well as vertically water has great power of dissolving most of the inorganic components in mixture form and in the pure elemental and ionic form. Water provides a medium for interaction among different compounds water is a great nurture for plants as well as for animals water helps in conducting of energy the form of heat helps in maintaining a soothing climate, water acts as a rejuvenator and medicament it self (Rigveda 1.23.19).

Chemically, water is the mono-oxide of Hydrogen i.e. (H.O.H). It freely disassociated into hydrogen and hydroxyl ions. The ionization product (H^+) and (OH^-) is about 10^{-14}. Water is a colourless liquid and possesses a high dielectric constant (81), and there for salts gets highly ionized when dissolved in water but not so in the other solvents. Due to this property, water is known as universal solvent present on the earth that is why the natural water contains many salts in dissolved form. On the basis of amount these slats dissolved in the earth only 3% of the total water (approximately 1.4 billion cubic kilometer) is fresh and suitable for human consumption of this, less than 0.01% is associated with rivers and streams (Bharti, 2012a).

Water Quality Standards

Water - the most abundant and vital natural resource is extremely essential for survival of all living organisms, but today clean water has become a precious commodity and its quality is threatened by numerous sources of pollution. Water pollution creates physical, chemical and biological changes in the water, and further affects the water quality for a long period of time. As the heavy metals enter in the food chains of aquatic ecosystem, ultimately affect the health of higher animals of that particular ecosystem. Different heavy metals like Mercury, Lead, Chromium, and Nickel, Cadmium etc. release from various sources like agriculture, urban and industrial uses, and these factors degrade the water quality.

To minimize the pollution load of water bodies various guidelines, quality standards and maximum permissible limits of pollutants have been set up in different countries. However, WHO standards are being applied in most countries of the world as they are considered as ideal. The Indian standards (BIS) or CPCB standards show relatively high deviation from the WHO standards for environmental quality. Maximum permissible limits for some water quality parameters are different than those of WHO. Limits for toxic metals (Cd, Cu, Hg, Mn, Ni, Pb, Zn) in drinking water are high in BIS or CPCB standards compared to WHO standards (Bharti, 2007a). Heavy metals are highly toxic and cause various health problems in humans and also affect cattle and vegetation. Thus, it is essential to control their migration to the unpolluted environment for the safety of human health and livestock.

The first sets of standards were published as Indian Standard, 2490 in 1963. These standards set the tolerance limits for Industrial Effluent discharged into inland surface water. The Indian Standard 2296 was also published in 1963, which set the tolerance limits for inland surface water subject to pollution (Kumar et al., 2012).

Table 2.2: Drinking Water Quality Standards (IS: 10500: 1991)

Sl. No.	Parameters	Unit	Permissible Limit	Desirable Limit
1.	Color	Hazen	5	—
2.	Odour	Unobjectionable	—	—
3.	Turbidity	NTU	5	10
4.	pH	—	6.5-8.5	—
5.	T. Hardness as $CaCO_3$	mg/l	300	600
6.	Iron (as Fe)	mg/l	0.3	1.0
7.	Chloride (as Cl)	mg/l	250	1000
8.	Fluoride (as F)	mg/l	1.0	1.5
9.	Total Dissolved Solids	mg/l	500	2000
10.	Magnesium as Mg	mg/l	30	100
11.	Calcium (as Ca)	mg/l	75	200
12.	Copper	mg/l	0.05	1.5
13.	Manganese as Mn	mg/l	0.1	0.3
14.	Sulphate as SO_4	mg/l	200	—
15.	Nitrate as NO_3	mg/l	45	—
16.	Phenolic Compound as C_6H_5OH	mg/l	0.002	—
17.	Mercury as Hg	mg/l	0.001	—
18.	Cadmium as Cd	mg/l	0.01	—
19.	Selenium as Se	mg/l	0.01	—
20.	Arsenic as As	mg/l	0.01	—
21.	Cyanide as CN	mg/l	0.05	—
22.	Lead as Pb	mg/l	0.05	—
23.	Zinc as Zn	mg/l	5	15
24.	Anionic Detergent (MBAS)	mg/l	0.2	—
25.	Chromium as Cr+6	mg/l	0.05	—
26.	Mineral Oil	mg/l	0.01	—
27.	Alkalinity as $CaCO_3$	mg/l	200	600
28.	Aluminium as Al	mg/l	0.2	—
29.	Phosphate as PO_4	mg/l	0.05	—
30.	Boron as B	mg/l	1.0	5
31.	MPN Coliform/100 ml	Cfu	10	—

The first attempts of water pollution control thus approached the problem using two independent concepts, one dealt with the control of pollution through specification of various parameters and their maximum concentration in the effluent itself. These could be referred to as 'Effluent Standards'. The other approach was to set standards for the receiving water body presumply after a reasonable opportunity for dilution. These standards could be called 'Receiving Water Body Standards' and were related to identified beneficial use to the receiving water body. It is extremely significant that the very first attempt of control of water pollution was through setting of standards simultaneously adopting the above two approaches.

Table 2.3: WHO's Guidelines for Drinking-water Quality, 2006, are the International Reference Point for Standard Setting and Drinking-water Safety

Element/ substance	Symbol/ formula	Normally found in fresh water/surface water/ground water	Health based guideline by the WHO
1	2	3	4
Aluminium	Al		0.2 mg/l
Ammonia	NH_4	< 0.2 mg/l (up to 0.3 mg/l in anaerobic waters)	No guideline
Antimony	Sb	< 4 μg/l	0.02 mg/l
Arsenic	As		0.01 mg/l
Asbestos			No guideline
Barium	Ba		0.7 mg/l
Beryllium	Be	< 1 μg/l	No guideline
Boron	B	< 1 mg/l	0.5 mg/l
Cadmium	Cd	< 1 μg/l	0.003 mg/l
Chloride	Cl		No guideline
Chromium	Cr^{+3}, Cr^{+6}	< 2 μg/l	0.05 mg/l
Colour			Not mentioned
Copper	Cu		2 mg/l
Cyanide	CN^-		0.07 mg/l
Dissolved oxygen	O_2		No guideline
Fluoride	F	< 1.5 mg/l (up to 10)	1.5 mg/l
Hardness	mg/l $CaCO_3$		No guideline
Hydrogen sulfide	H_2S		No guideline

1	2	3	4
Iron	Fe	0.5- 50 mg/l	No guideline
Lead	Pb		0.01 mg/l
Manganese	Mn		0.4 mg/l
Mercury	Hg	< 0.5 μg/l	0.006 mg/l
Molybdenum	Mb	< 0.01 mg/l	0.07 mg/l
Nickel	Ni	< 0.02 mg/l	0.07 mg/l
Nitrate and nitrite	NO_3, NO_2		50 mg/l and 3 mg/l
Turbidity			Not mentioned
pH			No guideline
Selenium	Se	< 0.01 mg/l	0.01 mg/l
Silver	Ag	5 – 50 μg/l	No guideline
Sodium	Na	< 20 mg/l	No guideline
Sulfate	SO_4		No guideline
Inorganic tin	Sn		Not mentioned
Total Dissolved Solids			No guideline
Uranium	U		0.015 mg/l
Zinc	Zn		No guideline

(**Source:** www.who.in)

Around 1976, the CPCB developed the concept of evolving industry specific effluent standards based on a comprehensive study of the problems of that particular industry relevant polluting parameters, their pollution potential, best pollution control technology available in the country and the cost of such a technology.

From these, comprehensive documentation evolved the idea of Minimal National Standards (MINAS). These standards were considered to be the minimum standards for specified industries. In the Environmental Protection Act (EPA), 1986, some of these standards were incorporated. Since these are the Minimal National Standards, the State Boards are only permitted to make them more stringent and in no case can relax them. It is essential that effluent standards satisfy three basic criteria namely Necessity, Implement ability and Enforceability. The stipulation of standards for a specific parameter is necessary when the effect of the parameters on the environment were thoroughly studied and established. No compromise, therefore, can be made with regard to concentration of toxic pollutants. By implement ability it should mean that with best pollution control technology currently available in this country, these parameters could be brought down to the specified limits. Enforceability means either the industry or the concerned authorities have the expertise to analyze, to monitor the wastewater discharged from the industry. Each of the parameters included in the MINAS must satisfy each of these three fundamental criteria. At the same time, the set of parameters chosen must ensure the primary objective of protection of environment. Keeping in mind the basic criteria, major polluting parameters from the industries and the performance of the treatment plants, the standards are evolved (Bharti, 2007b).

Table 2.4: Drinking Water Quality Standards

Parameters	BIS	CPCB	UPPCB	WHO
Temperature	40°C	±5°C than receiving water	40°C	-
SS	100 mg/l	100 mg/l	100 mg/l	5-25 mg/l
Ph	5.5-9.0	5.5-9.0	5.5-9.0	7.0-8.5
BOD_5 at 20°C	30 mg/l	30 mg/l	30 mg/l	-
COD	250 mg/l	250 mg/l	250 mg/l	-
Cl	-	-	-	75-200 mg/l
Ca	-	-	-	75-200 mg/l
Mg	-	-	-	30-150 mg/l
Cd	2.0 mg/l	2.0 mg/l	2.0 mg/l	0.1 mg/l
Cu	3.0 mg/l	3.0 mg/l	3.0 mg/l	0.05-1.5 mg/l
Fe	-	3.0 mg/l	-	0.1-1.0 mg/l
Pb	0.1 mg/l	0.1 mg/l	0.1 mg/l	0.1 mg/l
Mn	-	2.0 mg/l	-	0.05-0.5 mg/l
Ni	2.0 mg/l	3.0 mg/l	2.0 mg/l	-
Zn	5.0 mg/l	5.0 mg/l	5.0 mg/l	5-15.0 mg/l

Table 2.5: Recent Standards for Heavy Metals (in mg/l)

	Inland surface water		Drinking water		
	BIS / CPCB	WHO	WHO, 1993 Drinking water	WHO, 2006	
				Normal	Health based
Cd	2.0	0.1	0.003-0.005	<1µg/l	0.003
Cu	3.0	0.05-1.5	2.0	-	2.0
Fe	3.0	0.1-1.0	0.2	0.5-50	-
Mn	2.0	0.05-0.5	0.5-0.05	-	0.4
Ni	2.0	-	0.02	0.02	0.07
Pb	0.1	0.1	0.01	-	0.01
Zn	5.0	5.0-15.0	3.0	<20	-

Source: www.lenntech.com.

Water and Human Health

In Vedic literature, water is called as a medicine for human health. Nobody can imagine life without water. Water is our basic requirement even animal and plant can't survive without water. It is common statement that "Life is not possible without water". Thus life and water are inseparable faces of the same coin. Water is not only essential for life but predominant inorganic constituent of living matter forming in general nearly three quarters of the weight of living cells. It makes some 5 percent of the body weight of an adult human and can forms as 98% of the mass of certain jellyfish. Organisms that contain relatively small amounts of water are generally in dormant state or show very slow development; seeds and certain invertebrates that live in arid environments are examples. On the other hand high rainfall over a landmass in variably means a large biomass per unit area.

Next to oxygen, water is the most important substance for human existence and it is essential for everything on our planet to grow and prosper. Freshwater rivers, lakes and ground water are used to irrigate crops, to provide drinking water and to act as a sanitation system. Although we as humans recognize this fact, we disregard it by polluting our rivers, lakes, and oceans. Most of our water resources are gradually becoming contaminated due to the addition of foreign materials from the surroundings (Lokeshwari and Chandrappa, 2006). These include organic matter of plant and animal origin, land surface washing and industrial and sewage effluents. Rapid urbanization and industrialization with improper environmental planning often lead to discharge of industrial and sewage effluents into rivers. In addition to the process of desertification, pollution is also reducing the volume of safe fishing, irrigation and drinking water.

The problem of water pollution due to toxic metals has begun to cause concern now in most metropolitan cities. The toxic heavy metals entering the ecosystem may lead to geo-accumulation and biomagnifications. Metals like Fe, Cu, Zn, Ni and other trace elements are important for proper functioning of biological systems and their deficiency or excess could lead to a number of disorders (Ward, 1995). Food chain contamination by heavy metals has become a burning issue in recent years because of their potential accumulation in biological systems through contaminated water, soil and air. Therefore, a better understanding of heavy metal sources, their accumulation in the soil and the effect of their presence in water, soil and on plant systems seem to be particularly important issues of present day research on risk assessment. The main sources of heavy metals to vegetable crops are their growth media (soil, air, nutrient solutions) from which these are taken up by the roots or foliage.

Water is a resource circulated throughout all ecosystems and is one of the most important factors of them (Odum 1971). From the point of view of eco-hydrology, for the main elements of an ecosystem including inorganic and organic compound, producers and consumers both the quantity and the chemistry of water have a decisive impact on its biomass and biotic composition. Information obtained from current hydro-chemical analyses of water specimens is very important but it is sometimes difficult to Ganga the overall situation especially the occurrence of nutrient, which may be very important to an ecosystem.

Everything originated in the water and everything is sustained by water all life on earth depends on water. Water is very essential for the survival of all living organism there is a wide variety of beneficial uses of water. Man uses water for many purposes, drinking, irrigation, fisheries, industrial purposes, transportation and waste disposal. The origin of water on the earth is not clear so far. However, the current presumption is that the primordial earth had no oceans and perhaps volatile constituents bound in the earth crust oozing to the surface through volcanoes rock movements and hot springs, condensed to form the ocean and the atmosphere. This way come into being and eventually become an indispensable component of earth' environment.

Water quality includes all physical, chemical and biological factor that influence the beneficial use of water, Lotic habitats are those exiting in relatively fast running streams, springs, river and brooks. The lakes represent lentic habitats; marshes and swamps represent ponds and wetland. The above classification of fresh water environment is based on currents and ratio of the depth of surface area.

Groundwater is one of the major water resources for domestic, agricultural and industrial uses. Pollutants are being added to the ground water and soil system through various human activities and rapid growth of industrialization, which affects the human health directly or indirectly.

Environmental assessment in this context is concerned with groundwater concentrations of cadmium, zinc, lead and arsenic, the levels of which are often increased by the effects of human activity. Metals are spread via the atmosphere from smelters and other metal industrial plants. Significant increases in groundwater concentrations of metals from such sources may occur within a local radius of ca. ten kilometers; but their distribution through the atmosphere extends over far greater areas. Large quantities of lead have also been released into the atmosphere through the use of leaded petrol. Such releases have declined in recent years, but the greater portion of airborne lead pollution from previous years is still present in the surface layers of earth. Levels of cadmium, lead, zinc and arsenic in groundwater are often related to pollution or other human activities. Cadmium, lead and arsenic are dangerous to human health even in fairly low concentrations.

Metals have also entered land and water by more direct routes. In some areas, the use of cadmium-contaminated phosphate fertilizer has led to a doubling of cadmium levels in cropland during the past fifty years. Since zinc is often used for anti-corrosion purposes, it may enter the soil via galvanized steel products embedded in the ground. Both arsenic and zinc are included in many wood preservatives, and can be spread via waste spill at impregnating facilities or via the wood products themselves. Waste sites are another source of zinc and arsenic, which may leach out from discarded materials that include those metals. Still greater quantities of polluting metals may leach from dumps of mining waste (Bharti, 2012b).

Naturally high levels of cadmium and arsenic can occur in areas where the bedrock contains high concentrations of metals; this applies to many types of shale and slate. Lowering the water table, for example by pumping out water, may lead to increases in the amounts of naturally-occurring metals that enter the groundwater. This is because metals in bedrock are often bound in sulfide minerals. The addition of oxygen results in oxidation of the sulfide compounds and the release of their metallic components. In some cases, however, arsenic may also be released as the result of a rise in the water table. It is with redox class 3 that the risk of water-soluble arsenic is greatest.

The solubility of cadmium and zinc increases significantly with a decline in pH value, which means that acidification, can lead to increased levels of those metals in groundwater. Normally, lead is very tightly bound to humus and clay, but it may dissolve more readily if the pH value declines. In the case of arsenic, the reverse usually applies: Solubility increases concurrently with rising pH values. Zinc is an element that is essential to life for most organisms, and humans can tolerate high concentrations. Aquatic organisms, on the other hand, are much more sensitive to zinc. Increased levels in groundwater indicate that concentrations of other metals may be above normal. This is especially true of cadmium, which is often present concurrently with zinc. In most cases, cadmium levels are, at most, one percent higher than those of zinc; but cadmium can be harmful even at such low concentrations. Lead is another heavy metal, which is toxic at low concentrations. If pregnant women are exposed to lead concentrations above medically established threshold levels, there is an increased risk of birth defects. The toxicity of arsenic is comparatively moderate, but over longer periods of time it may produce changes in skin tissue, even at levels below medically established thresholds (Bharti, 2012b).

Threshold Levels of Heavy Metals

In several cases, the limits for the above five classes correspond with those of the National Food Administration's threshold levels (see table below). For all metals, the boundary between class 2 and class 3 is defined as the level at which effects on organisms in lakes and watercourses begin to occur.

Table 2.6: Threshold Levels of Heavy Metals

Class	Level	Cadmiumµg/l	Zincµg/l	Leadµg/l	Arsenicµg/l
1	Very low	< 0.05	< 5	< 0.2	< 1
2	Low	0.05-0.1	5-20	0.2-1	1-5
3	Moderate	0.1-1	20-300	1-3	5-10
4	High	1-5	300-1000	3-10	10-50
5	Very high	> 5	> 1000	> 10	> 50

Table 2.7: Different Types of Threshold Levels of Heavy Metals

Type of threshold level	Cadmium µg/l	Zinc µg/l	Lead µg/l	Arsenic µg/l
Warning based on technical grounds; survival of aquatic organisms is affected even with brief exposure		> 300		
Warning based on technical and aesthetic grounds; risk of taste changes and turbidity		> 1000		
Medically-established threshold; use with caution	> 1			> 10
Medically-established; unsuitable for drinking	> 5		> 10	> 50

Source: National Food Administration.

Reference Values

Reference values have been set so high that uncontaminated groundwater has low concentrations of metals in the majority of cases. Such water may, however, include pollutants that have traveled lengthy distances through the atmosphere.

Table 2.8: Reference Values of Heavy Metals

Metal	Reference value, µg/l
Cadmium	0.1
Zinc	100
Lead	1
Arsenic	1

Table 2.9: Deviations from Reference Values of Heavy Metals

Class	Extent of deviation	Cadmium µg/l	Zinc µg/l	Lead µg/l	Arsenic µg/l
1	None or insignificant	< 0.1	< 100	< 1	< 1
2	Moderate	0.1-0.5	100-200	1-1.5	1-2
3	Significant	0.5-2	200-400	1.5-2.5	2-5
4	Large	2-5	400-700	2.5-5	5-10
5	Very large	> 5	> 700	> 5	> 10

The five classes indicate the extent to which measured levels of metals in groundwater deviate from the reference values, which are relatively unaffected by non-natural causes. The upper limit of class 1, separating it from class 2, is the same as the reference value. The values of class 5 indicate the strong possibility of a local source of contamination. But in isolated cases, there may be another cause of the unusually high levels, for example: Class 5 levels of cadmium may occur naturally in extremely acid water ($pH < 5$); likewise, high arsenic levels occur naturally at a number of locations in the regions of Bergslagen and Skellefteå, as well as other parts in certain deep-drilled wells with high levels of iron (redox class 3) and high pH values.

Soil Pollution

Soil pollution is defined or can be described as the contamination of soil of a particular region. Soil pollution mainly is a result of penetration of harmful pesticides and insecticides, which on one hand serve whatever their main purpose is, but on the other hand, bring about deterioration in the soil quality, thus making it contaminated and unfit for use. Insecticides and pesticides are not to be blamed alone for soil pollution, but there are many other leading causes of soil pollution too.

Table 2.10: Soil Quality Characteristics and Methodology

Sl.No.	Parameters	Unit	Protocol/Method
1	2	3	4
1.	pH	-	IS:2720 (Part-26)
2.	Conductivity	µS/cm	Conductivity meter
3.	Sodium as Na_2O	% by mass	ICP-OES
4.	Potassium as K_2O	% by mass	ICP/AAS/APHA 21st Ed.
5.	Calcium as CaO	% by mass	ICP/AAS/APHA 21st Ed.
6.	Magnesium as MgO	% by mass	ICP/AAS/APHA 21st Ed.
7.	Iron as Fe_2O_3	% by mass	ICP/AAS/APHA 21st Ed.
8.	Aluminium as Al	% by mass	ICP/AAS/APHA 21st Ed.
9.	Phosphorus as P_2O_5	Mg/kg	ICP/AAS/APHA 21st Ed.

1	2	3	4
10.	Cadmium as Cd	Mg/kg	ICP/AAS/APHA 21st Ed.
11.	Chromium as Cr	Mg/kg	ICP/AAS/APHA 21st Ed.
12.	Zinc as Zn	Mg/kg	ICP/AAS/APHA 21st Ed.
13.	Manganese as Mn	Mg/kg	ICP/AAS/APHA 21st Ed.
14.	Copper as Cu	Mg/kg	ICP/AAS/APHA 21st Ed.
15.	Chloride as Cl	% by mass	Volhard method
16.	Sulphate as SO_4	% by mass	IS: 2720 (Part-27)
17.	Radiation contamination as Cs-137	Bq/kg	AERB Guidelines

Soil pollution results from the buildup of contaminants, toxic compounds, radioactive materials, salts, chemicals and cancer-causing agents. The most common soil pollutants are hydrocarbons, heavy metals (cadmium, lead, chromium, copper, zinc, mercury and arsenic), herbicides, pesticides, oils, tars, PCBs and dioxins.

The intensity of all these causes on a local or regional level might appear very small and you may argue that soil is not harmed by above activities if done on a small scale! However, thinking globally, it is not your region or my place, which will be the only sufferer of soil pollution.

Noise Pollution

Noise pollution is a type of energy pollution in which distracting, irritating, or damaging sounds are freely audible. As with other forms of energy pollution, noise pollution contaminants are not physical particles, but rather waves that interfere with naturally-occurring waves of a similar type in the same environment. Thus, the definition of noise pollution is open to debate, and there is no clear border as to which sounds may constitute noise pollution. In the easiest sense, sounds are considered noise pollution if they adversely affect wildlife, human activity, or are capable of damaging physical structures on a regular, repeating basis.

Table 2.11: Standards for Noise Level in different Countries

Sl.No.	Country	Ind. Area Day/Night	Comm. Area, Day/Night	Residential Area Day/ Night	Silent Area Day/ Night
1.	Australia	65/55	55/45	45/35	45/35
2.	India	75/70	65/55	55/45	50/40
3.	Japan	60/50	60/50	50/60	45/35
4.	U.S. (E.P.A.)	70/60	60/50	55/45	45/35
5.	WHO (E.C.)	65	55	55/45	45/35

Effect of Noise on Human Health

Noise health effects are both health and behavioral in nature. The unwanted sound is called noise. This unwanted sound can damage physiological and psychological health. Noise pollution can cause annoyance and aggression, hypertension, high stress levels, tinnitus, hearing loss, sleep disturbances, and other harmful effects. Furthermore, stress and hypertension are the leading causes to health problems, whereas tinnitus can lead to forgetfulness, severe depression and at times panic attacks. Chronic exposure to noise may cause noise-induced hearing loss. Older males exposed to significant occupational noise demonstrate significantly reduced hearing sensitivity than their non-exposed peers, though differences in hearing sensitivity decrease with time and the two groups are indistinguishable by age 79. A comparison of Maaban tribesmen, who were insignificantly exposed to transportation or industrial noise, to a typical U.S. population showed that chronic exposure to moderately high levels of environmental noise contributes to hearing loss.

High noise levels can contribute to cardiovascular effects and exposure to moderately high levels during a single eight hour period causes a statistical rise in blood pressure of five to ten points and an increase in stress and vasoconstriction leading to the increased blood pressure noted above as well as to increased incidence of coronary artery disease. Noise pollution is also a cause of annoyance (Sangal, 2002).

Environmental protection is a practice of protecting the environment, on individual, organizational or governmental level, for the benefit of the natural environment and humans. Due to the pressures of population and our technology the biophysical environment is being degraded, sometimes permanently. This has been recognized and governments began placing restraints on activities that caused environmental degradation. Since the 1960s activism by the environmental movement has created awareness of the various environmental issues. There is not a full agreement on the extent of the environmental impact of human activity and protection measures are occasionally criticized.

For environmental protection to become a reality it will be important for societies to develop each of these areas that together will inform and drive environmental decisions. Although environmental protection is not simply the role of government agencies they are however generally seen as being of prime importance in establishing and maintaining basic standards that protect both the environment and the people interacting with it.

Environmental ethics should be created among the industrialists, workers and the inhabitants for feel responsibilities to maintain, preserve, protection and healthy environment through sustainable, holistic environment friendly activities.

REFERENCE

Bharti, Pawan K. (2004): Limnological study of Sahastradhara hill-stream, Dehradun, M.Sc. Thesis, *Gurukula Kangri University, Hardwar, India.* pp: 102.

Bharti, Pawan Kr. (2007a): Why are Indian standards not so strict?, *Current Science*, 93(9): 1202.

Bharti, P.K. (2007b): Effect of textile industrial effluents on ground water and soil quality in Panipat region (Haryana), Ph. D. thesis, *Gurukula Kangri University*, Hardwar, India. pp: 191.

Bharti, Pawan K. (2012a): Hill-stream Ecology, *Biotech Books*, Delhi, pp: 246.

Bharti, Pawan K. (2012b): Groundwater Pollution, *Biotech Books*, Delhi, pp: 243.

http://www.lenntech.com

http://www.who.in

Kataria, H.C.; Gupta, S.S. and Jain, O.P. (1995): Water quality of bore wells in B.H.E.L. area of Bhopal, *Poll. Res.* 14 (4): 455-462.

Kumar, P.; Singh, V. and Bharti, P.K. (2012): Environmental Pollution, In: Environmental Pollution and Biodiversity (Eds.- Bharti, P.K; Chauhan, A. and Kumar, P.), Discovery Publishing House, Delhi, pp: 326.

Lokeshwari, H., and Chandrappa, G.T. (2006): Imapct of heavy metal contamination of Bellandur lake on soil and cultivated vegetation. *Current Science*, 91(5), pp: 622-27.

Odum, E.P. (1971): Fundamentals of Ecology. *W.B. Saunders and Co.* New York.

Ward, N.I. (1995): In: Environmental analytical chemistry-Trace elements. (Eds.- F.W. Fifield, and P.J. Haines.), *Blackie Academic and Professional*, UK, pp: 320-328.

Sangal, P.P. (2002): Little noise about noise pollution, Financial Daily from THE HINDU group of publications, Oct. 08, 2002.

3

Hydro-geochemical Evaluation of the Groundwater Sustainability in and around Weishui Campus of Chang'an University, Xi'an, China

— *Li Peiyue, China*
— *Qian Hui, China*

ABSTRACT

The domestic water supply in the Weishui Campus of Chang'an University is disrupted from time to time by the incidents such as water pipe spilt occurring in the city construction process. To solve the problem, the director of the university has decided to construct one its own water supply well. The present study investigated the possibility of building a new well from the point of view of groundwater quality in the area. The groundwater protection strategies for safe water supply were also provided in the paper. The study shows that it is possible to dig and construct a new well in the campus from the water quality point of view. The well should be constructed at the selected well location and use the lower confined aquifer as the water source.

The comprehensive assessment results show that the groundwater quality near the campus is generally suitable for domestic uses and the factors influencing water quality are F^-, NH_4^+, SO_4^{2-}, Mn, total dissolved solid (TDS) and total hardness (TH). The entire area was divided into three sub-zones and the campus belongs to the fair quality zone. During the well construction, the standard construction process and the necessary requirements by the related regulations must be met and some human activities should also be regulated after the well is constructed.

Key words: *groundwater, hydrogeochemistry, groundwater pollution, safe water supply, groundwater suitability, groundwater quality.*

Introduction

Groundwater, as an essential resource for human beings and various animals and plants, is regarded as the most reliable and important source for fresh water supply in many countries and regions where surface water is scarce (Delgado et al. 2010; Ravikumar et al. 2011). However, groundwater pollution is becoming more and more serious in many parts of the world due to the ever growing population, extensive human activities, rapid industrialization and uncontrolled urban expansion etc (Reza and Singh 2010; Li et al. 2010; Jamshidzadeh and Mirbagheri 2011). Hydrogeochemical evaluation of groundwater quality provides instructions and suggestions for groundwater quality control, management and protection. Furthermore, it is also the basis for safe water supply which is close with residents' health. Numerous studies concentrated on groundwater quality evaluation for domestic use have been carried out over the globe. Nagarajan et al. (2010) and Jain et al. (2010) carried out a research on the groundwater quality assessment for drinking and agricultural usage in Thanjavur city and District Nainital, India, respectively. Al-Ruwaih et al. (2010) determined the best blending ratios in the blending plants of Kuwait for getting the best quality of drinking water according to the WHO guidelines. Li et al. (2011) proposed a method based on rough sets reduction and TOPSIS for water quality assessment. A study conducted by Li and Qian (2011) also focused on the human health risk related with drinking groundwater in a local area of China. The work conducted by these researchers is important for groundwater quality protection and groundwater management in those areas.

The Weishui Campus of Chang'an University, located in the northwest of Xi'an City, China, is a newly constructed campus in 2003. Its domestic water mainly relies on the water supply from the Weibin Water Source of the Xi'an Water Supply Company. In recent years, with the rapid development of the northern suburb of Xi'an, construction sites in various size can be seen everywhere. Because the area is currently under development and construction, such incidents as water pipe spilt during the construction process will directly affect the normal water supply in the Weishui Campus of Chang'an University. The losses can be very great when the number of students has reached over 20 thousand. Therefore, to meet their urgent needs, the director of the university has decided to dig and construct one its own water supply well in its campus in case of such emergency. However, the area has been irrigated by contaminated water from the Weihe River for a long time, which has caused the shallow groundwater pollution and the shallow groundwater quality can not meet the domestic requirements.

This research was carried out to assess the groundwater quality and to provide the theoretic basis for the well location identification and well construction. The study will answer the following two questions:

(1) From the water quality point of view, is it proper and possible to dig and construct a well in the campus area at the selected well location? If possible, which aquifer should be used for water supply?

(2) When the well is constructed, how should it be operated and assist the Water Supply Company to meet the daily water consumption requirement and what kind of measures should be taken to protect the water quality?

Study Area

Location

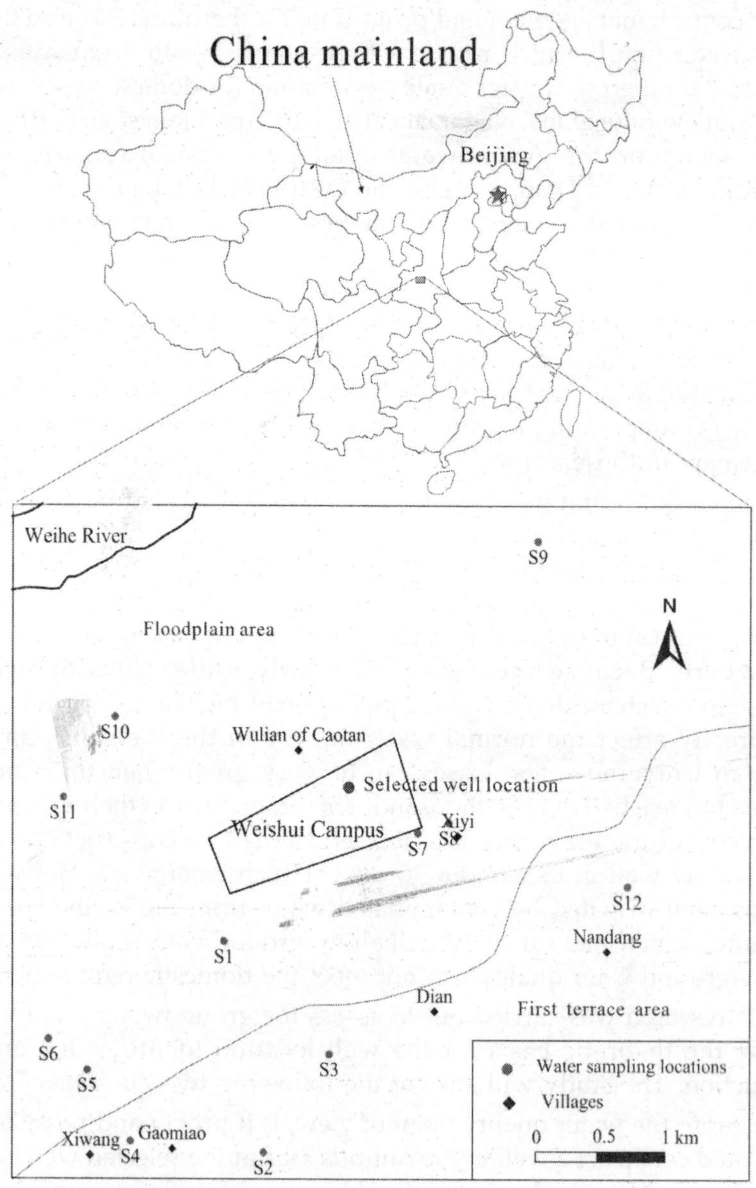

Fig. 3.1. Location of the Study Area

The total study area is 30 km^2, which ranges from 108°522 283 E to 108°562 173 E and from 34°202 573 N to 34°232 353 N (Figure 1). The Weishui Campus of Chang'an University is located in the middle of the study area which is about 30 km away from the center of Xi'an city. The Weishui Campus of Chang'an University, located in the floodplain area of the Weihe River, is about 1.13×10^6 m^2. There are more than 20 thousand students living and studying here currently.

The landforms in the study area can be generally divided into three regions (Figure 1). In the northwest pole of the study area, the Weihe River runs across from southwest to northeast, and it is about 2 km away from the Weishui Campus. In the middle part where the Weishui Campus located is the floodplain area formed by the Weihe River. The floodplain area is about 4 km wide. The first terrace area is adjacent to the floodplain area in the southeast, and many villages are located in the first terrace area. The study area is flat and the elevation ranges from the 375.2 m to 370.2 m above mean sea level with a gradient of about 0.06%.

Xi'an belongs to the warm semi-humid continental monsoon climate zone with four distinct seasons. Summer is hot and rainy, winter is cold and dry, spring and autumn is cool with moderate rainfall. The annually average temperature is about 13.3!, the coldest month is January with an average temperature of -0.9!, and the hottest month is July with an average temperature of 26.4!. The extreme minimum temperature is -20.6! occurred on January 11th, 1995, and the extreme maximum temperature is 43.4 ! on June 19th, 1966. The annual rainfall is 558-750 mm, and increases from north to south. The seasonal distribution of rainfall is uneven. Seventy eight percent of the rainfall concentrates in May to October, and the rainfall in July to September accounts for 47% of annual rainfall.

Hydrogeology

Influenced by the sinking of the crust and river flood, thick deposits with sand and clay have been deposited since the Pleistocene of the Quaternary. Vertically, Clay-like layers form impermeable layers and sands form aquifers. The aquifers are composed of sands and gravels from the Holocene, Pleistocene and the middle Pleistocene. Based on the depth, three aquifers are classified, namely, the phreatic aquifer, upper confined aquifer and the lower confined aquifer. The general characteristics of the three aquifers can be outlined as follows:

(1) **Phreatic aquifer**: The phreatic aquifer is formed by river in the Holocene and the Pleistocene periods and its lithology is sand and gravel. The aquifer is thick with shallow groundwater level. The depth to water table is less than 10 m, and the hydraulic conductivity is typically 10-30 m/d. Water chemistry type is usually HCO_3·SO_4·Cl-Na·Ca type with salinity higher than 0.9 g/L.

(2) **The confined aquifers**: The confined aquifers are formed by alluvial deposits, too. The lithology of the confined aquifers is characterized by fine, medium and coarse sand or gravels. General depth of the upper confined aquifer is 75-170 m, and the depth of the lower confined aquifer is 180-300 m. Hydrochemical type in the upper confined aquifer is HCO_3-Na with salinity of 0.5-0.6 g/L, and in the lower confined aquifer the HCO_3-Na type with salinity of 0.25-0.5 g/L is prevalent.

Materials and Methods

Sample Collection and Physiochemical Analysis

A total of 12 groundwater samples were collected for the research and two were from phreatic aquifer and 10 were from confined aquifers. The sampling locations were shown in Figure 1. S1 and S8 were phreatic water, being

Table 3.1 : Chemical Index of Groundwater Samples

Sample No.	S1	S8	S2	S3	S4	S12	S5	S6	S7	S9	S10	S11
Landforms	Floodplain		First terrace		Floodplain							
Aquifers	Phreatic aquifer		Confined aquifer									
K^+	5.77	7.16	0.22	0.26	0.28	0.27	0.48	0.81	0.73	0.31	0.42	0.86
Na^+	177.29	147.62	83.05	69.73	52.67	91.24	52.67	56.38	57.86	48.22	56.38	88.27
Ca^{2+}	139.64	55.23	6.25	11.46	13.55	11.46	35.64	38.56	27.82	10.42	18.24	34.91
Mg^{2+}	68.58	84.7	1.26	2.21	3.48	1.9	10.62	41.4	11.25	4.11	6.32	42.03
Fe	**0.61**	**0.4**	0.04	0.08	0.04	0.04	**0.69**	0.23	0.1	0.04	0.1	0.21
NH_4^+	**2.4**	**1.45**	**0.35**	**0.43**	**0.44**	0.09	0.16	0.12	0.13	0.12	0.04	0.2
Cl^-	165.46	128.23	21.37	11.03	8.27	20.68	16.55	33.78	14.48	7.58	12.82	60.67
SO_4^{2-}	**282.15**	176.66	22.02	12.55	8.84	18.52	16.46	47.12	21.19	7.82	15.23	67.71
HCO_3^-	516.09	524.47	182.64	179.29	152.82	207.78	227.88	328.42	213.47	130.03	175.94	320.04
CO_3^{2-}	41.2	11.54	13.18	13.18	8.9	14.83	14.83	21.42	18.13	18.13	11.54	29.66
NO_3^-	0.85	3	0	0	0	0.68	1.36	0.58	0	0	0.72	0
NO_2^-	0	0	0	0	0	0.01	0.01	0.05	0.01	0	0	0
F^-	0.69	0.55	**1.9**	**1.43**	**1.08**	**1.61**	0.56	0.4	0.69	0.65	0.61	0.44
Pb	<0.05	<0.05	<0.05	<0.05	<0.05	<0.05	<0.05	<0.05	<0.05	<0.05	<0.05	<0.05
Cd	<0.01	<0.01	<0.01	<0.01	<0.01	<0.01	<0.01	<0.01	<0.01	<0.01	<0.01	<0.01
Mn	**1.1**	**0.8**	0.03	0.04	0.03	0.02	0.09	0.06	0.1	0.04	0.01	0.06
As	<0.05	<0.05	<0.05	<0.05	<0.05	<0.05	<0.05	<0.05	<0.05	<0.05	<0.05	<0.05
Cr^{6+}	0.02	0.01	0.01	0.01	0.01	0.01	0.01	0.01	0.01	0.01	0.01	0.01
H_2SiO_3	25.87	17.73	15.73	16.51	1.85	15.18	16.93	17.5	16.47	17.5	17.03	16.46
TDS	**1202**	942	273	297	269	258	292	444	269	226	227	535
TH	**631.07**	**486.64**	20.82	37.73	48.14	36.43	132.71	266.74	115.8	42.94	71.56	260.23
pH	**8.61**	7.44	8	8.1	8.06	8.32	7.83	7.73	8	8.06	7.95	7.84

Note: The numbers in bold are values beyond the permissible limits of the drinking water standard of China.

located to the west and east, respectively, S2, S3, S4 and S12 were confined water collected from the first terrace area within depth of 180-280 m and S5, S6, S7, S9, S10 and S11 were confined water collected in the floodplain area of Weihe River within the depth of 150-210 m. All the samples were collected in white plastic bottles and the sampling method, sampling procedures and the conservation were done following the standards (APHA 2005). The samples were analyzed by the laboratory of School of Environmental Science and Engineering, Chang'an University. The indices analyzed include pH, sodium (Na^+), potassium (K^+), calcium (Ca^{2+}), magnesium (Mg^{2+}), carbonate (CO_3^{2-}), bicarbonate (HCO_3^-), chloride (Cl^-), sulphate (SO_4^{2-}), phosphate, chemical oxygen demand (COD), total dissolved solid (TDS), total hardness (TH), nitrate (NO_3^-), nitrite (NO_2^-), ammonium (NH_4^+), fluoride (F^-), total iron (Tfe), color, arsenic (As), manganese (Mn) and chromium (Cr^{6+}), etc. The results of theses analyzed indices are listed in Table 1.

Methods

As per the Quality Standard for Groundwater (GB/T14848-93, Bureau of Quality and Technical Supervision of China 1994), the groundwater is classified into five grades: excellent (Grade I), good (Grade II), fair (Grade III), poor (Grade IV), and polluted (Grade V). The standard is listed in Table 2.

Table 3.2: Standards of Groundwater Quality of China

Sl.No.	Items	Standard values				
		Grade I	Grade II	Grade III	Grade IV	Grade V
1.	pH	6.5-8.5	6.5-8.5	6.5-8.5	5.5-6.5, 8.5-9	<5.5, >9
2.	Total hardness (as $CaCO_3$) (mg/L)	≤150	d'300	d'450	d'550	>550
3.	TDS (mg/L)	≤300	≤500	≤1000	≤2000	>2000
4.	Sulfate (mg/L)	≤50	≤150	≤250	≤350	>350
5.	Chloride (mg/L)	≤50	≤150	≤250	≤350	>350
6.	Fe (mg/L)	≤0.1	≤0.2	≤0.3	≤1.5	>1.5
7.	Mn (mg/L)	≤0.05	≤0.05	≤0.1	≤1.0	>1.0
8.	Nitrate(as N) (mg/L)	≤2.0	≤5.0	≤20	≤30	>30
9.	Nitrite(as N) (mg/L)	≤0.001	≤0.01	≤0.02	≤0.1	>0.1
10.	NH_4 (mg/L)	≤0.02	≤0.02	≤0.2	≤0.5	>0.5
11.	Fluoride (mg/L)	≤1.0	≤1.0	≤1.0	≤2.0	>2.0
12.	As (mg/L)	≤0.005	≤0.01	≤0.05	≤0.05	>0.05
13.	Cd (mg/L)	≤0.0001	≤0.001	≤0.01	≤0.01	>0.01
14.	Cr^{6+} (mg/L)	≤0.005	≤0.01	≤0.05	≤0.1	>0.1
15.	Pb (mg/L)	≤0.005	≤0.01	≤0.05	≤0.1	>0.1

- Grade I: The water samples with excellent quality represent the natural low background and they are suitable for all uses.
- Grade II: The water samples with good quality represent the natural background and they are suitable for all uses.
- Grade III: The water with fair quality can be used for drinking, irrigation, and industrial production.
- Grade IV: The poor quality water is mainly used for irrigation and industrial production, and may be used as drinking water after proper treatment.
- Grade V: The polluted water is not suitable for drinking, and can be used for other uses partially.

The Quality Standard for Groundwater is the basic guidance to classify and evaluate the quality of groundwater in China (Li et al. 2009). The assessment procedures are as follows:

(1) According to the standard and the various observed index values of the samples, for a given water sample j (j=1, 2, 3, ..., m), the ith (i=1, 2, 3, ..., n) index of sample j will be assign a evaluation value according to Table 3.

Table 3.3: Evaluation values of single indices

Grade	I	II	III	IV	V
F_{ij}	0	1	3	6	10

(2) To comprehensively assess the quality of water sample j, the comprehensive evaluation value will be calculated according to formulas (1) and (2).

$$F_j = \sqrt{\frac{\overline{F}_{ij}^2 + \overline{\overline{F}}_{ij}^2}{2}} \quad (i = 1, 2, 3, \ldots, n) \tag{1}$$

$$\overline{F}_{ij} = \frac{1}{n}\sum_{i=1}^{n} F_{ij} \quad (i = 1, 2, 3, \ldots, n) \tag{2}$$

Where,

F_j The comprehensive evaluation value of sample j,

F_{ij} The evaluation value of ith index of the jth water sample

$\overline{F}_{ij}$ The average value of F_{ij} for n indices of the jth water sample

$\overline{\overline{F}}_{ij}$ The maximum value of F_{ij} for n indices of the jth water sample

n The numbers of index for sample j

(3) Based on the calculated comprehensive evaluation value, the groundwater quality is classified according to Table 4.

Table 3.4: Standards of Groundwater Quality Classification

Grade	Excellent	Good	Fair	Poor	Polluted
F_j	$F_j < 0.8$	$0.8 < F_j \leq 2.50$	$2.50 < F_j \leq 4.25$	$4.25 < F_j \leq 7.20$	$F_j > 7.20$

Results and Discussion

General Groundwater Quality

It can be seen from the Table 1 that the phreatic water in the study area has already been contaminated to some degree. The concentrations of NH_4^+, F^-, Mn, Fe and TH are beyond the permissible limits of drinkingwater standard of China. Besides, the SO_4^{2-} and TDS in S1 are also beyond the permissible limits. Therefore, it can be concluded that the phreatic water is not suitable for drinking purpose.

Table 1 also shows an obvious difference between samples from different landforms. The indices contents of samples collected from the confined aquifers of the first terrace are all within the permissible limits of the standard of China except F^- and NH_4^+ contents. The F^- contents of the four samples collected from the first terrace all exceed the permissible limit (1.0 mg/L), and the highest is 1.9 mg/L, the lowest is 1.08 mg/L. The maximum value of NH_4^+ is 0.44 mg/L which is over 2 times higher than the permissible limit (0.2 mg/L). Three of four samples are exceeding the permissible limit regarding to NH_4^+. On the contrary, F^- and NH_4^+ contents in the 12 samples collected from the floodplain area, within the ranges of 0.4-0.69 mg/L and 0.04-0.2 mg/L, respectively, are within the permissible limits. However, the Fe content in S5 is a little beyond the permissible limit, which may affect the water quality near the selected well location. Overall, in all samples collected from the confined aquifers, the concentrations of all indices except the indices discussed above are within the limits of the drinking water standard.

Hydrochemical concepts can help to elucidate mechanisms of flow and transport in groundwater systems, and unlock an archive of pale environmental information (Vasanthavigar 2010). In this research, A Piper diagram (Piper 1953) was used to infer hydrogeochemical facies of groundwater (Figure 2). It can be seen from the diagram that the two phreatic water samples are $HCO_3{\cdot}SO_4{\cdot}Cl$ type water with respect to anions, and the confined water samples are HCO_3 type. For the cations, Na takes a big portion and Mg and Ca only take a small portion. It can be inferred from the diagram that the groundwater type is mainly determined by Na and HCO_3 contents.

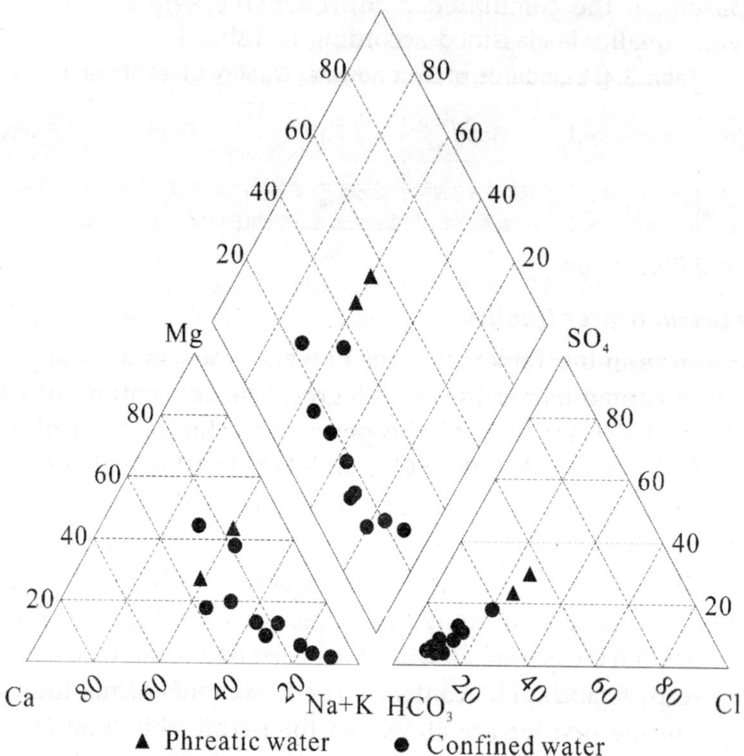

Fig. 3.2. Piper Diagram for Groundwater Samples

Groundwater Quality Comprehensive Assessment

The groundwater quality was assessed using the method introduced in the paper, and the results were shown in Table 5. It can be seen from Table 5 that the two phreatic water samples (S1 and S8) are both classified into polluted water category which indicates that they are unsuitable for human drinking and the samples (S2, S3, S4, and S12) collected from the first terrace area are poor water with the calculated comprehensive evaluation value higher than 4.25. It can also be seen from the table that the poor quality is mainly attributed to some indices classified into grade IV which assigns them a value of 6. This can be proved by the comparison of S5 and S11. The average value of single index ($\overline{F}_{ij}$) for S11 is bigger than that for S5, but the maximum value ($\overline{\overline{F}}_{ij}$) is only 3 for S11, which makes the final result (F_j) is 2.303, being good water quality. On the other hand, the maximum value for S5 is 6, and the final result is 4.309, being poor quality. It can be inferred from the results that the comprehensive assessment results are influenced to a large degree by the most seriously polluted indices. All confined water samples collected from the floodplain area where the campus located, except S5, are good quality water which is suitable for human drinking.

Table 3.5: Results of Groundwater Quality Comprehensive Assessment

Landforms	Aquifers	Sample No.	Numbers of index used for assessment	$\overline{F}_{ij}$	$\overline{\overline{F}}_{ij}$	F_i	Grade	Water quality
Floodplain	Phreatic	S1	15	4.333	10	7.706	V	Polluted water
Floodplain	Phreatic	S8	15	2.600	10	7.306	V	Polluted water
First terrace	Confined	S2	15	1.067	6	4.309	IV	Poor water
First terrace	Confined	S3	15	1.067	6	4.309	IV	Poor water
First terrace	Confined	S4	15	1.067	6	4.309	IV	Poor water
First terrace	Confined	S12	15	1.067	6	4.309	IV	Poor water
Floodplain	Confined	S5	15	1.067	6	4.309	IV	Poor water
Floodplain	Confined	S6	15	1.000	3	2.236	II	Good water
Floodplain	Confined	S7	15	0.667	3	2.173	II	Good water
Floodplain	Confined	S9	15	0.667	3	2.173	II	Good water
Floodplain	Confined	S10	15	0.667	3	2.173	II	Good water
Floodplain	Confined	S11	15	1.267	3	2.303	II	Good water

A map showing the distribution of groundwater quality in confined aquifers was illustrated in Figure 3. It can be seen that the whole study area

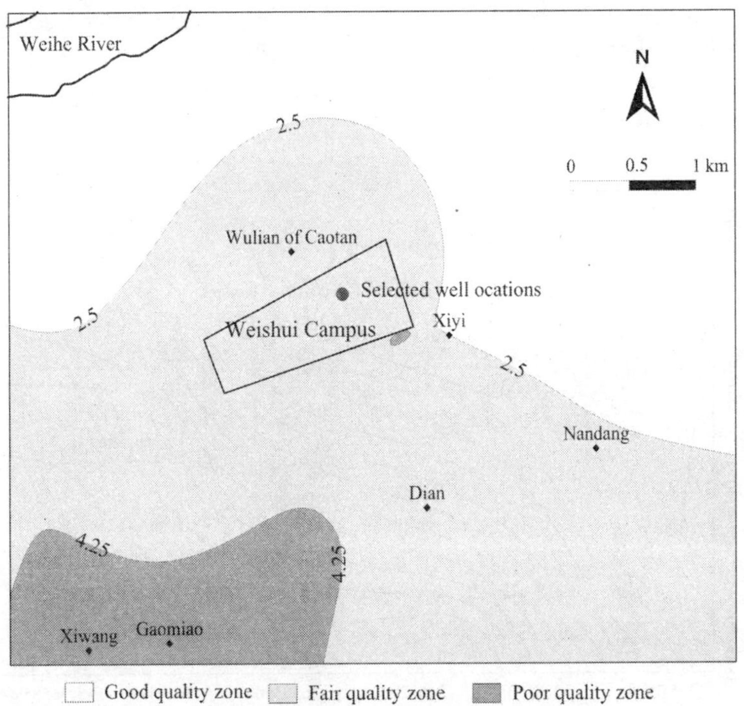

Fig. 3.3: Distribution of Groundwater Quality

can be divided into three sub-zones, good quality zone, fair quality zone and poor quality zone. The poor water zone distributes on the southwest of the area locally, the good quality zone distributes in the north part of the study area, and the middle zone where the Weishui Campus located belongs to fair quality zone. The poor quality for the water samples in the first terrace is caused by the F^- and NH_4^+ contents, because only F^- and NH_4^+ contents are beyond the permissible limits in the samples. The poor quality in S5 is deemed to be caused by the excessive Fe content. That is to say, as long as one index is beyond the permissible limit, the water quality will be classified into grade c! or worse according to the comprehensive results.

Groundwater Quality at the Selected well Location

It is our most concern that how the confined water quality is at the selected well location. To predict the water quality at the well location, several contour maps were drawn to show the spatial distribution of concerned indices including NH_4^+, F^-, Fe, SO_4^{2-}, TDS and TH. These maps are shown in Figure 4 to Figure 9. It can be seen from Figure 4 that F^- content shows an increase tendency southeastwards, and the predicted concentration of F^- at the selected well location is about 0.65 mg/L which is within the permissible limit of the standard. The Fe content is beyond the permissible limit in the southwest of the study area and shows a decrease trend from southwest to northeast. At

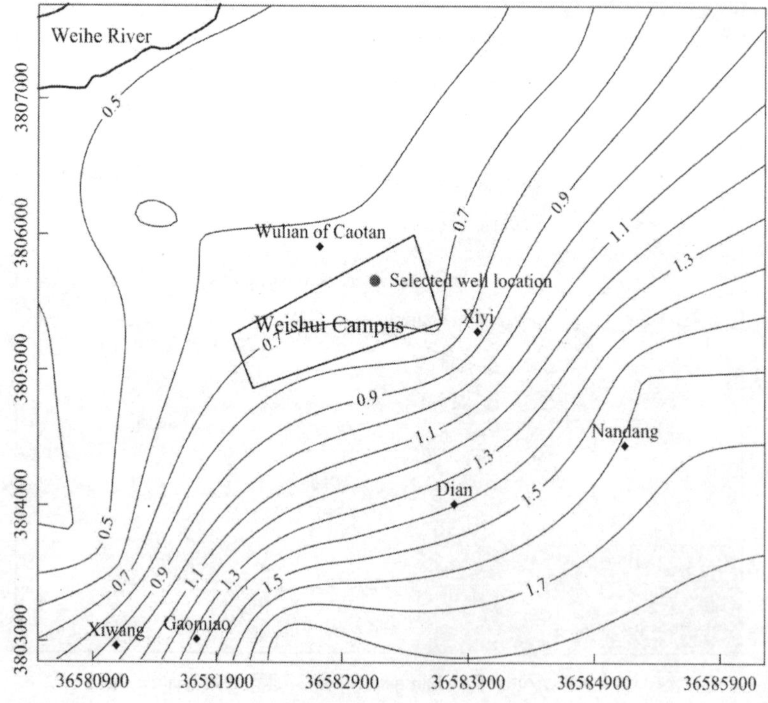

Fig. 3.4. Map of F^- distributions

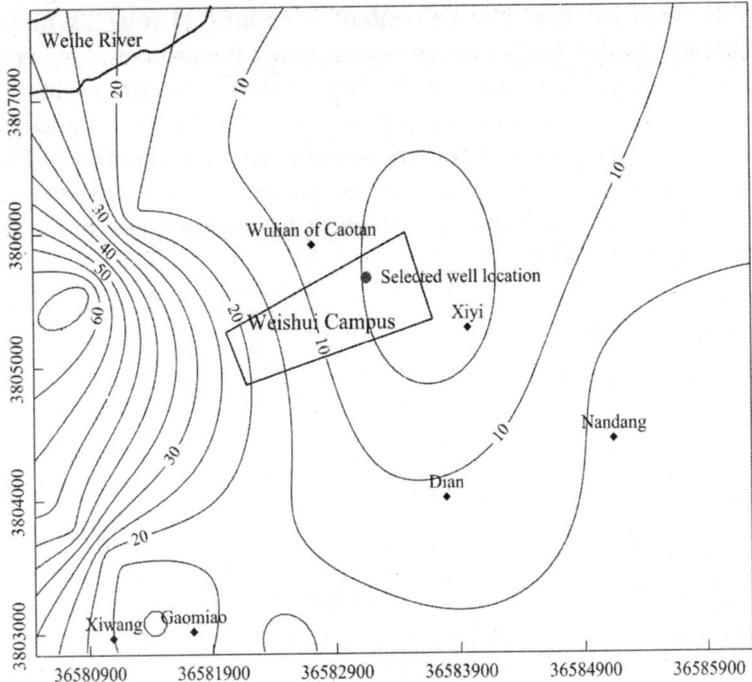

Fig. 3.5. Map of Fe distributions

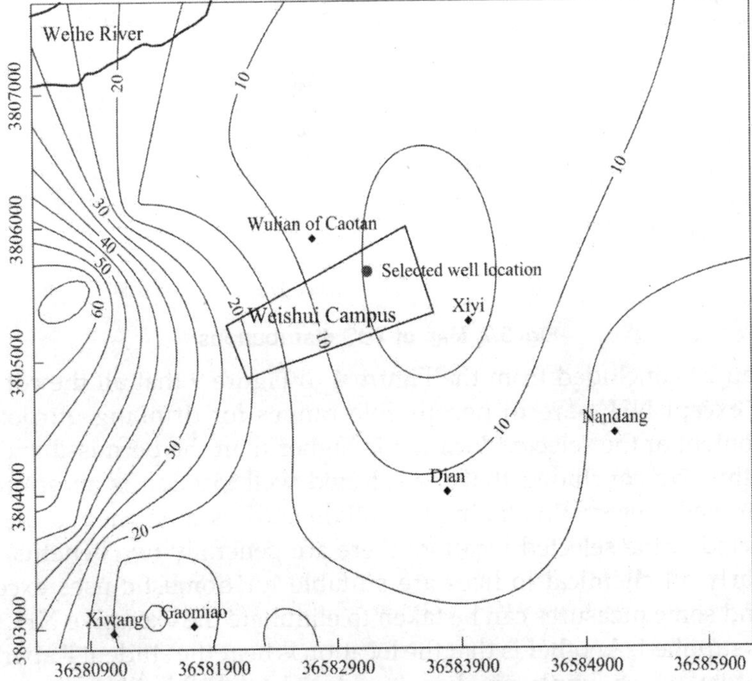

Fig. 3.6. Map of SO_4^{2-} distributions

the selected well location, the Fe content is about 0.11 mg/L which is well below the permissible limit. Figure 6 shows that the predicted concentration of SO_4^{2-} at the selected location is 5.0 mg/L and is acceptable for drinking purpose. The TDS and TH contents predicted from Figures 7 and 8 are 265 and 95 mg/L, respectively. They are suitable for domestic uses. However, the NH_4^+ content showed in Figure 9 is not suitable for drinking, because the predicted value from Figure 9 at the selected location is 0.36 mg/L which is beyond the permissible limit.

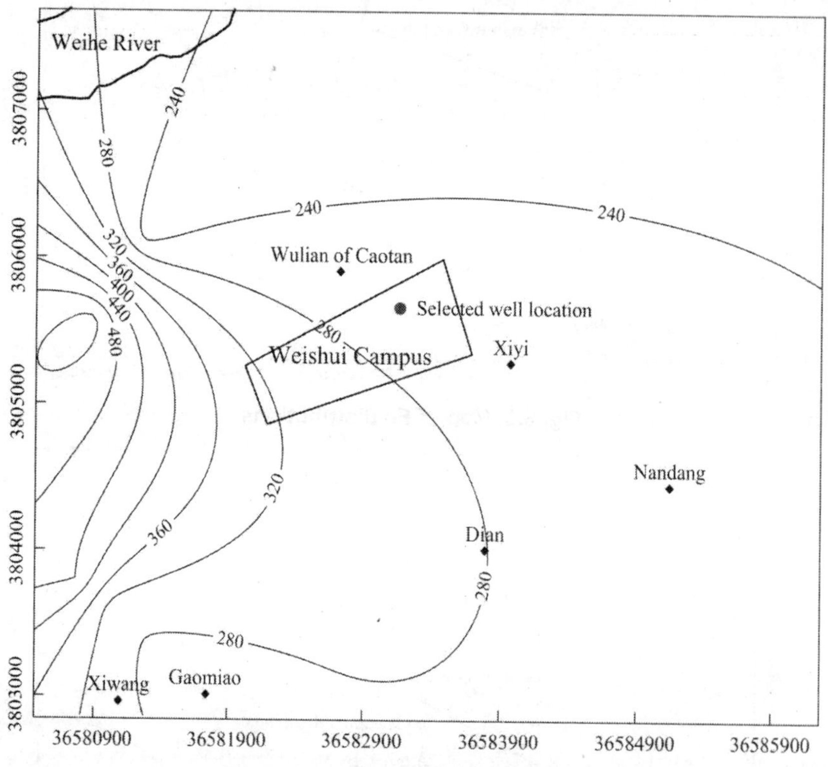

Fig. 3.7. Map of TDS distributions

It can be concluded from the Figure 4 to Figure 9 that all the concerned indices except NH_4^+ are in permissible ranges for drinking purpose. The NH_4^+ content at the selected location is higher than the permissible limit. In spit of this, we concluded that the selected well location is an appropriate place for well construction taking into all the indices concerned. If the well is constructed at the selected location, there are generally two benefits. One is that nearly all chemical indices are suitable for domestic uses except the NH_4^+ and some measures can be taken to eliminate the excessive NH_4^+ when water is supplied. Another is that the location is near the students' apartments and the total water supply pipelines are shortest, which will be economically beneficial.

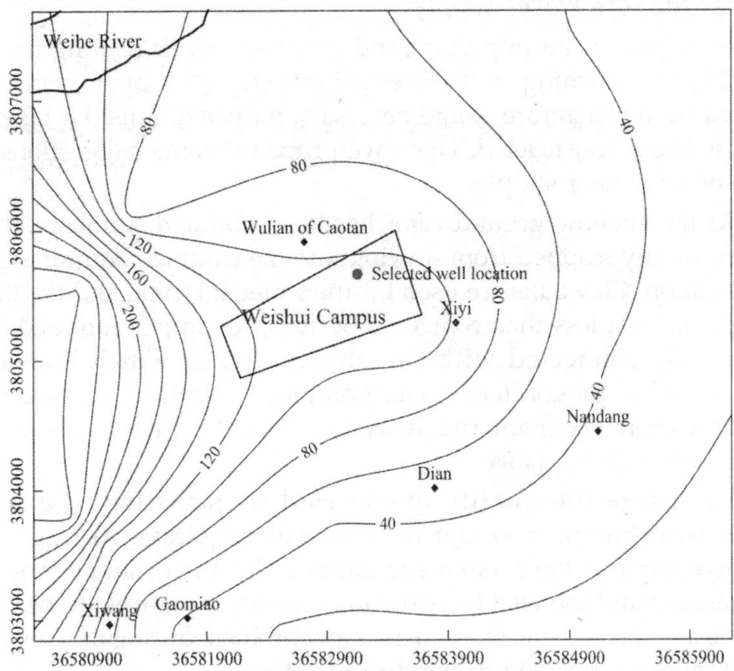

Fig. 3.8. Map of TH distributions

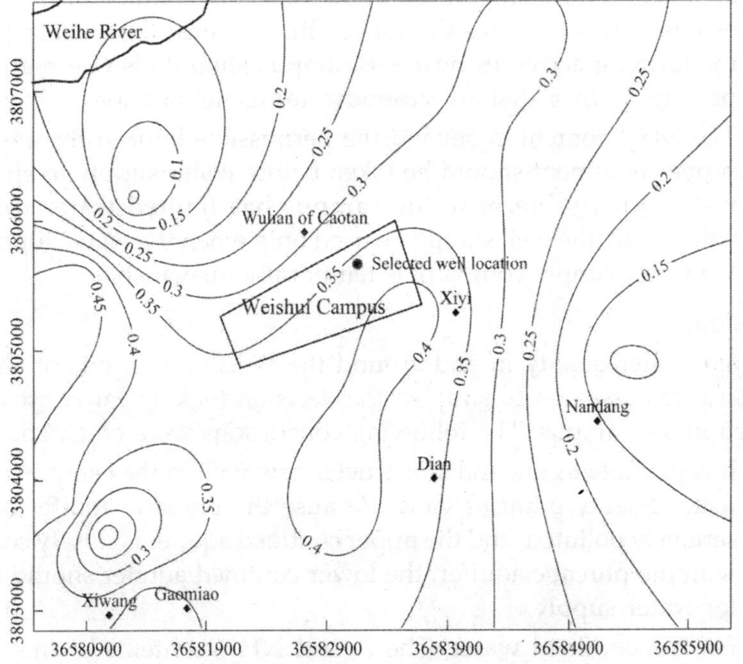

Fig. 3.9. Map of NH_4^+ distributions

Strategies for Safe Water Supply

Safe water supply is an important and necessary work relating the normal campus life and teaching, and the emotional stabilities of students are also influenced by it. Therefore, some necessary measures must be taken when the well is being constructed. Here, we proposed some suggestions for the purpose of safe water supply.

- As the shallow groundwater has been polluted seriously, it should be strictly stopped from flowing into the confined aquifer at the well location. Clay balls are used for the water stopping and the thickness should not less than 8 meters. Besides, the upper confined water is closely connected with the phreatic water which increases the possibility for confined water pollution. Therefore, the water should be extracted from the lower confined aquifer to ensure the groundwater quality.
- To ensure the quality of the well construction, the standard construction process and the necessary requirements must be done according to the related regulations. All the original construction records and the well construction report are required to be accurate, clear and complete. Once there is any problem during the construction, it must be reported to the director at once.
- After the well is constructed, groundwater quality protection must be taken into consideration. In the range of 50 m, no latrines should be built, and no wastes should be pilled up near the well. In addition, the farming activities near the campus should also be regulated to prevent further shallow groundwater contamination.
- The NH_4^+ content is beyond the permissible limit in the area, some proper treatment should be taken before water supply to ensure the water quality. Because the campus has limited water treatment equipment, the well should be used only when the water supply from the water supply company is temporally unavailable.

Conclusions

The groundwater quality in and around the Weishui Campus of Chang'an University was assessed to support the decision making for constructing a new well in the campus. The following conclusions were obtained.

(1) It is possible to dig and construct a new well in the campus from the water quality point of view. Because the phreatic aquifer has been seriously polluted, and the upper confined aquifer is closely connected with the phreatic aquifer, the lower confined aquifer should be used for water supply.

(2) For the confined water, The F^- and NH_4^+ contents of the samples collected from the first terrace area exceed the permissible limits,

while their contents are within the permissible limits in the samples collected from the floodplain area. Fe content in S5 is a little beyond the permissible limit, which may affect the water quality near the selected well location.

(3) The comprehensive water quality assessment results show that the phreatic water has been contaminated and can not be used for water supply. The entire study area can be divided into three sub-zones, good quality zone, fair quality zone and poor quality zone according to the water quality assessment results of confined water. Weishui Campus is located in the fair quality zone. The groundwater quality at the selected location is generally fit for domestic uses and the location is an appropriate place for well construction taking into all the indices concerned.

(4) Some strategies for groundwater quality protection and safe water supply were provided. During the well construction, the standard construction process and the necessary requirements must be done according to the related regulations. Some human activities should also be regulated after the well is constructed.

Acknowledgement

The research was supported by the National Natural Science Foundation of China (40772160). The authors are thankful to Prof. Yang S K for his assistance in laboratory experiments, and the anonymous referees are also highly acknowledged for their useful comments on the original manuscript.

REFERENCES

APHA (2005) Standard methods for the examination of water and wastewater (21st edition). American Public Health Association, Washington.

Al-Ruwaih FM, Alhumoud JM and Al-Mutairi SM (2010) Quality of Potable Water in Kuwait. American Journal of Environmental Sciences 6 (3): 260-267.

Bureau of Quality and Technical Supervision of China (1994) National Standard of the People's Republic of China: Quality Standard for Groundwater, GB/T 14848-93.

Delgado C, Pacheco J, Cabrera A, Batllori E, Orellana R, and Bautista F (2010) Quality of groundwater for irrigation in tropical karst environment: The case of Yucatán, Mexico. Agricultural Water Management 97: 1423-1433. DOI: 10.1016/j.agwat.2010.04.006

Jamshidzadeh Z and Mirbagheri SA (2011) Evaluation of groundwater quantity and quality in the Kashan Basin, Central Iran. Desalination 270: 23-30. DOI: 10.1016/j.desal.2010.10.067

Jain CK, Bandyopadhyay A and Bhadra A (2010) Assessment of ground water quality for drinking purpose, District Nainital, Uttarakhand, India. Environ Monit Assess 166: 663–676. DOI: 10.1007/s10661-009-1031-5

Li PY, Qian H and Wu JH (2010) Groundwater Quality Assessment Based on Improved Water Quality Index in Pengyang County, Ningxia, Northwest China. E-J Chem 7(S1): S209-S216.

Li PY and Qian H (2011) Human health risk assessment for chemical pollutants in drinking water source in Shizuishan city, Northwest China. Iranian Journal of Environmental Health Science & Engineering, 8(1): 41-48.

Li PY, Wu JH and Qian H (2011) Groundwater quality assessment based on rough sets attribute reduction and TOPSIS method in a semi-arid area, China. Environ Monit Assess Online first, DOI: 10.1007/s10661-011-2306-1

Li YF, Song GH, Wu YG, Wan WF, Zhang MS and Xu YJ (2009) Evaluation of water quality and protection strategies of waterresources in arid–semiarid climates: a case study in the Yuxi RiverValley of Northern Shaanxi Province, China. Environ Geol 57: 1933-1938. DOI: 10.1007/s00254-008-1483-x

Nagarajan R, Rajmohan N, Mahendran U, Senthamilkumar S (2010) Evaluation of groundwater quality and its suitability for drinking and agricultural use in Thanjavur city, Tamil Nadu, India. Environ Monit Assess 171: 289–308. DOI: 10.1007/s10661-009-1279-9

Piper AM (1953) A Graphic Procedure in the Geochemical Interpretation of Water Analysis. Washington D.C.: United States Geological Survey.

Ravikumar P, Somashekar RK and Angami M (2011) Hydrochemistry and evaluation of groundwater suitability for irrigation and drinking purposes in the Markandeya River basin, Belgaum District, Karnataka State, India. Environ Monit Assess 173: 459-487. DOI: 10.1007/s10661-010-1399-2

Ramakrishnaiah C R, Sadashivaiah C and Ranganna G (2009) Assessment of Water Quality Index for the Groundwater in Tumkur Taluk, Karnataka State, India. E-J Chem 6(2), 523-530.

Reza R and Singh G (2010) Assessment of Ground Water Quality Status by Using Water Quality Index Method in Orissa, India. World Appl Sci J 9 (12): 1392-1397.

Vasanthavigar M., Srinivasamoorthy K., Vijayaragavan K., Rajiv Ganthi R., Chidambaram S., Anandhan P., Manivannan R., and Vasudevan S (2010) Application of water quality index for groundwater quality assessment: Thirumanimuttar sub-basin, Tamilnadu, India. Environ Monit Assess 171, 595-609. DOI: 10.1007/s10661-009-1302-1

4

Impact of dyeing units on Environment and Health Hazards of Dyeing Workers

—*Meenu Srivastava, India*
—*Saroj Palawat, India*

ABSTRACT

The textile industry is the second largest industry in India and India has a long rich tradition of producing variety of textile. Sanganer town and Bagru village situated at Rajasthan, famous for printing and dyeing industries. "Chippa" community has been engaged in dyeing and printing of textiles. At present due to industrialization the textile industries in India are using harmful substance either for enhancing aesthetic appeal or for improving certain desirable characteristics. About more than 8000 chemical substances are used in several textile processes such as sizing bleaching, scouring, dyeing, printing and finishing. A study stated that the industry used about 17 million litres per day of water and about 75% of the effluents is discharged into the Gullar dam near the Sanganer town. Disposal of industrial waste is the major problem responsible for soil and water pollution. An increasing number of these substances is today known or suspected to be harmful to human health as well as the animals, plants, soil and water quality and environment. The present study "Impact of dyeing units on environment and health hazards of dyeing workers of Jaipur district" was conducted in Sanganer and Bagru area of Jaipur district.

Laboratory testing was carried out to assess 15 different parametric like – Odour, Colour, Temperature, pH, TDS, NO_3^-, SO_4^{2-} *and content of other heavy metals like Zn, Cu, Cd, Pb, Ni, Mn, and Fe in soil and water. Sample collected from Bagru and Sanganer area 60 workers comprised of 30 males and 30 females were selected as sample subjects, through purposing sampling technique for assessment of the health status of dyeing workers. Interview cum questionnaire technique was used for collecting desired information about health of the subjects and impact on environment. The data were statistically analyzed through frequencies and percentage.*

The major finding showed that textile dyeing effluents is highly polluting in nature. Almost all parameters in water and soil samples collected form Sanganer exceeds the prescribed limits, therefore it was necessary to treat it properly before discharging it. On the other hand soil sample of Bagru village also exceeds the prescribed limits as for as heavy metals contents were concerned. This affects the vegetative growth of that area. Water sample did not show much deviation although it was found to be slightly acidic in nature.

There was vast difference in health status of the dyeing workers of both Bagru and Sanganer area and in neighborhood community. The study revealed that majority hundred percent of respondents from Sanganer were suffering from different disease like skin, eye, heart, and respiratory problems, while the 80 percent respondents of Bagru were not facing any problems related to health. 70 percent respondents from Bagru and 100 percent of respondents form Sanganer admit that dyeing effluents had adverse effect on other people's health and environment also. Thus the study emphasized the need of waste water minimization, treatment of waste water before disposal, recycling of waste, awareness of common health hazards and problems among textile dyeing workers to take due precautions and safety measures at work place.

Key words: *environment, soil, water, pollution, dye industry, workers, health.*

Introduction

India has a long and rich traditional of producing variety of textiles. The textile industry is the second largest industry, after agriculture in terms of number of person's employed. Rajasthan in famous in India as well as all over world for traditional clothing especially that of women folk, displaying brilliant colours and intricate design printed on it. The famous centre of traditional dyeing & printing in Rajasthan are Sanganer and Bagru village, which have number of industries providing employment to about 3000 families. The chippa community has been engaged in dyeing and printing of textiles. Different dyes are being used on silk and cotton material. Dye units release a large amount of waste water during printing and dyeing process. This waste water causes ground water pollution besides causing a number of adverse effects an agriculture products, animals, and health of the people in that areas. Rough estimate is that 70% of water becomes waste. The waste water contains not only a large amount of colour, but also organic compounds, nitrogen compounds as well as salt and heavy metals. Disposal of industrial waste is the major problem causing soil pollution. The use of polluted ground water for irrigation of agriculture field severely damage crops decrease grain production and affect soil fertility.

An industry worker may be exposed to different types of hazards depending upon occupation. Dyeing industrial hazards are chemical, biological and physical hazards. Poisoning may occur in three ways:

1. Inhalation.

2. Ingestion and
3. Skin.

About more than 8000 chemicals substances are used in several processes such as sizing, scouring, bleaching, dyeing and finishing. Textile waste water is contains excessive amount of oil, grease, detergent, other organic matter, suspended solids and heavy metals like Hg, Cr, As, Cd, Fe, Zn, Ni, Ca, etc. due to this it is highly polluting in nature. Exposure to these toxic chemicals like arsenic, lead, mercury, cause various skin problems like burns, itching, allergies, dermatitis, depigmentation etc. Most of dyes are carcinogenic in nature and pose a specific threat to the environment. Some chemical agents cause disability and respiratory illness. The present study was undertaken to assess the Impact of dyeing units on Environment and health hazards of dyeing workers of Jaipur District of Rajasthan State (India).

Methods of Investigation

The present study was conducted in Sanganer and Bagru areas of Jaipur district. The grab sampling technique was used for analysis of industrial effluents in waste water and soil. The pH and Electrical conductivity were measured using portable meters. Colour, and odour was observed by visual and TDS, NO^{3-} SO_4^{2-} were measured with the help of water and soil analysis kit. Atomic absorption spectrophotometer (DTPA) extractable method described by Alan Wahh (1955) was used for determination of heavy metals like Zn, Ca, Ni, Mn, Pb, Cd, and Fe.

Selection of samples of assess the health status of dyeing workers was done through purposive sampling technique. 60 workers comprised of 30 males and 30 females from Sanganer and Bagru areas of Jaipur district were sample subject. Interview cum questionnaire technique was used for collecting desired information about health of the subjects and impact an environment. The interview schedule was comprised of four parts- General information about socio-economic variables of respondents, dyeing related information, impact on environment and health hazards of dyeing workers. The data were statistically analyzed through frequencies and percentage.

Results and Discussion

Effect of Dyeing Effluents

This section contains the data procured form respondents about-effect of dyeing effluents on human, health, animals, water, soil and vegetative growth.

Most of the questions got similar response. Areas wise, the majority of the respondents of Bagru did not suffer from major health problems due to soil or water contamination as compared to workers from Sanganer area.

Effect on Human Health

The respondent of Sanganer area told about frequent occurrence of common disease like stomach pain, diarrhea, vomiting, headache, waist pain, skin disease etc.

Water Borne Disease

An observation of table- 1 reveals the occurrence of water borne diseases from dyeing effluents. All the male and female respondents of Bagru group were not having any water borne diseases, while all the male and female respondents of sanganer suffered from different digestive problems.

Table 4.1: Frequency and Percentage distribution of the Respondents by Occurring of Water Born Diseases

N = 60

Water born disease	Bagru				Sanganer			
	Male		Female		Male		Female	
	F	%	F	%	F	%	F	%
(a) Cholera		-		-	1	6.67	1	6.67
(b) Typhoide		-		-		-	3	20
(c) Digestive problems		-		-	15	100	15	100
(d) Do not occure	15	100	15	100	1	6.67	2	13.33

The findings of the present study are in accordance with those of Sharma and kaur (1997), and Gupta (2002), who analyzed that polluted ground water was the major cause for the spread of epidemic and chronic diseases in human beings. The waste water contains several pathogenic and non-pathogenic microorganisms and viruses. Apart from this other water borne diseases like cholera, typhoid, paratyphide, colitist, tuberculois and hepatitis etc. also exists.

Effect on Animals

The respondents provided the information about the effect of water pollution on animals. The respondents of Sanganer said that milk production of animals has declined and problems of bone deformation etc. exist in these animals.

Effect on Water

The respondents were asked about ill effect of dyeing effluents on drinking water, the subjects reveals that the water had bitter taste, typical offensive odour and slight change in colour. Boiling of drinking water has become a common phenomenon at these places.

Effect on Soil

The respondents of Sanganer total about – the change of soil quality- change in colour (dark black to brown), cracking the soil, deposition of chemical layer on surface of soil, decrease fertility of soil, low production, burning of crops etc.

Effect on Vegetative Growth

Majority of the respondents informed about the low yield per hectare beside these, change in taste of ripe vegetables and fruits, falling of the leaves, burning of the leaves etc. are some of the major changes visible in plants and crops irrigated with polluted water.

The above mention findings are in tune with Gupta (2000), who reported that the metal toxicity of plants and crops was below:

Fe- Reduction in growth and browing of roots.

Mn- Chlorotic leaves, also the leaf sheaths and the lower part of the stem in cereals often develop minute brown spots. In broad-leaved legumes, the leaf margins may develop brown or purple sports.

Cu- Leaves become dried and withered.

Zn- The affected leaves show the rolling of leaf margines roots turn brown and often nectotic. Cereals are generally resistant.

Dyeing Effluents Treatment

The researcher also made efforts to find out the treatment given to waste water before finally disposal in both the study areas. It was evident from table- 2 that respondents of Bagru (95 percent) were reusing the dyeing effluents. While all the respondents of Sanganer (100 percent) drained the last products waste directly into sewage line. As such no treatment is given to dye effluents prior to disposal.

Table 4.2: Frequency and Percentage distribution of the Respondents by Dyeing Effluents Treatment

N = 60

Dyeing effluents treatment	Bagru				Sanganer			
	Male		Female		Male		Female	
	F	%	F	%	F	%	F	%
(*a*) Drain in sewage line		-	1	6.67	15	100	15	100
(*b*) Reuses	15	100	13	86.67		-		-
(*c*) Other		-	1	6.67		-		-

The table- 2 further discloses the problems from these dyeing effluents. The respondents (90 percent) of Bagru were not facing problem because they were reusing it. While respondents (100 percent) from Sanganer reported existence of different problems due to the untreated dye effluents disposal.

Causative Factor for the Pollution

The table-3 points out that approximately all the respondents (100 percent) thought the cause of this pollution or these pollutants from the dyeing effluents. However 30 percent respondents of Sanganer group were also of the view that these might be some other causes.

All the respondents of Bagru, although they did not use synthetic dyes but still they were aware of the fact that synthetic dyes and chemicals used in various processes are harmful and admitted that it causes different health hazards. All the respondents (100 percent) of Sanganer also reported that synthetic dyes were responsible for health problems.

Health Problems due to Dyeing Work

The investigator was keen to know whether the health problems develop due to dyeing work. It was evident-from the table- 3 that 40 percent respondents of Bagru gave negative answer, while 100 percent-respondents from Sanganer respond in affirmation.

Table 4.3: Frequency and Percentage distribution of the Respondents by Causative Factors for the Pollution

N = 60

Causative factors	Bagru				Sanganer			
	Male		Female		Male		Female	
	F	%	F	%	F	%	F	%
Causative factors for the pollution								
(*a*) Dyeing/printing work		-	1	6.67		-		-
(*b*) Effluents of dyeing/ printing	14	93.33	14	93.33	14	93.33	15	100
(*c*) Other reasons	1	6.67	1	-	1	6.67		-
Synthetic dyes causes health hazards								
(*a*) Yes	10	66.67	9	60	15	100	15	100
(*b*) No	5	33.33	6	40				
Health problems due to dyeing work								
(*a*) Yes	5	33.33	3	20	15	100	15	100
(*b*) No	10	66.67	12	80		-		-

The finding of present study seek support from research conducted by Decan Heraled (2003), who revealed his paper "Dyeing out" the screen printing units are the main polluting units in the township but in the absence of an exemption from the state government, the hand block printers using only azo free dyes and working in their homes. Also reported by the survey was conducted by the National productivity council, New Delhi and German Technical Corporation (2003), who reported that the dyeing industries used about – 17 million liter per day of water and about -75 percent of the effluents discharged into the Gullar dam near the township (Sanganer).

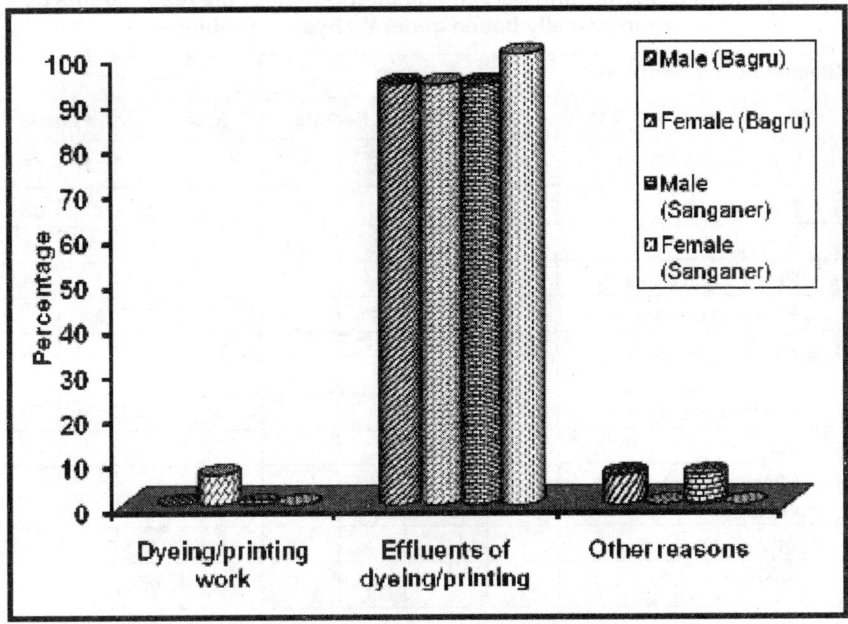

Fig. 4.1. Percentage distribution of the respondents by causative factors for the pollution

Since the sandy soil in Sanganer is porous, untreated effluents tend to percolated and pollute ground water, said another study, which warned against consuming vegetables cultivated in the area through irrigation from the Gullar dam.

Health Hazards of Dyeing Workers

General Health Problems

There was vast difference in health status of the dyeing workers of both Bagru and Sanganer area. The investigator inquired about existence of ergonomically based physical problems among respondents of both the groups.

Table- 4 clearly indicated that in the respondents of Bagru only 20 percent female suffered from waist pain. While the majority of respondents of Sanganer suffered from various health related problems. The female respondents (90 per cent) were suffering from back pain and fatigue and the male respondents (73.33 percent) had physical fatigue.

The results are in coordination with Chouhan (1999), who identified major health problems of women in selected occupation. The major health problems related to abnormal work posture are the "problem of aches" or the "musculoskeletal" problems. These problems included low back pain, pain in joints and muscles of the upper and lower extremities.

Table 4.4: Frequency and percentage distribution of the respondents by ergonomically based general physical problems

General health problems		Bagru				Sanganer			
		Male		Female		Male		Female	
		F	%	F	%	F	%	F	%
(*a*)	Fatigue		-		-	11	73.33	13.	86.67
(*b*)	Back pain		-	3	20	7	46.67	14	93.33
(*c*)	Pain in hand & legs		-		-	2	13.33	1	6.67
(*d*)	Pain in shoulders		-		-		-		-
(*e*)	Pain in hand, leg & plams		-		-	4	26.67	1	6.67
(*f*)	Vomiting and nossaia		-		-		-	1	6.67
(*g*)	Fant		-		-		-		-
(*h*)	Effect on hearing capacity		-		-		-		-
(*i*)	Other		-		-	11	73.33	7	46.67
	Average		-		20		46.67		41.11

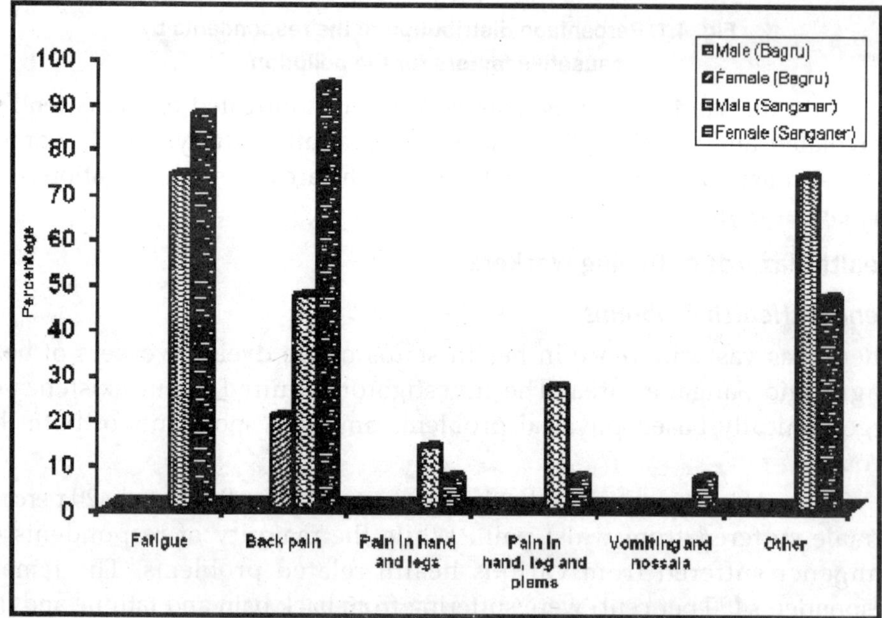

Fig. 4.2. Percentage distribution of the Respondents by Ergonomically based General Physical Problems

The author Roe and Lundgren 1955, and Sarkar et al., 2004, reported that the common physical hazards in dyeing and other industries are heat. The direct effect of heat exposure were burns, heat exhaustion, heat stock etc., the indirect effect were decreased efficiency, increase fatigue and enhance accidents rates. The major health hazards in textiles mills are mainly due to air, water and sound pollution.

Skin Disease

The data pertaining to various skin problems that occurred while doing the dyeing work have been given in Table-5. The respondents (30 percent) of

Table 4.5: Frequency and Percentage Distribution of the Respondents by Skin Diseases

N=60

Skin diseases		Bagru				Sanganer			
		Male		Female		Male		Female	
		F	%	F	%	F	%	F	%
(*a*)	Burning sensation hand, legs, plams	1	6.67	3	20	2	13.33	4	26.67
(*b*)	Itching in hand, legs & plams	3	20	3	20	9	60	9	60
(*c*)	Cracking & scaling of skin	1	6.67	4	26.67	12	80	10	66.67
(*d*)	Any types of allergy	2	13.33	2	13.33	6	40	7	46.67
(*e*)	Skin disease (dermatitis)		-		-	9	60	8	53.33
(*f*)	Other problems	5	33.33	6	40	13	86.67	13	86.67
	Average		**15.96**		**23.98**		**56.67**		**56.67**

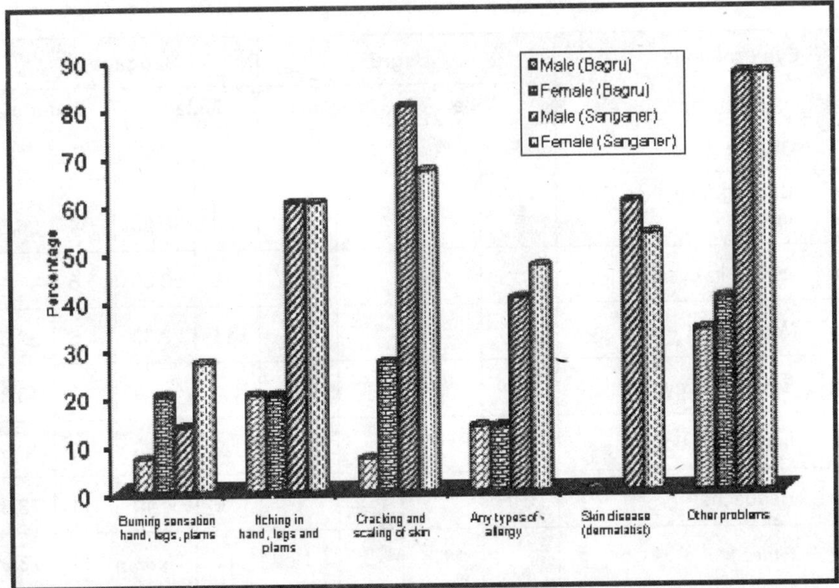

Fig. 4.3. Percentage distribution of the Respondents by Skin Diseases

Bagru and 56.67 percent respondents of Sanganer were found to be suffering from various skin problems. Majority of respondents (70 percent) had the problems of cracking and scaling of the skin and 60 percent itching problems also. 86.6 percent respondents of Sanganer suffered from other types of skin problems (like ureticaria, Axima, dermatitis, multiple boil etc.).

The findings seek Support from the research conducted by Ranganayaki (2000), who reported that, the exposure to toxic chemical like As, Pb, Hg cause various skin problems like burns, itching, allergies, hemorrhages, dermatitis, depigmentation and syphilis. Prolonged exposure to various detergents and water results in Eczema.

Occupational dermatitis as reported by Park (2002) may be caused due to, cold, moisture, friction, pressure, X-rays and other rays, chemical-acids, alkalies dyes, solvent, grease, far, phenols etc.

Eye Problems

Table-6 points out that none of the respondents of Bagru had any eye related infection or problem, while 100 percent respondents from Sannganer were suffering from one or other eye related problems. The majority of (73.33 percent) respondents of male group from Sanganer were facing problems of watering of eye and female respondent's headache problems.

Table 4.6: Frequency and Percentage distribution of the Respondents by eye Problems

N = 60

Eye Problems	Bagru				Sanganer			
	Male		Female		Male		Female	
	F	%	F	%	F	%	F	%
(*a*) Burning sensation in eyes		-		-	3	20	4	26.67
(*b*) Itching in eyes		-		-	8	53.33	6	40
(*c*) Watering of eyes		-		-	11	73.33	5	33.33
(*d*) Swelling of eyes		-		-		-	2	13.33
(*e*) Impaired vision		-		-	2	13.33	2	13.33
(*f*) Headache		-		-	6	40	11	73.33
(*g*) Other		No		No	11	73.33	11	73.33
Average		-		-		**45.56**		**39.05**

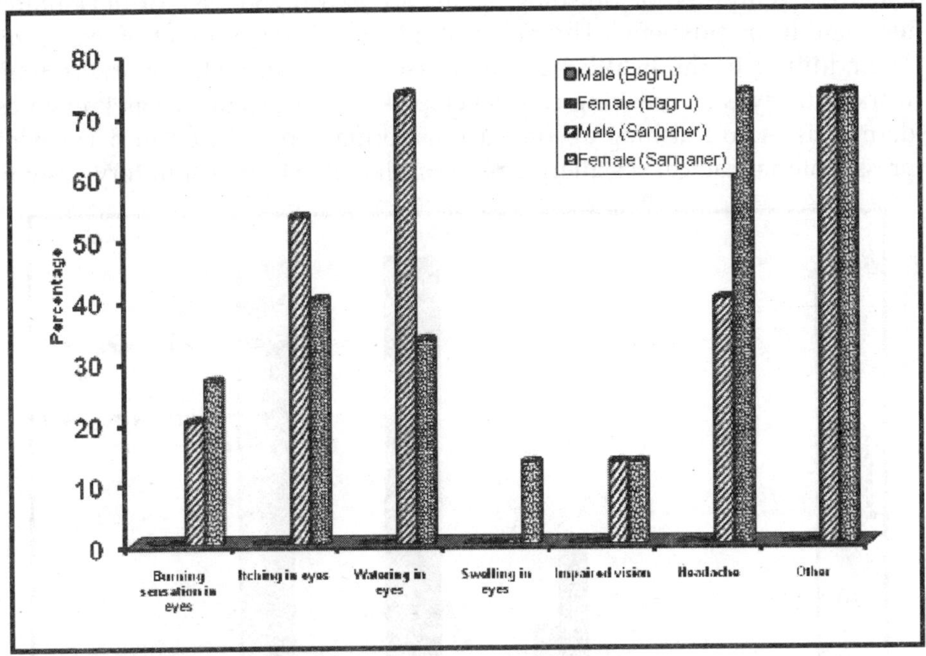

Fig. 4.4. Percentage distribution of the Respondents by Eye Problems

Heart Problems

As evident from the Table the respondents of Bagru (100 percent) did not have any heart problems. While 30 percent respondents of Sanganer group suffered from heart disease. The Table-7 further indicates that the 6 respondents (40 percent) of both male and female group from Sanganer were having problem of blood pressure and heart burn sensation.

Table 4.7: Frequency and Percentage distribution of the Respondents by Heart Problems

N = 60

Heart troublems		Bagru				Sanganer			
		Male		Female		Male		Female	
		F	%	F	%	F	%	F	%
(*a*)	Chest pain		-		-		-		-
(*b*)	Heart burn		-		-	2	13.33	1	6.67
(*c*)	Blood pressure		-		-	6	40	6	40
(*d*)	Other problems		-		-	6	40	6	40
	Average		**-**		**-**		**31.11**		**28.89**

The results of the study are in conformity with the finding of Sarker et al., (2004), who analyzed that the textile workers who are regular smokers and work with dust or finishing agents are at a higher risk of developing lung and heart problems. The risk multiplies with the amount of exposure. The addition to the health hazards caused by dust, textile workers who work with dyes or finishing can develop skin allergies or rashes known as dermatitis. Also finishing agents such as formaldehyde used in permanent press material can causes allergic reaction that affect the respiratory system.

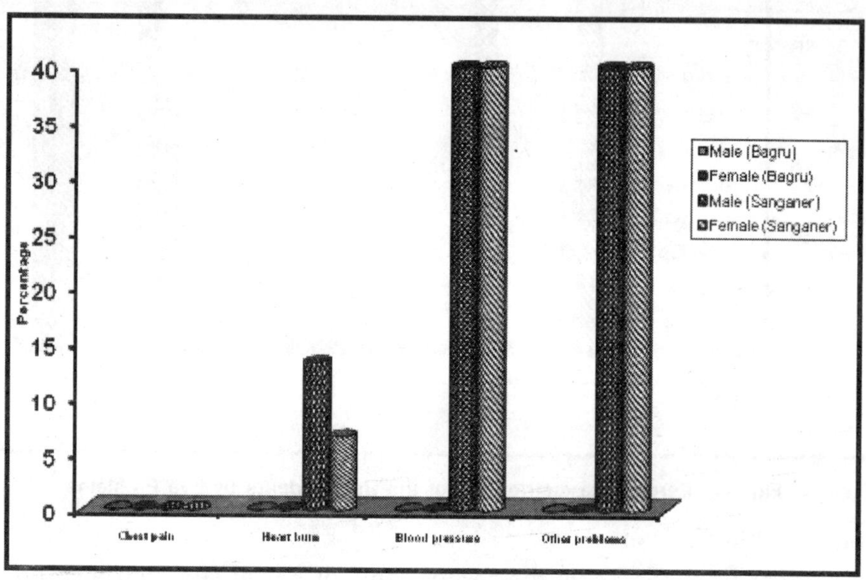

Fig. 4.5. Percentage distribution of the Respondents by Heart Problems

Respiratory Problems

Table-8 provides information about respiratory infection among respondents. The total respondents of Bagru group were not having any respiratory illness, whereas, 40 percent respondents of Sanganer were found to be asthmatic and had other infection in respiratory tract also.

Table 4.8: Frequency and Percentage distribution of the Respondents by Respiratory Infection

N = 60

Respiratory infection	Bagru				Sanganer			
	Male		Female		Male		Female	
	F	%	F	%	F	%	F	%
(*a*) Breathing problems		-		-	2	13.33	3	20
(*b*) Dry cough		-		-	3	20	3	20
(*c*) Asthma		-		-	7	46.67	6	40
(*d*) Other problem		-		-	8	53.33	8	53.33
Average		-		-		**33.33**		**26.67**

The result of present study are in tune with Paramesh (2002), who reported that in his observation on asthma in the city of Bangalore in 20,000 children has shown a prevalence of 9%, 16.5%, 18.5%, 24.5% and 29.5% in the year 1979, 84, 89, 94 and 99 respectively and it is correlated with the change of demography of city, increase industries, density of population and increase number of automobile and exhaust.

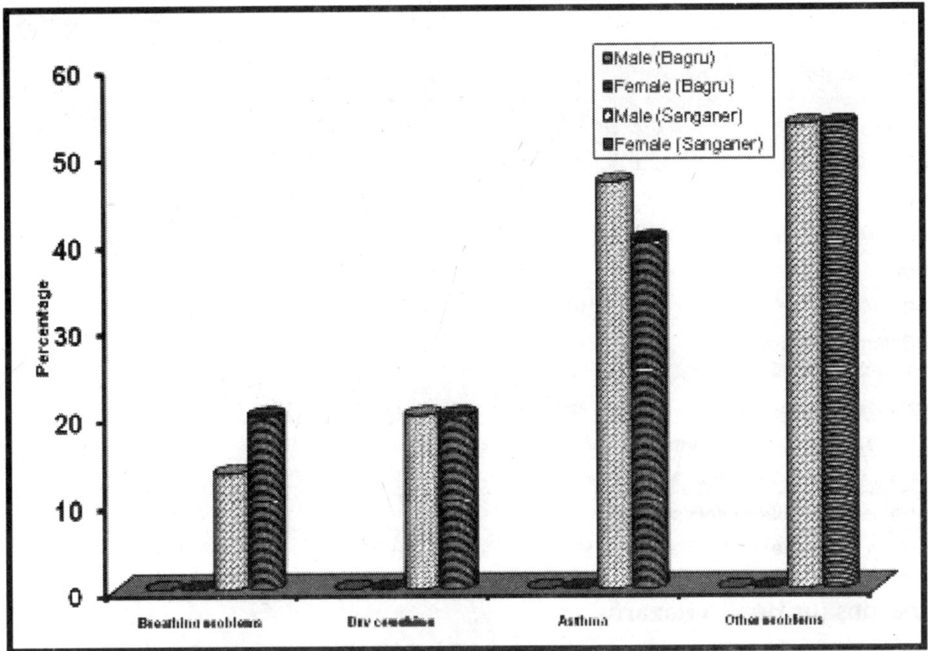

Fig. 4.6. Percentage distribution of the respondents by respiratory problem

Prevalence of Disease in Neighborhood

Table-9 depicts the status of respondents neighbourhood who suffered from different health problems due to dyes and dyeing effluents. The respondent (80 percent female and 66.67 percent male) from Bagru gave negative answer where as in Sanganer 100 percent respondents committed that dyeing effluents had affected other people's health also.

Further inquiry was made to assess the types of disease (like skin, eye, heart, and respiratory) most prevalent among these persons. Problems related to eye, heart, lungs, skin were found to be prevalent in Sanganer area whereas in Bagru there were few cases of skin disease as reported by 20 percent female and 33.33 percent male respondents.

Elaborating on the heavy metal pollution threat to human being Gupta (2002), who emphasized that arsenic leads to liver damage ulcers and some kidney problems. Whereas lead poisoning can do havoc in children by affecting central nervous system malfunctioning and other disorder. Copper leads to mental stress and disturbances, coma, and tension vis-va-vis uremia, Cadmium leads to suppression of growth bone deformation problems, blood less ness and anemia, while accumulation of zinc leads to kidney problems, pain in legs and even vomiting, selenium in an agent for lever, problems in teeth, blood pressure fall and problems in liver and spleen.

Table 4.9 : Frequency and percentage distribution of the Respondents by Prevalence of Disease in Neighborhood

N = 60

Prevalence of disease	Bagru				Sanganer			
	Male		Female		Male		Female	
	F	%	F	%	F	%	F	%
Prevalence of disease in neighbourhood								
(a) Yes	5	33.33	3	20	15	100	15	100
(b) No	10	66.67	12	80		-		-
Different disease in neighbour hood								
(a) Skin disease	5	33.33	3	20	15	100	15	100
(b). Eye problems		-		-	15	100	15	100
(*c*) Heart problems		-		-	15	100	15	100
(*d*) Respiratory infection		-		-	15	100	15	100
Average		**33.33%**		**20%**		**100%**		**100%**

Reasons for Health Hazards

Table-10 points out that more that 80 percent respondents of all group assumed that the causes of these problems were dyeing effluents.

Table 4.10 : Frequency and percentage distribution of the Respondents by Reasons for Health Hazards

N = 60

Prevalence of disease	Bagru				Sanganer			
	Male		Female		Male		Female	
	F	%	F	%	F	%	F	%
(*a*) Dyeing/printing	1	6.67	1	6.67		-	1	6.67
(*b*) Dyeing effluents	12	80	13	86.67	15	100	14	93.33
(*c*) Others reasons	2	13.33	1	6.67		-		-

With respect to present study Chinta et al., (1998), who reported that more than 25 percent of our workers employed in the textile industry, it is obvious that the majority of health hazards are associated with this industry. This observation in well-supported by many studies which indicates that more than 50% of total industrial accidents occure in textile industry.

Sharma (1997) also reported chemical industries, textiles, paper and pulp industries discharge maximum amount of polluted water. An estimate indicates that about 140 m3/tone water is required per 1000 meter of cotton cloth. The waste consist of a variety of chemicals which are extremely toxic to living beings. These toxicants are transferred to different organisms in their food chain causing a number of undesirable effects.

Hospital Record of Patients from Sanganer Area (during 2004-05)

In order to assess the health status of these dyeing workers, the investigator also visited the general hospital situated in Sanganer area and consulted the doctors about frequency of occurrence of various problems in the patients from these areas.

Table-11 portrays a clear picture of the common health problems found from the hospital record in the patients from Sanganer area in the year 2004-05.

Table 4.11 : Hospital record of patients from Sanganer area during 2004-05

Disease	No. of patients	
	Male	Female
Eye problems or disease:		
Glauecoma	3	7
Cataract	5	7
Confunctivitis	711	739
Blindness and low vision	3	5
Heart diseases:		
Hyper tension, B.P.	37	69
Respiratory infection:		
(*a*) T.B. and acute bronchitis.	775	855
(*b*) Pneumonia, influenza, bronchitis chronic and unspecified emphyseme and asthama.	899	631
(*c*) Indoor asthama patient (serious condition)	71	43
Skin diseases:		
Skin and subcutaneous	4313	4147
Total indoor patient	**1427**	

The worker name and existing problems as identified by the doctor has been given in appendix V. The above Tables throws light on the fact that the dye effluents has adverse effect on soil, water and health of workers along with neighboring community in Sanganer area due to untreated disposal of dye effluents in sewage line.

Strategies Adopted to cope up with the Problems

The researcher tried to find out from the respondents about what strategies they adopted at the time of illness and precaution taken to avoid the reoccurrence of such problems.

(1) Treatment taken:

Table-12 indicates that approximately 95 percent respondents took medical treatment to cope up with the existing problems, while (33.33 percent) female respondents of Sanganer also used home based treatment like application of oil, grease etc.

Table 4.12: Frequency and percentage distribution of the Respondents by Treatment Taken

N=60

Treatment of diseases	Bagru				Sanganer			
	Male		Female		Male		Female	
	F	%	F	%	F	%	F	%
How do you cope up there problems and disease								
(a) Home base treatment		-		-		-		-
(b) No attempt		-	1	6.67		-		-
(c) Consult the doctors	15	100	14	93.33	15	100	15	100
Do you take medical treatment for their problems								
(a) Yes		-		-	12	80	11	73.33
(b) No	15	100	15	100	3	20	4	26.67
How do you cope up these problems at home								
(a) Use of oil, greases		-	1	6.67		-	5	33.33
(b) Use of meditional plants		-		-		-	1	6.67
(c) Medicines	15	100	14	93.33	14	93.33	15	100
(d) Cleaning of wounds		-		-	3	20	6	40
(e) Others		-	1	6.67	1	6.67		-

Table-12 further shows that the all respondents (100 percent) of Bagru both male and female group did not take medical treatment as they did not have serious health problems. The respondents of Sanganer group (60 percent) used to take medicine for different health problems.

2. Precautions taken:

It is evident from Table-13 that all the respondents of Bagru and Sanganer were taking some precautions to make them safe. Gloves were used by 100 percent respondents of both the group.

Table 4.13: Frequency and percentage distribution of the respondents by used precaution during dyeing work.

N=60

Precaution during dyeing work	Bagru				Sanganer			
	Male		Female		Male		Female	
	F	%	F	%	F	%	F	%
Do you take any special measure to make yourself safe								
(*a*) Yes	5	33.33	3	20	12	80	13	86.67
(*b*) No	10	66.67	12	80	3	20	2	13.33
Do you take precaution during dyeing works								
(*a*) Yes	15	100	12	80	15	100	15	100
(*b*) No		-	3	20		-		-
Do you take following precaution								
(*a*) Use of gloves	15	· 100	15	100	15	100	15	100
(*b*) wraping the face by cloth	1	6.67			11	73.33	8	53.33
(*c*) Covering body by cloth	11	73.33	5	33.33	13	86.67	13	86.67
(*d*) Less contact b/w hand & colour		-		-	1	6.67	2	13.33
(*e*) Use of any equipment		-		-		-	1	6.67
(*f*) Others	12	80	10	66.67	15	100	15	100

It was further noted that for a vast majority of respondent (80 percent) were using precautions like wraping face, covering body and other precaution of Bagru and Sanganer dyeing area.

Suggestions for the Improvement of Health Status of Dyeing Workers

The researcher made extensive efforts to know the ways & means to improve the health status, the suggestive measures are as follows:

- There is an imperative need to take proper steps to encourage the workers towards traditional activity of using natural resources for dyeing and printing of textile which not only protects the rich heritage of Indian culture but also serve to solve the employment problems to a great extent among the youth.

- Technical training is important to improve the efficiency and ultimately the quality of life. The need arises to organize more training to impart knowledge and develop skills in dyeing/printing.
- Strengthening of National Policies for health at work. Updating of legislation and standards. Emphasis on the primary responsibility of the employer for health and safety, education, training and information available to employers and workers enhancement of occupational health services.
- Use of protective clothing, foot wear, head cover, gloves, mask etc. while preparing colours for dyeing and printing.
- Daily change of clothes and a bath after dying works.
- Medical screening of every worker in the hazardous area periodically.
- Adequate protection may be given against chemicals used in dyeing, printing and fabric processing section.
- Implementation of appropriate technologies for dyeing and printing work.
- Use of standardarized technique for dying and washing operation. Reducing the number of washing in the sequence and use of hot water in washing. Recycling of less contaminated wash water. In this manner reduction of 20-40% in the volumes of waste water generated.
- Reduction of the volume and toxicity of discharge. Adoption of alternative processing methods and chemicals and recycling and reuses of water, chemicals and colorants.
- Not to employ the persons suffering from any disease, as dyer and chemists, as it can cause allergic reactions and may further cause adverse effect on the health status of the workers.

Impact on Environment: Analysis of Physico-chemical Properties of Water and Soil

In order to assess the soil and water quality for different selected parameters, two water sample from Bagru and Sanganer each, and 3 soil sample one from Bagru and two from Sanganer (one from nearby dyeing area and another from washing area) were collected. The laboratory analysis was done for the assessment of following 15 parameters-pH, electrical conductivity, colour, odour, temperature TDS, SO_4^{2-} , NO^{3-} and heavy metals like Zn, Cu, Fe^{+2}, Mn, Pb^{+2}, Cd^{+2}, Ni, The results obtained are presented here:

Table 4.14: Impact on environment: Analysis of physio-chemical properties of water and soil samples

Sample No.	0	1	2	3	4	5
	Water sample			Soil sample		
	ISI standard Based	Bagru W-I	Sanganer W-II	Bagru S-I	Sanganer-IS-II	Sanganer-IIS-III
pH	6.5 to 8.5	7.89	8.44	7.95	3.4	5.45
Acidic/Alkanity	-	Alkaline	Alkaline	Alkaline	Extremely acidic	Highly acidic
Colour	-	No	Yellowish green	Orange	Yellow green	Lemon yellow
Odour	-	No	Chemical	No	Chemical	Chemical
Zn (mg/dl)	5	-	0.131	4.226	2.946	1.348
Cu (mg/dl)	0.05	0.016	0.038	5.636	62.358	29.858
Fe (mg/dl)	0.3	0.256	0.70	59.285	58.979	37.174
Mn (mg/dl)	0.10	0.106	0.188	103.248 72	6.336	2.52
Pb (mg/dl)	0.10	0.040	0.041	0.89	2.376	1.168
Cd (mg/dl)	0.01	0.001	0.003	0.008	0.022	0.016
Ni (mg/dl)	0.02	0.0085	0.082	0.506	0.410	0.228
SO_4^{2-} (mg/dl)	150	133	245	-	-	-
NO^{3-} (mg/dl)	45	35	50	-	-	-
TDS (mg/dl)	1000	880	1211.5	-	-	-
Electrical conductivity	-	2.92	1.87	2.03	2.95	2.45

W-I water sample from Bagru

W-II water sample from Sanganer

S-I Soil sample from Bagru

S-II Soil sample from Sanganer (Dyeing effluents)

S-III Soil sample from Sanganer (Processing waste)

Colour

The table- 14 indicates that the water sample collected from Bagru did not show any change in the colour, while water sample collected from Sanganer were yellowish green in colour. The colour of the soil was orange, yellowish green and lemon yellow in the samples collected from Bagru, and nearby areas of dyeing and washing areas of Sanganer respectively.

The above mentioned finding are in tune with Saroya (2003) and Bhole (1997) who, stated that textile mill waste water in highly coloured due to presence of dyes used as colouring materials. The waste water containing dye stuffs with intensive colour and toxicity was introduced into the aquatic systems.

Odour

Odour pollution in water and soil samples is usually present due to both chemical and biological agents. Soil and water samples of Bagru did not have any offensive smell while both the sample from Sanganer possessed chemical odour. Finding of the present study get support from the Sharma and Kaur (1997), who reported, the presence of unpleasant odour and dissolve organic in the water, makes the water unlit for drinking and domestic are.

Temperature

Temperature of the water and soil samples recorded during collection time varied from 20ºC to 25ºC

pH

The table- 14 further indicated the pH of the soil and water samples. The pH of water sample from both areas was within the permissible limit i.e. 6.5 to 8.5 while the pH of soil samples from Bagru was in prescribed limit but the soil sample of Sanganer- I was found acidic and Sanganer-II strongly acidic in nature.

Electrical Conductivity

The value of EC in all fine sample of water and soil samples was out of range. The standard EC rating for soil should be below 0.5 ds/m and for water less than 0.25 as described in table- 15.

EC Rating for Soil and Water

Table 4.15: Standard EC rating of Water and Soil for Comparison

EC soil (ds/m)	Suitability for crops	EC water ds/m	Water class
0 to 0.8	Normal for most crops	Less than 0.25	C1
0.8 to 1.6	Injurious to some crops	0.25 to 0.75	C2
1.6 to 3.2	Injurious to most crops	0.75 to 2.25	C3
3.2 to above	Injurious to all crops	2.25 to above	C4

The data in table 15 depicts that the EC in water sample of Bagru was 2.92 ds/m and in Sanganer it was found to be 1.87 ds/m. All the three soil samples also showed higher (2.03 to 2.95 ds/m) rating as compared to the standard EC rating.

Table 4.16: EC Rating of Water and Soil Samples from Bagru and Sanganer area

Sample No.	1	2	3	4	5
	Water sample		Soil sample		
	Bagru W-I	Sanganer W-II	Bagru S-I	Sanganer–I S-II	Sanganer-II S-III
Electrical conductivity (ds/m)	2.92	1.87	2.03	2.95	2.45

Hence these samples are highly unsuitable and injurious for proper growth of plants and production of crops.

NO^3 and SO_4^{2-}

Table-14 shows the sulphate and nitrate levels in Sanganer water sample. The sulphate content was 245 mg/l and nitrate 50 mg/l which have crossed the permissible limit hence found harmful for human beings. The water of Sanganer area in not found suitable for drinking purpose.

TDS

Table-14 reveals that the TDS of effluent was found to be 12.11.5 mg/l in the water samples collected from Sanganer. TDS rating crossed the range of prescribed limit and found harmful for human beings.

The finding of present study seek supports from the research conducted by Sharma and Kaur (1997), who analysized that the high values of sulphate and total dissolve solid (TDS) in drinking water are generally not harmful to human but high concentration of these may affect persons who are suffering from kidney and heart disease. The author also stated that the nitrate above 20 mg/liter is reported to cause methemoglobin in infants. The disease cyanossish which haemoglobin becomes incapable of transporting oxygen in who attributed to high level of nitrate in drinking water and nitrate are harmful to fermentation process and courses disagreeable taste to bear.

Heavy Metals

The table-14 further depicts the content of different heavy metals in selected water and soil samples. The content of all the heavy metals in Bagru water sample were almost in prescribed limit. Parameters Zn, Cu, Pb was within permissible limit but the Fe, Mn, Cd, Ni was in high range and found harmful for surrounding. On the other hand soil sample from Bagru as well as Sanganer showed higher limits when compared with the prescribed limit hence there is every likelihood of evidence of harmful effect on environment.

The results of the physico-chemical analysis of soil samples collected from disposal of effluents area. Shows that textile dyeing effluents is highly polluting in nature. Almost all parameter in soil samples of Sanganer exceeds the permissible limit therefore it is necessary to treat it properly before discharging it. On the other hand soil sample of Bagru village also exceeds the prescribed limit as for as heavy metal content was concerned. This affects the vegetative growth of that area. Water sample did not show much deviation although it is found to be slightly acidic in nature.

The results are in coordination with Sharma and Kaur, 1997; Gupta, 2000, and Park, 2002, who reported that the effect of heavy metal pollution on environment and also the colour, odour, TDS, SO_4^{2-}, NO^{3-} etc. had harmful effect on the environment.

WHO standard for cadmium in water is 0.005 mg/L. It is highly toxic and its traces are responsible for adverse renal arterial change in kidneys in man. Copper salt (0.1 to 0.5 mg/L are toxic to microorganisms and causes fishy, fatty and oily tastes in milk products. Arsenic is extremely toxic in drinking water. It is a cumulative poison and exhibit carcinogenic properties. It is occur in water as a results of industrial discharges. Lead is who cumulative poison and it tends to deposit in the bones. Inorganic Pb salts is irrigation water are toxic to plants organic matter present in acidic wastes increases the plumbo-solvency.

The physio-chemical analysis of water and soil samples from disposal of effluents area clearly depicts table-14 that textile dyeing effluents were highly polluting in nature. Almost all parameters in water and soil samples of Sanganer exceed the permissible limits, it is necessary to treat it properly before discharging it. On the other hand soil samples of Bagru village also exceed the prescribed limits as for as heavy metal contents are concerned. Water sample did not should much deviation although it was found to be slightly acidic in nature.

Regarding heavy metal pollution threat to human being, animal, vegetation growth, due to soil & water pollution are major issues to be given due consideration. The heavy metal content was found much beyond permissible limits in both soil & water samples of selected sites. The soil was found unfit for vegetation growth and water unfit for drinking purposes.

Conclusion

Hence it can be concluded that workers who are working with different of dyeing and finishing scouring etc. are at a higher risk of developing skin, eye, heart and respiratory problems. The risk multiplies with the amount of exposure of different chemicals further heavy metal pollution threat to human being, animals and vegetation growth due to soil and water pollution are major issues to be given consideration. The heavy metal content was found much beyond permissible limits in both soil and water samples of selected sites. The soil was found unfit for vegetation growth and water unfit for drinking purposes.

Thus the present study has been a effort to describe features and risk factors of hazards to dyeing workers and apply these findings towards prevention of occupational disease and injury among workers as well as their families and environment.

Thus, the initiative through present research has been conducted to describe the features, risk factors and hazards on environment and dyeing workers as well as suggested strategies towards prevention of occupational disease and injury among the workers and their families. This would be beneficial for health and safety of professional and others in a position to improve the health and safety of dyeing workers.

REFERENCE

Agarwal, S.K. and Sharma, L. (2003). Environmental Scenario for 21st century. APH Publishing Corporation, New Delhi: 439-448.

Ansari, A.A. and Dr. Thakur, B.D. (1999). Red listed dyes and chemicals used in textiles: Health hazards, International norms and possible remedies, Colourage, November. pp: 21-32.

Bahl, A.K. (2004). Writing occupational health and safety policy. standards India, Vol-18, No. 1, April : 13-15.

Boob, J.M. (2004). Textile industry in Rajasthan. The present Scenario. Colourage, Oct. : 57-60.

Desai C. (1993). Waste minimization in synthetic textiles process house. colourage Aug.

Glover, B. (2005). Reactive dyes for textile printing. Colourage annual: 67-81.

Grover, I. (1988). Occupational hazards of rural working women. Social welfare 35 (2) : 12.

Gupta P.K. (2000). Methods in Environmental Analysis-water, soil and air. AGROBIOS (India), New Delhi.

Gupta, R.O. (2002). Heavy metal pollution threat to human life. Environ. & people, Vol-9, No. 2 & 3, July & August: 32-35.

Gupta, S., Kumar A., Ojha C.K., & Seth G. (2004). Chemical Analysis of Ground water of Sanganer Area, Jaipur in Rajasthan. J.of Environ. Science & Engg. Vol.46, No.1, Jan.: 74-78.

http: // www.indiaprofile.com / fashion / blockprinting.htm_blockprinting. ercating cotton cloth block by block.

http://www.deccanherald.com/deccanherald/july06/s15.asp.

http://www.rajchamber.com/htm/rcci_sdc_interventions/textiles/effluent_treatment_plant_htm.

http://www.rajtourism.com/htm/raj_tour/art_craft/textiles.htm.

Lal, R. A. (1998). Environmental protection through waste management colourage TEX INDIA FAIR '98 special Nov: 29-34.

Resources Conservation and Recovery Act (RCRA) (2000). Annual report of badan Solid waste management authority.

Riganti, V., Gallotti, E., and Gallotti, L. (1998). The degrading action of NOx on wool dyed with natural dyes. (1997) 94/12: 38-42, 1998 95/2: 32-39 and 1998 95/3: 63-71.

Sarkar, M.K., Sahu, S.K., Agnihotri, V. & Paul, R. (2004). Safety and pollution control in textile industry. TAE (Mumbai Unit) Chemical processing seminar-10th Jan. Colourage: 29-37.

Sathe, C.N. & Kulkarni P.S. (2001). Application of Biotechnology in waste water treatment. Environment & people. March-April, Vol-7, No. 10 & 11: 3-6.

Satyanarayana, Y.V.V. (2004). Total water management in Cotton Textile Industry. India time 2004 special, Colourage: 75-81.

Shroff J. J. (2001).Textiles and Ecology, Colourage July: 17-18.

Shukla S.R. (2005). Environmental aspects of textile wet processing. Environ Talk, Colourage, January, Feb, March, April: 51-54.

Srivastava U.C. and Pal N.K. (2004). Standardization in the field of occupational health and safety (OH & S) management System. Standards India, Vol 18, No.1, April: 6-12.

5

Air Pollution and Its Impact on Human Health

—*S.P. Kaushik, India*
—*Archana Tyagi, India*
—*Pankaj Tyagi, India*

ABSTRACT

The present study deals with the quantitative effect of vehicular emission on ambient air quality during January, 2010 in urban area of Panipat city. In this study, SPM, RSPM, SO_2, NO_x were estimated at 4 locations in urban area. Beside this, air quality index (AQI), impact of pollution in human health was assessed. The 24 hr mean of SPM and RSPM at each location of commercial areas were found to be higher than prescribed limit of National Ambient Air Quality Standard (NAAQS) as compare to residential areas. These results indicate that ambient air quality in the commercial areas is affected adversely due to emission and accumulation of SPM, RSPM, SO_2 and NO_x. Since the main source of the pollutants in the commercial areas is motor vehicular traffic as well as smoke release to industries, there is a clear need to decongest such traffic in these areas. These pollutants may pose detrimental effect on human health, as exposure of these are associated with cardiovascular and respiratory diseases respiratory problems like cough, dry cough, cold, runny nose, nose block, bronchitis, wheezing, pneumonia and asthma along with eye problems, skin diseases and heart diseases. The average percentage disease occurrences (APDO) observed higher in commercial areas due to high concentrations of air pollutants and lower in residential areas to low concentrations of air pollutants. It shows that for every ailment, except the chronic ones bronchitis and asthma, the APDO is significantly higher in the commercial areas, with higher concentrations of air pollutants, than in the residential areas. The maximum number of respondents suffering from eye diseases and acute respiratory illnesses (correlate strongly with air pollution levels) in commercial area residents as compare to residential area residents.

Key Words: *Air pollution, Air quality index, Commercial areas, Eye diseases and APDO*

Introduction

Panipat is situated on Shershah Suri Marg (now known as G.T. road or NH-1), 90 KM north of Delhi. On three sides, Panipat district boundaries touch other districts of Haryana Karnal in the north, Jind in the west and Sonipat in the south. Panipat also has heavy industry with include three major public sector projects: the Indian Oil Corporation oil refinery, the National Fertilizers Limited plant and the thermal power station and the biggest centre in the country for producing shoddy (recycled) yarn, a large consumer of rags for reprocessing and producing low priced blankets. A traditional supplier of barrack blankets to the armed forces. Biggest centre in the country engaged in export of cotton durries, made-ups, throws and mats. Samalkha, a small town near Panipat, is known for foundry work and supply of agricultural machinery to neighbouring Uttar Pradesh. Relatively high wages compared to the Indian national average – a worker earns Rs.300/- to 450/- per day on Handloom/ Powerloom. The town has infrastructure such as rail, road and inland container depots well suited to industry and export. The main source of air pollution is heavy traffic load of NH-1 highway and uncontrolled exhaust smoke release by vehicles and Industries.

The impact of industrial and vehicle pollution on human health in urban areas is at peak level as vehicle emissions are near the ground level where people live and work. Atmospheric pollutants exist in both gaseous and pollutants forms. Diesel exhaust, in addition to generating pollutants like hydrocarbons, oxides of nitrogen and carbon is a major contributor to particulate matter in most places of the world. Symptoms like chronic cough, wheezing and breathlessness have been reported on exposure to these pollutants (Chabra et al., 2001). The respirable particles are responsible for the cardiovascular as well as respiratory diseases (Sagai et al., 1996) of human being because these particles can penetrate deep into the respiratory system, and studies indicates that the smaller the particle, more severe the health impacts (Dockery et al., 1993; Pope et al., 1995; Schwartz et al., 1996). Ambient particulate matter may be carriers of acidic or toxic species (e.g., heavy metals, acids and carcinogenic organic compounds) and may have detrimental effects on human health and ecosystems. Besides the effect of particulate matter, literature also suggests that there is a strong relationship between higher concentration of SO2 and NOx and several health effects (Curtis et al., 2006), like cardiovascular diseases (Zanobetti and Schwartz, 2002; Peters et al., 2004; Chen et al., 2005; Dockery et al., 2005) respiratory health effects such as asthma and bronchitis (Ye et al., 2001; Barnett et al., 2005) and reproductive and developmental effects such as increased risk of preterm birth (Liu et al., 2003).

Acute Effects or Short term Effects due to Air Pollution

Acute effects are immediate and short-term effects on the body. The effects of irritant particles in the respiratory tract depend upon their solubility, size, and their penetration, deposition and clearance mechanisms in the respiratory tract. Fine particles may cause bronchospasm, pulmonary oedema and allergic alveolitis. Three types of acute effects which may result from inhalation of gases and vapors are asphyxiation, irritation of respiratory organs and harcosis. Other acute effects of particulate air pollution are stuffy or runny nose, sinusitis, sore throat, wet cough, head cold, hay fever and burning or red eyes (Dockery D.W and Pope C.A. III, 1994).

Chronic Effects or Long term Effects due to Air Pollution

Chronic effects are long-term ailments due to a certain trigger. Chronic Obstructive Pulmonary Diseases (COPDs) include bronchitis or emphysema, which are long term and serious conditions. More typical chronic responses include damage to lungs, to blood, nervous system, liver, kidneys, bones and skin (Dockery D.W and Pope C.A. III, 1994).

The objective of the present study was to cheek the adverse health effects of exposure to ambient air pollution in different areas of Panipat Cityof Haryana and examine the relationship between the levels of air pollution in Industrial areas as well as residential areas. The reasons for faster urbanization of Panipat city may be due to its being very near to Delhi. Panipat has seen tremendous increase of industries with uncontrolled exhaust. Air pollution in Panipat city is increasing day by day due to vehicular exhausts. Hence ambient air quality of the city and impact on human health has been monitored and was to cheek the adverse health effects of exposure to different pollutants in the present study.

Material of Methods

Study area and Sample Collection

Panipat City of Haryana, India located at 29.39°N 76.97°E in 90 KM north of Delhi. In 2011, Panipat had population of 1,202,811 of which male and female were 646,324 and 556,487 respectively. There was change of 24.33 percent in the population compared to population as per 2001. In the previous census of India 2001, Panipat District recorded increase of 38.58 percent to its population compared to 1991. Panipat is a city of textiles and carpets. It is the biggest centre for quality blankets and carpets in India and has a handloom weaving industry. Panipat also has heavy industry; with include Indian Oil Corporation oil refinery, the National Fertilizers Limited plant and the thermal power station. Panipat Cityalso the biggest centre in the country for producing shoddy (recycled) yarn, and a large consumer of rags for reprocessing and producing low priced blankets, a traditional supplier of barrack blankets to the armed forces. Keeping of these points we are monitoring of SPM, RSPM, SO2 and NOx were done in the ambient air of Panipat city at four location in which two are commercial (Lord Shiva Woolen Mills near Toll Plaza and Pan Foods Ltd. G.T. Road) and two are residential (Residential Sector 24, HUDDA near M. J. R. School Panipat and Residential Sector 7, HUDDA).

Air Quality Monitoring and Analysis

Air monitoring was conducted during the month of January 2010 for 24 hrs of SPM, RSPM, and 8 hrs for SO_2 and NO_X. Monitoring of SPM and RSPM was carried out using Respirable Dust Sampler (Model-415, Envirotech, New Delhi) at a flow rate of 1.0- 1.2 m3 min-1 for 24 hr (6.0 A.M. to 6.0 A.M.) and SO2 and NOx 8 hr (6.0 A.M. to 2.0 P.M, 2.0 P.M to 10:00 P.M. and 10 P.M. to 6 A.M) .

SPM and RSPM Analysis

The Respirable Dust sampler has been provided with a cyclone for the separation of RSPM. The suspended particles enters the cyclone, coarse non-respirable dust is separated from the air stream by centrifugal forces. The suspended particulate matter falls through the cyclone's conical hopper and gets collected in the cyclonic-cup. The fine dust comprising the respirable fraction of SPM passes through the cyclone and gets collected on filter paper. Pre-weighed cellulose filters, Whatman paper (EPM-2000) of 20 x 25 cm size were used and reweighed after sampling in order to determine the mass of the particles collected (RSPM). The concentration of the particulate matter in the ambient air was then computed on the net mass collected divided by the volume of air sampled. The amount of non-respirable suspended particulate matter (NRSPM) was summed up with respirable particulate matter (RSPM) for calculation of SPM (Suspended Particulate Matter). The sampling instruments were fixed at a breathing height of 1.5 m above the ground level.

SO_2 and NO_X Analysis

The analysis of SO_2 and NOx was done by Bureau of Indian Standard methods IS 5182 (Part II): and IS 5182: (Part VI) (IS: 2001 and 1975) respectively. A known quantity of air was passed through the impinger containing known volume of absorbing solution; SO_2 was absorbed in absorbing solution, sodium tetrachloromecurate. A dichlorosulphitomercurate complex was formed which was made to react with para-rosaniline and methysulphonic acid. The absorbance of the solution was measured at a wavelength of 560 nm on spectrophotometer (JASCO V-530, UV/Vis). Whereas, Nitrogen oxides (NOx) as nitrogen dioxide (NO_2) was absorbed in absorbing solution, sodium hydroxide which formed a stable solution of sodium nitrite. The nitrite ion so produced, was determined colorimetrically at wavelength 540 nm by reacting the exposed absorbing reagent with phosphoric acid, sulphanilamide and N (1-naphthyl) ethylenediamine dihydrochloride.

Air Quality Index (AQI)

The Air Quality Index (AQI) was calculated using the method suggested by Tiwari and Ali (1987) and followed by Kaushik et al., (2006). For AQI, the air quality rating of each pollutant was calculated first by the following formula.

$$Q = 100\frac{V}{V_s}$$

Where, Q represents quality rating, V the observed value of the pollutant and Vs the standard value recommended for that pollutant. The Vs values used are the recommended national ambient air quality standards (CPCB 1994), for different areas.

Health Risk Analysis

A survey (Based on questioners) of 525 individuals was conducted in the selected areas of local residents shopkeepers, hawkers, auto rickshaw drivers are expends at least 12 hrs times in a day in these study areas due to their residence, to perform duties, business work and others reason. Data taken from primary health centers (Civil Hospitals) and survey questioners etc. were asked to list the occurrence of respiratory problems like cough, dry cough, cold, runny nose, nose block, bronchitis, wheezing, pneumonia and asthma along with eye problems, skin diseases and heart diseases. Information regarding respondent's age, sex, occupation, residence etc. was also collected for subsequent analysis but in this study we are only work male sex. The number of respondents in the four sites is given in Table 1.

Results and Discussion

Air Monitoring and level of SPM and RSPM, SO2 and NOX

In residential areas, the average concentration of SPM and RSPM, were found to be 197.7 (196.7-198.7) and 79.98 (65.1-94.8) μg m^{-3} respectively whereas, SO2 and NOx were found to be 13.5 (10.2-16.8), 19.75 (15.5-24.0) μg m^{-3} respectively. In Commercial areas, the average concentration of SPM and RSPM, were found to be 605.0 (558.7- 652.0) and 377.4 (319.0-435.0) μg m^{-3} respectively whereas, SO2 and NOx were found to be 22.1 (21.2-23.0), 31.2 (30.0-32.5) μg m^{-3} respectively (Table 2). The mean concentration of air pollutants (SPM, RSPM, SO2 and NOx) found in the reducing order of Residential area < Commercial area. The 24 hr mean concentration of SPM and RSPM, at all the locations in Commercial areas were found higher than the respective prescribed National Ambient Air Quality Standards (NAAQS). On the other hand the Air Quality Index (AQI) based on the calculation of 24 hr average concentration of SPM, RSPM, SO2 and NOx at different locations showed to polluted (V) category at all the commercial areas, whereas, the residential areas showed fairly clean (III) for residential sector 24, HUDDA and clean (II) category in residential sector 7, HUDDA (Table 2). Higher index values indicate higher health risks and maximum value was found in the commercial area. Urban air pollution due to vehicular emission is a matter of concern because of exposure of large number of people to it. Vehicular emission is responsible for higher level of air pollutants like SPM, RSPM,

SO2, NOx and other organic and inorganic pollutants including trace metals and their adverse effects on human and environmental health (Caselles et al., 2002; Kaushik et al., 2006; Maitre et al., 2006 ; Curtis et al., 2006; Sharma et al., 2006; Jayaraman, 2007). The only industrial area showed fairly clean category because of higher NAAQS. The concentration of RSPM at all the commercial and residential areas showed higher than the permissible values and based on AQI, all the locations are either in polluted or moderately polluted category and might be due to the harmful effect of the RSPM dwelling in the area.

Table 5.1: Numbers of respondents in four different study sites in Panipat City of Haryana, India

Sl. No.	Study site	No. of respon-dents	Age Group (Years)	Occupation
1.	Lord Shiva Woolen Mills near Toll Plaza	150	18-60	local residents, shopkeepers, hawkers, auto rickshaw and drivers
2.	Pan Foods Ltd. G.T. Road, Panipat	130	18-60	local residents, shopkeepers, hawkers, auto rickshaw and drivers
3.	Residential Sector 24, HUDDA near M.J.R. School	125	18-60	local residents, shopkeepers, hawkers, auto rickshaw and drivers
4.	Residential Sector 7, HUDDA	120	18-60	local residents, shopkeepers, hawkers, auto rickshaw and drivers

Table 5.2: Mean concentration (μg m^{-3}) of air pollutants (SPM, RSPM, SO_2 and NO_x) and air quality index (AQI) at different locations

Sl. No.	Air Monitoring locations	Pollutants in μg/ m^3				AQI Category/ Description
		RSPM	SPM	NO_x	SO_2	
1.	Lord Shiva Woolen Mills near Toll Plaza	319.10	652.40	32.5	21.2	V / Polluted
2.	Pan Foods Ltd. G.T.Road, Panipat	435.70	558.70	30.0	23.0	V / Polluted
3.	Residential Sector 24, HUDDA near M. J. R. School	65.10	196.70	24.0	16.8	III / Fairly Clean
4.	Residential Sector 7, HUDDA	94.85	198.70	15.5	10.2	II / Clean
CPCB Standard*		100	200	80	80	
EPA Rules 1996*	Industrial/ Commercial areas	150	500	120	120	
	Residential areas	100	200	80	80	

***Source:** CPCB, National Ambient Air quality Monitoring series, NAAQMS/22/2001-02.

Table 5.3: Percentage of Respondents Reporting Specific Ailments in Panipat City of Haryana

Sl.No.	Disease	Lord Shiva Woolen Mills	Pan Foods Ltd.	Residential Sector 24, HUDDA	Residential Sector 7, HUDDA
1.	Eye problems	47.6	40.4	14.0	12.0
2.	Cough	48.0	42.4	28.0	32.0
3.	Dry cough	13.5	14.0	7.7	5.9
4.	Sneezing	26.7	26.8	15.0	13.0
5.	Nose block	24.0	18.4	15.0	11.0
6.	Running nose	11.5	13.6	5.2	4.9
7.	Wheezing	20.9	18.2	14.5	8.1
8.	Bronchitis	8.1	7.2	4.3	4.3
9.	Asthma	6.1	1.8	2.8	1.6
10.	Skin disease	4.7	10.0	1.7	0.6
Total number of respondents		**150**	**130**	**125**	**120**

Table 5.4: A comparison between commercial and residential areas disease patterns in Panipat City of Haryana

Sl.No.	Diseases	APDO* in commercial areas with high level of air pollution (%)	APDO* in residential areas with low level of air pollution (%)
1.	Eye problems	44.0	13.50
2.	Cough	45.20	30.0
3.	Sneezing	26.75	14.0
4.	Nose block	21.20	13.0
5.	Wheezing	19.55	12.0
6.	Dry cough	13.75	6.80
7.	Running nose	12.55	5.05
8.	Bronchitis	7.65	4.30
9.	Skin diseases	7.35	1.15
10.	Asthma	3.95	0.88

* ADPO: Average Percentage Disease occurrence

Impact of Pollution in Human Health

At elevated levels, all the pollutants have adverse effects on human and environmental health. Accumulation of pollutants in the human body through inhalation of air is an important route. Results of present study revealed that higher level of particulate matter especially the RSPM, is more dangerous for human health and responsible for several cardiovascular and respiratory problems like cough, dry cough, cold, runny nose, nose block, bronchitis, wheezing, pneumonia and asthma along with eye problems, skin diseases and heart diseases. Information was collected from the respondents about the incidence of eye problems, acute and chronic respiratory diseases and skin diseases. In many cases incidence of multiple diseases in a single respondent was reported. Table 3 presents an account of the percentage occurrence of various diseases in respondents interviewed at the different study locations. Keeping in view this fact and considering NAAQS as a standard we perform the comparison of the average percentage disease occurrence (APDO) in the commercial areas (with high concentrations of air pollutants) and the residential areas (with low concentrations of air pollutants) is presented in Table 4. It shows that for every ailment, except the chronic ones – bronchitis and asthma, the APDO is significantly higher in the commercial areas, with higher concentrations of air pollutants, than in the residential areas. Since the main source of the pollutants in the commercial areas is motor vehicular traffic as well as smoke release to thermal, Refinery and NFL, there is a clear need to decongest such traffic in these areas. Similar study was done in 1996 in Mumbai in which, the exposure to air pollution and its consequent health effects by IIT-Bombay CPCB reported findings of a similar nature (Ghosh C.2001). The maximum number of respondents suffering from chronic cough was from the high pollution areas (18.4%), followed by those living in medium pollution zones (10.2%) and finally the low pollution zones (6.9%). The results of the present study were compared with earlier study during pre monsoon, 2005 (ITRC report 2005; Sharma et al., 2006) during the year 2005 and it was found that the average concentration of air pollutants like SPM and RSPM at ten locations of urban area, showed slightly higher value in commercial areas as compare to residential areas in 2006. The results of the epidemiological study indicate that air pollution in Panipat city of Haryana is seriously affecting the health of the people, especially lived in commercial areas as compare to people lived in residential areas. Increased day by day air pollution is a serious problem and need to immediate reduce traffic congestion in Panipat commercial areas.

Acknowledgement

We are thankful to the Editor and Reviewers of this paper for his valuable comments and also highly thankful to 525 individuals of local residents, shopkeepers, hawkers, auto rickshaw drivers which are highly cooperate during the time of survey periods.

REFERENCES

Barnett, A.G., G.M. Williams, J. Schwartz, A.H. Nekker, T.L.: (2005) Best and A.L. Petriescgevsjt: Air pollution and child respiratory health: A casecrossover study in Australia and New Zealand. Am. J. Respir. Crit.Care Med., 171: 1272-1278.

Caselles, J., C. Colliga and P. Zornoza: (2002) Evaluation of trace elements pollution from vehicle emissions in Petunia plants. Water Air Soil Pollut. 136, 1-9.

Chen, L.H., S.F. Knutsen, D. Shavlik, W.L. Beeson, F. Peterson and M. Ghamsary: (2005) The association between fatal coronary heart disease and ambient particulate air pollution: Are females at greater risk? Environ. Hlth. Persp., 113: 723-1729.

CPCB: (1994) National Ambient Air Quality Standards, Central Pollution Control Board, Gazette Notification, New Delhi.

Curtis, L., W. Rea, P. Smith-Willis, E. Fenyves and Y. Pan: (2006) Adverse health effects of outdoor air pollutants. Environ. Intern., 32 : 815-830.

Dockery, D.W., H. Luttnabb-Gibson, D.Q. Rich, M.L. Link, M.A. Mittleman, D.R. Gold: (2005) Association of air pollution with increased incidence of ventricular tachyarrythmias recorded by impanted cardioverter defibrillators. Environ. Hlth. Persp., 113: 670-674.

Dockery, D.W., C.A. Pope, X. Xu, J.D. Spengler, J.H. Ware, M.E. Fay, B. G. Ferris and F.E. Speizer: (1993) An association between air pollution and mortality in six US cities. New Eng. J. Med., 329: 1753-1759.

Dockery D.W and Pope C.A. III: (1994) "Acute Respiratory Effects of Particulate Air Pollution", Annual Review of Public Health, v.15, pp: 107-132.

Ghosh C. : (2001) "Clear as Air", Down to Earth. V.10 No.8, September.

Jayaraman, G.N.: (2007) Air quality and respiratory health in Delhi. Environ. Monit. Assess DOI 10.1007/s 10661-007-9651-0.

Kaushik, C.P., K. Ravindra and K. Yadav: (2006) Assessment of ambient air quality in urban centres of Haryana (India) in relation to different anthropogenic activities and health risk. Environ. Monit. Assess., 122: 27-40.

Liu, D, S. Knewski, Y. Shi, Y. Chen and R.T. Burnett: (2003) Association between gaseous ambient air pollutants and adverse pregnancy outcomes in Vancouver, British Columbia. Environ. Hlth. Persp., 111: 1773-1778.

Maitre, A., V. Bonneterre, L. Huillard, P. Sabatier and R. Gaudemaris: (2006) Impact of urbanatmospheric pollution on coronary disease. European. Heart J., 27: 2275-2284.

Peters, A, S. Von Klot, M. Heier, I. Trentinaglia, A. Horman and E. Wichmann: (2004) Exposure to traffic and the onset of myocardial infarction. New Eng. J. Med., 351: 1721-1730.

Pope, C.A., M.J. Thyb and M.M. Namboodiri: (1995) Particulate air pullution as a predictor of mortality in a prospective study of US adults. Am. J. Respir Crit. Care Med., 151: 669-674.

Sagai, M., A. Furuyama and T. Ichinose: (1996) Biological effects of diesel exhaust particles (DEP). III. Pathogenosis of asthma like symptoms in mice. Free Rad. Biol. Med., 21: 199-209.

Schwartz, J., D.W. Dockery and L.M. Neas: (1996) Is daily mortality associated specifically with fine particles? J. Air Waste Manage. Asso., 46: 927-939.

Sharma, K., R. Singh, S.C. Barman, D. Mishra, R. Kumar, M.P.S. Negi, S.K. Mandal, G.C. Kisku, A.H. Khan, M.M. Kidwai and S.K. Bhargava: (2006) Comparison of trace metals concentration in PM10 of different location of Lucknow city. Bullet Environ. Contam. Toxicol., 77: 419-426.

Ye, F., W.T. Piver, M. Ando and C.J. Portier: (2001) Effects of temperature and air pollutants on cardiovascular and respiratory diseases for males and females older than 65 years of age in Tokyo, July and August 1980-1995.Environ. Hlth. Persp., 109: 355-359.

Zanobetti, A. and J. Schwartz: Cardiovascular damage by airborne particles: (2002) Are diabetics more susceptible? Epidemiol., 13: 588-592.

6

Environmental Impact of Human Activities on Coastal Erosion, Coastal Ecosystem and Marine Biodiversity in India

—G.C. Kisku, India

ABSTRACT

Coastal erosion and accretion is a natural phenomenon all along the coastal zone of peninsular India and Andaman Nicobar & Lakshadweep islands. The basic purpose of this paper is to understand the short and long term consequences on Coastal Erosion & Accretion, Coastal Ecosystem and Marine Biodiversity due to the interferences and activities of human either in the coastal areas or in the inland areas. Fragile Coastal ecosystems includes coral reefs, mangrove forests, sea grass beds, estuaries, hydrothermal vents, sea mounts and soft sediments on the ocean floor deep below the surface area. Both the ecosystem and the biodiversity are adversely affected because of indiscriminate destructive fishing practices, habitat destruction, the over-exploitation of living resources, transportation, disposal of untreated or partially treated domestic sewage & industrial effluents, organic & chemical pollution, oil pollution, agricultural runoff containing persistent pesticides & nutrients, coastal development & tourism, the introduction of exotic species and global climate change. Measurable irreversible damages have already been noticed on some of the atolls of Lakshadweep and coral reefs of the Andaman and Nicobar groups of islands because of oil pollution. Coal fired power plants, along with factories and vehicles all emit SO2 and NOx. These mildly acidic gases react with the atmospheric water vapours and create acidic compounds; sulfurous acid & sulfuric acid and nitric acid that precipitate as acid rain. Coal is the dirtiest carbon intensive of all fossil fuels and the leading contributors to climate change. Burning of coal releases the huge amounts of solid waste residue, massive amounts of gaseous pollutants such SO_2, including green house gases CO_2, NOx and water vapors. Besides, these pollutants, it also releases substantial amount of direct heat into the atmosphere either through discharge of hot flu gases (50-70 °C) from chimney, diffusion of hot stream from *various points or waste heat to atmosphere from the cooling water system. Global climate and global warming change will make seas and coastal levels will rise, water temperature will increase, oceans will acidify and there will be more storms and natural disasters. Detailed information and monitoring about the changes occurred along the Indian coast is a prime need at certain time interval due to the human activities and climate change to prepare and develop "Coastal Management Plan".*

Key words: *Environmental Impact, Human Activities, Coastal Erosion, Coastal Ecosystem, Marine Biodiversity*

Introduction

India's coast is ~7517 km long spanning 13 maritime mainland states and Union Territories; of this 5423 km belong to peninsular India and 2094 km to the Andaman Nicobar and Lakshadweep islands. According to the Indian naval hydrographic charts, the mainland coast consists of 43% sandy beaches, 11% rocky coast including cliffs and 46% mudflats or marshy coast. It also supports almost 30% of its human population being dependent on the rich exploitable coastal and marine resources [(8)]. More than just a valuable source of food, the ocean is one of the largest natural reservoirs of carbon. It stores about over 15 times more CO_2 than the terrestrial biosphere and soils and plays a significant role in climate moderation.

Oceans cover 70% of our planet and represent over 95% of the biosphere. Oceans are seriously under-protected, with only about 0.8% of the oceans and 6% of territorial seas being in protected areas [(11)]. Coastal erosion depends on natural conditions and human actions. The most significant natural conditions are the marine climate (mainly storms), the geology and morphology of the littoral and recently climate change. The most significant human influences include the regulation of the river sediment flux in the hinterland and intervention on the coast: harbours, coastal defences sand nourishment and urban and infrastructure development in the coastal zone.

Human activities along the coast (land reclamation, port development, shrimp farming), within river catchments and watersheds (river damming and diversion) and offshore (dredging sand mining) in combination with these natural forces often exacerbate coastal erosion in many places and jeopardize opportunities for coasts to fulfil their socio-economic and ecological roles in the long term at a reasonable societal cost.

Five major social driving forces affecting coastal ecosystem in India are urbanization, intensive aquaculture and agriculture, industrial activity, port activity and tourism. A number of coastal areas and ecosystems in India are under stress due to growing aquaculture and agriculture activities. The coastal ecosystem is a very complex one and is always under stress because of industrial and domestic pollution. Along the Maharashtra coast luxuriant growth of seaweed was observed in verdant areas, whereas species diversity diminishes considerably in areas affected by pollution.

Shoreline changes induced by erosion and accretion are natural processes that take place over a range of time scales. They may occur in response to smaller-scale (short-term) events, such as storms, regular wave action, tides and winds, or in response to large-scale (long-term) events such as glaciation or orogenic cycles that may significantly alter sea levels (rise/fall) and tectonic activities that cause coastal land subsidence or emergence. Hence, most coastlines are naturally dynamic and cycles of erosion are often an important feature of their ecological character. Wind, waves and currents are natural forces that easily move the unconsolidated sand and soils in the coastal area, resulting in rapid changes in the position of the shoreline.

Marine and coastal habitats include coral reefs, mangrove forests, sea grass beds, estuaries, hydrothermal vents, sea mounts and soft sediments on the ocean floor deep below the surface. Fragile Coastal ecosystems are simultaneously attacked by organic and chemical pollution and degradation of natural recourses is some times irreversible. In fact Coastal zones are vulnerable areas in different parts of the world but in developing countries the impact of degradation can be worse than in others countries.

The basic purpose of this paper is to understand the short and long term consequences on Coastal Erosion & accretion, Coastal Ecosystem and Marine Biodiversity due to the interferences and activities of human either in the coastal areas or in the inland areas.

Extent of Coastal Erosion and Accretion

According to Gibb (1978) [6] coastal erosion is the process of removal of material at the shoreline which leads to loss of land as the shoreline retreats landward. Accretion is the product of deposition of material at the shoreline which leads to gain of land as the coast advances seaward. The coastal erosion and accretion indicator measures changes in shoreline dynamics and efforts to directly counteract the adverse effects of those dynamics. Detailed monitoring of these changes is very important, especially if we take into account that the effects of climate change could increase substantially in the next 100 years. Information on shoreline changes can help to predict future changes and to prepare and develop adaptation policies for climate change effects. Coastal erosion, related flood and landslide phenomena normally generate very high economic, social and environmental costs. In order to prevent and to avoid these costs it is necessary to have very good and detailed information about the real impacts in the past and in the present. The indicator has 3 set of measurements (1) The length of protected and defended coastline, (2) the length of dynamic coastline and (3) the area and volume of sand nourishment to achieve the goals for coastal sustainability set out in the EU Recommendation concerning the implementation of ICZM - "To recognise the threat to coastal zones posed by climate change and to ensure appropriate and ecologically responsible coastal protection".

Coastal Erosion: Extent and Causes

Coastal erosion and accretion are natural processes; however, they have become anomalous and widespread in the coastal zone of Asia and other countries in the Indian Ocean owing to combinations of various natural forces, population growth and unmanaged economic development along the coast, within river catchments and offshore. This type of erosion has been reported in Bangladesh, China, India, Indonesia, Japan, Sri Lanka, Thailand, Vietnam and Malaysia [2].

Marine and Coastal Biodiversity

Marine and coastal biodiversity encompasses the enormous number of marine and coastal species and their genetic variety. Coastal ecosystems, such as estuaries, wetlands, and mangrove forests, also contain significant diversity and are important to the economies of coastal communities. Highest diversity of corals has been recorded in Andaman and Nicobar islands. India is one among 17 mega biodiversity countries in the world and also ranked 14th among the 22 countries which contain the world's major mangrove areas. About 844 species of marine algae are recorded from India (Venkataraman and Wafar, 2005) [14]. Five of the seven species of sea turtles found world wide are reported to occur in Indian coastal waters. About 25 species of marine mammals known to occur in Indian water (Venkataraman and Wafar, 2005) [14].

The reef biocomposition is quite significant and includes 180 species of benthic algae, 14 species of seaweeds, 12 species of sea grasses, 108 species of sponges, 4 species of lobsters, 103 species of echinoderms, 600 species of fin fishes and also a good number of species of crabs, bivalves, gastropods and cephalopods each in Lakshadweep and Andaman and Nicobar islands. In India, 208 species of hard corals belonging to 60 genera have been so far described however, UNEP reported the presence of 342 species of coral reefs belonging to 76 genera from the seas around India[13]. Furthermore, coral reefs provide habitat for a rich diversity of marine life (3). Several reef organisms build their skeletons and shells out of calcium carbonate. When these organisms die, their skeletal remains are transported to the beach or are cemented into the framework of the reef. Most of the light-colored sand on beaches derives from coral reefs [3].

Threats to Coastal and Marine Biodiversity

Coastal and marine ecosystems are among the most biologically and economically productive ecosystems in the world and the same is true for India where these ecosystems are both a source of livelihood as well as of a range of ecological services that are critical for the day to day well-being of millions of people particularly coastal communities. Today, human activities around the world are depleting marine and coastal living resources and degrading marine and coastal ecosystems in ways that are harmful and sometimes irreversible. Numerous direct and indirect pressures arising from different types of faster economic development and associated activities are having adverse impacts on coastal and marine biodiversity across the country are posing major challenges for conservation of marine biodiversity and are greatly threatening the seas and coasts through overfishing, destructive fishing practices, habitat destruction, indiscriminate fishing and the over-exploitation of living resources, transportation, the effects of pollution & sewage waste disposal, agricultural runoff containing excessive nutrients and pesticides, coastal development and its side effects, the introduction of exotic species, tourism and global change, in particular climate change but also including ozone depletion. Loss of biodiversity and the attendant decimation of stocks of living resources, widespread appearance of ecosystem imbalances and impairment of ecological processes may well undermine the adaptive potential of species and ecosystems and their ability to meet future human needs.

Impact of Global Warming and Climate Change on Coastal and Marine Landscape and Biodiversity

Additionally, climate change is likely to have a growing impact on coastal and marine ecosystems, including a likely increase in extreme weather events e.g. storminess as well as sea level rise, warming of the sea surface temperatures and ocean acidification. The effect of global climate change and global warming brings changes in trophic dynamics, abundance and distribution of fauna in various tropic levels and it also one of the causative for coral bleaching phenomena.

Environmental Laws to Protect Marine Life

The Coastal Regulation Zone Notification, 1991; National Biodiversity Act, 2002 and the Environment (Protection) Act, 1986 have been enacted by India for the conservation of coastal and marine environment along with the Wildlife (Protection) Act, 1972 which also provides for the establishment of wildlife protected areas by State Governments. So far, about 25 Marine Protected Areas have been established. The Gulf of Kutch Marine National Park, the Gulf of Mannar National Park and Wandoor Marine National Park are some of the important MPAs of India.

Coastal Erosion Problems in India

Sagar Island in West Bengal

The rapid erosion of the coast of Sagar Island in West Bengal, India, is caused by several processes that act in concert; these are natural processes that occur frequently (cyclones, waves and tides that can reach 6 m in height) and anthropogenic activities such as human settlement and aquaculture that remove mangroves and other coastal vegetation. The erosion rate from 1996 to 1999 was calculated to be 5.47 square kilometres/year (Gopinath and Seralathan, 2005) [7]. The areas that are severely affected by erosion are the northeasterns, southwestern and southeastern faces of the island. Malini and Rao (2004) [10] reported coastal erosion and habitat loss along the Godavari Delta front owing to the combination of the dam construction across the Godavari and its tributaries that diminishes sediment supply to the coast and continued coastal land subsidence[2].

Problems of Coral reefs and Mangroves

Coral reefs and mangroves (including macroalgae and seagrasses) occur widely in Indian coastal areas. Damages that can occur to these ecosystems as a result of over exploitation of the reefs of mangroves or because of pollution are quite extensive.

Coral reefs in the Lakshadweep and other Coastal Zones

Coral reefs of the tropical Indian ocean include, fringing and barrier reefs; sea-level atoll; and elevated reefs. Around India coral reef formations are found in the Palk bay, gulf of Mannar, Gulf of Kutch, Central West coast of India, Lakshadweep atolls and Andaman & Nicobar Islands and Maldives Islands. Both, the coral atoll and the fringing coral reefs are of utmost significance in Indian water. Nine genera of coral reefs from Lakshadweep have been reported. Most of the coral reefs in this region have been declared as endangered ecosystems. Several coral reefs have almost disappeared because of the collection of coral debris and live corals for use as a raw material in the cement industry, while others have died due to their constant exposure to pollutants, particularly oil viz. the region of Kavaratti reef in the Lakshadweep [13].

It has been observed that dead as well as live coral beds are exploited for the Carbide industry and for white cement. Large scale exploitation of corals in the Gulf of Kutch has been checked to a great extent due to timely warning. Development of Tuticorin harbor and associated industrial activities as well as oil pollution has resulted in large scale destruction of coral reefs around the islands of Tuticorin. Andaman-Nicobar fringing reefs and Lakshadweep coral atolls are comparatively free from such problems.. However, the recent data of Minicoy and Kavaratti atolls and Great Nicobar Island indicate that there is a definite effect of oil pollution on coral of these areas.

Apart from this, use of corals for ornamental and decorative purpose is yet another serious threat to this sensitive ecosystem. Local people of Lakshadweep also use corals for construction and white washing of houses and as mortar.

Reefs are natural breakwaters; they absorb much of the incoming wave energy and help protect the shoreline from wave attack. Without the wave buffering and sand production that coral reefs provide, rates of coastal erosion and beach loss would be significantly higher.

Climate Change and Coral reefs Marine Working Group

This need is particularly critical for coral reef ecosystem, which are both highly vulnerable to climate change and also vital to the welfare of large human population throughout the tropical world. The International Union for the Conservation of Nature (IUCN) recognizes this need to promote the integration of resilience science and coral reef ecosystem management [(3)].

Mangroves in Sundarbans and Deltas

Mangroves (viz. Rhizophora sp., Xylocarpus sp., Cenocarpus sp., Cariops sp.,.) occur in profusion along NE coast of India. Mangroves constitute an important resource in the region and form spawning grounds, nurseries and feeding grounds for economically important fishes and crustaceans. They act as a buffer zone and offer protection to vulnerable communities like coral reefs. They also stabilize the bottom sediments, control the local mean water level and the direction of flow. Mangroves constitutes a significant portion of the coastal wetland in many countries and a fairly large percentage of the human population is dependent on them. Due to ever increasing demand for land and fuel, many mangroves areas of the Indian Ocean region have been and are being destroyed. This has led to heavy siltation in the near shore region and with no protective cover of mangrove, the devastation of men and material caused during cyclones in coastal areas is immense [(13)].

Assessment of Possible Impacts of Pollutants on the on Coastal Areas and Marine Environment

Industries remain one of the major competitors for the use of coastal areas. For industries, the major advantages of the location on the coast are transportation, water use and waste disposal. The importance of the industrial sector in the Indian economy has risen over the years. The contribution of industries to the gross domestic product has improved, along with a rise in the share of employment in the secondary sector. The New Economic Policy, with its package of globalisation, liberalisation and privatisation, changed the entire scenario of the Indian industrial sector. Thus the coastal states together represented 55% of the foreign investment in India during this period.

In India, industrial activity has concentrated in certain specific areas, causing a regional imbalance. Cities like Mumbai, Ahmedabad, Chennai and Calcutta had large-scale industrialization during the colonial period and even now also. Many of the highly polluting industries are located in the coastal areas. Dumping industrial waste is common in many parts of those areas.

Some of the industrial effluents are toxic and can remain in the sea for a long time and bioconcentrated in the organisms. Several pollutants have detrimental effects on most life forms and affect their breeding, growth, reproduction and survival (Jorge et al, 2002) [9].

Industrial and port activity tend to affect coastal ecosystems due to a number of reasons : wrong location can be the most obvious reason; choice of technology that is not environmentally friendly; no preventive approach to pollution in place, the tendency is always to look for end of pipe solutions; poor enforcement of standards and rules and sometimes poor ability to judge whether they comply to norms.

The coastal areas attract an increasing number of industrial investments, resulting in an increase in terms of economic activity. Industries draw foreign exchange, improve the standard of living and create employment. However, the adverse impacts of industries on the coastal ecosystems cannot be neglected. Adequate legal structure for coastal zones and strict implementation of the existing laws are required to collect the benefits without compromising ecology.

The oil pollution problem is almost common to all countries. Because of the transportation of a large volume of oil through the Indian Ocean, many areas are getting damaged. The worst affected ecosystems are the coral reefs and sandy beaches. Significant damage has already been noted on some of the atolls of Lakshadweep and coral reefs of the Andaman and Nicobar groups of islands. In India, the disposal of untreated or partially treated domestic sewage and industrial effluents generally discharges into the river which find its way into the seas. The excess and indiscriminate use of fertilizers, pesticides, herbicides and insecticides in agricultural practices can also pose significant problems. Apart from toxic industrial effluents discharges from thermal power plants have also been reported to be harmful to the general productivity.

Potential of Coal Power Plant to Climate Change and Its Possible Impact on Seas

Coal is the dirtiest carbon intensive of all fossil fuels and the leading contributors to climate change. Burning of coal releases of huge amounts of solid waste residue, massive amounts of gaseous pollutants SO_2, including green house gases CO_2, NOx and water vapors.

Besides, these solid, liquid and gaseous pollutants, it also releases substantial amount of direct heat into the atmosphere either through discharge of hot flu gases (50-70 °C) from chimney, diffusion of hot stream from various points or waste heat to atmosphere in the cooling water system. The cooling water has used to condense the steam in the condenser and returns to its source without having been changed other than having been warmed up to 35 - 55 °C which may create thermal shock when discharged into the receiving water body if the hot water is not tempered with cool raw water. Fossil fueled power stations are major emitters of Green House Gases (GHG) which according to the consensus of scientific organization are a major contributor to the global warming observed over the last 100 years. Brown coal emits 3 times as much as GHG as Natural gas, black coal emits twice as much.

Electricity generation using carbon based fuels is reasonable for a large fraction of CO_2 emissions world wide and for 41% of U.S. anthropogenic CO_2 emission. Of fossil fuel, coal combustion in thermal power station resulting greater amount of CO_2 emission per unit of electricity generated (2249 lbs/MWh) while oil produce less 1672 lbs/MW h are 211 kg/GJ) and natural gas produced the least 1135 lbs/MWh or (143 kg/GJ). The Intergovernmental Panel on Climatic Change (IPCC) states that CO_2 is a green house gas and that increased quantities within the atmosphere will "very likely" lead to higher average temperature on a global scale (global warming) concerns regarding the potential for such warming to change the global climate prompted IPCC recommendations calling for large cut to CO_2 emission worldwide [(5)].

The world organizations and international agency, like the International Energy Agency (IEA), are concerned about the Environmental impact of burning fossil fuel and coal in particular. Global climate and global warming change will make seas and coastal areas worse. Sea levels will rise, water temperature will increase, oceans will acidify, and there will be more storms and natural disasters.

Impact of Air Pollution and Acid Rain

The combustion of coal contributes the most to acid rain and air pollution and has been connected with global warming and climatic change. Power plants, along with factories and vehicles that also burn fossil fuels, all emit SO_2 and NOx. These mildly acidic gases react with the atmosphere and create acidic compounds viz. sulfurous acid & sulfuric acid and nitric acid that fall as acid rain (De, 2007) (4). Acid precursors can easily be absorbed in by the seas water and may be the cause of acidification and ultimately impair the marine biodiversity.

$$SO_2 + \frac{1}{2}O_2 \xrightarrow[\text{or merit oxide}]{\text{Soot dust}} SO_3 + \xrightarrow{H_2O} H_2SO_3 \longrightarrow \underset{\text{Aerosol Droplet}}{(H_2SO_4)} \quad (i)$$

$$NO_2 + O_3 \longrightarrow NO_3 + O_2$$

$$NO_2 + NO_3 \longrightarrow N_2O_5 + \xrightarrow{H_2O} 2HNO_3 \quad (ii)$$

Conclusion

More focus should be given to ecologically sensitive coastal areas such as coral reefs, mangroves, turtle nesting beaches, sand dunes, mud flats, estuaries etc. Planning and managing of the coastal zone must consider the effect of human intervention on costal erosion but must also take into account the natural erosion/accretion trends. Unless measures to minimize the pollution along the coastal area are adopted some of the unique flora and fauna of the Indian coastline may be lost for ever. The increasing threats associated with climate change and increased population pressure is driving an urgent need to accelerate developments in resilience science and its incorporation into realistic and meaningful management strategies. Restoration and proper management of coastal ecosystems is an immediate need of the mankind for long term sustainable development.

Acknowledgements

The technical assistance of Ms. Poonam Pandey is highly acknowledged.

REFERENCES

1. Bhupathy, S. and S. Saravanan Status Survey of Sea Turtles along the Tamilnadu Coast. *Kachhapa* 7(2002) :7-13.
2. Chapter 4 Protection From Coastal Erosion (Thematic paper: The role of coastal forests and trees in protecting against coastal erosion) available at http://www.fao.org/docrep/010/ag127e/AG127E09.htm
3. Coastal Ecosystems available at http://www.soest.hawaii.edu/SEAGRANT/ bmpm/coastal_ecosystems.html.
4. De AK, 2007. Environmental Chemistry, 6th Edition, New Age International (P) Limited, Publishers, New Delhi.
5. Fossil fuel power station available at <http://en.wikipendia.org/wiki/Fossil_Fuel_power_ plant>
6. Gibb J.G., Rates of coastal erosion and accretion in New Zealand, *N.Z. Journal of Marine and Freshwater Research 12 (4):* 429-56 December 1978
7. Gopinath, G. and P. Seralathan. 2005. Rapid erosion of the coast of Sagar island, West Bengal–India. *Environment Geology*, 48: 1058–1067.
8. India available at http://en.wikipedia.org/wiki/india
9. Jorge, M.R., Lourenco N., Nelson, Machado C.R. and Rodrigues, L. Measuring, monitoring and managing sustainability in Indian coastal areas: the socioeconomic dimension, Littoral (2002), 22- 26.
10. Malini, B.H. & K.N. Rao. 2004. Coastal erosion and habitat loss along the Godavari delta front – a fallout of dam construction. Current Science, 87 (9): 1232–126.
11. Marine and Coastal Biodiversity available at www.cbd.int/marine
12. A. Charlotte de Fontaubert, David R. Downes, and Tundi S. Agardy. 1996. *Biodiversity in the Seas: Implementing the Convention on Biological Diversity in Marine and Coastal Habitats.* Gland, Switzerland: IUCN- The World Conservation Union available at Web: http://www.econet.apc.org/ciel/
13. UNEP regional Seas Reports abd studies No. 59. Environmental problems of the marine and coastal area of India: National Report.
14. *Venkataraman, K and Mohideen Wafar*, M. Coastal and marine biodiversity of India, Indian J. of Mar. Sc., 34 (2005): 57-75.

7

Environmental Pollution during Election

—Shreerup Goswami, India
—Swati Pattanayak, India

ABSTRACT

Now election and politics at all levels are inevitable in our society. By this process, we generally select our new leader. However, now-a-days elections intensify societal and environmental problems such as noise pollution, vehicular pollution (air pollution), colour pollution (water and soil pollution), paper pollution, (air, water and soil pollution), health hazard and adverse socio economic impact. We must pay for the evil we do. Nevertheless, the election is the only way to form the Government in a democratic country. Hence, one and all including the political leaders irrespective of parties should be aware of our natural environment. The present ways and means of promoting and publicizing own political parties in the election should be restrained. The different societal and environmental hazards associated with the election are discussed in this article to make aware the people and politicians.

Keywords: *Environmental pollution, vehicular pollution, Election, Noise pollution*

Introduction

The planet earth houses animals, insects, birds, plants and other living beings and a number of non living objects made up of five basic elements such as water, air, fire, sky and soil (The Pancha Mahabhut). Man, an appealing creation of nature has been living with these members of his environment since its origin leading a peaceful life. Man influences and is influenced by all these living and non-living creations of nature. Each member supports the existence of the other on the planet -one complements the other, with no contradictions. Thus, man and its society help each other for their survival. This is an intrinsic harmony between man and societal environment (Goswami et al., 2007; Bapat and Rao, 2004; Anderson, 2001).

From the day, when man started living in group instead of living individually, they began to select the group leader. Subsequently election and politics in the society started. As civilization progressed and science advanced, man started creating his own 'artificial' environment such as nasty politics, malicious political beliefs and malevolent political affairs to fit them into the sanctified societal environment. As a result the harmony in the society is disturbed. Man's unplanned behaviour and repulsive gestures during the election have worn purity of the earth. In one hand, civilization and living style has reached its peak, but in the other hand the ethical values of life and wholesomeness of environment and society have besmirched. Now all the living beings are living in a venomous world and taking up poison in their breath, drink and food. Election also has a major role in polluting the natural environment. The activities involved in the election are the cause of societal and environmental pollution such as water, air, soil pollution (colour pollution, paper pollution), noise pollution, health hazard and have serious socio economic impact. As India is the largest democratic country in the world, general election here in India is conducted in many phases and continues for several months. Besides our general election, interestingly our nation is conducting several elections throughout the year, which are polluting our environment.

It is evident that technological progress, and the way it progressed, had a disastrously negative impact on our environment (Aswathanarayana, 2003; Dash, 2004; Santra, 2004). As civilisation progressed and science advanced, we became a pollution loving nation and gradually forgot minimum civic sense. We need wholesome oxygen. However, we pollute air by bursting crackers on the occasions of wining of an election, and in many other such occasions. We worship many animals as they are associated with many God and Goddess, but our wildlife is on the verge of extinction. We are primarily a vegetarian nation, but kill goat, sheep and other animals and birds for festivities during election. We are lovers of cleanliness and thus broom out all pushing cards and banners etc. in the public streets during election. We equally enjoy noise pollution. Our election campaign and processions must be accompanied by bands, twists and must use loud speakers.

Vehicular Pollution

Due to unlimited and excessive running of thousands of vehicles for election campaigning, different gaseous pollutants are released during, before and after elections. In India, during election, air pollution is widespread where vehicles are the major contributors. The exhaust gas of vehicle contains mainly CO_2, CO etc., which released in the air and pollute the atmosphere. Carbon monoxide is emitted in considerable quantity, when petrol is completely oxidized in the environment. When CO is in the air, it rapidly accumulates in the blood, causing symptoms similar to the flu, such as headaches, fatigue, nausea and dizzy spells. As levels increase, vomiting, loss of consciousness and eventually brain damage or death can result (Pattanaik and Goswami, 2008).

Apart from the products of incomplete or partial combustion of petrol, lead and lead compounds are also present in the exhaust. It has been reported that some 3000 tons of lead are emitted with the exhaust gases of automobiles, especially cars. This has been found to accumulate in the vegetations and soil. In addition, some oxides of nitrogen are also emitted from the engine. All these chemical products are expelled as exhaust gas. The diesel exhaust contains some carcinogens like benjopyrene, which cause cancer in human body (Pattanaik and Goswami, 2008). Apart from the concentration of vehicles during election, other reasons for increasing vehicular pollution are the types of engines used, age of vehicles, congested traffic, poor road conditions, and outdated automotive technologies and traffic management systems. Though under the National Ambient Air Quality Monitoring (NAAQM) network, three criteria air pollutants, namely, SPM, SO2, and NO2 have been identified for regular monitoring at different stations spread across the country by CPCB, air monitoring during election should be conducted and compared with that of other time of the same station.

The important pollutants present in the exhaust gas produced by automobiles are given below (Pattanaik and Goswami, 2008; Das, 2004; Santra, 2004; Sharma, 2005).

Pollutant	
Water vapour CO_2 Unburnt petrol	Not considered as serious pollutants.
CO Nitrogen oxides Lead compounds Sulphur oxides Carbon particles (smoke) Carcinogens (Benjopyrene etc.)	Considered as serious pollutants.

Different automobile parts also cause air pollution (Pattanaik and Goswami, 2008; Das, 2004; Santra, 2004; Sharma, 2005).

During election, different political conflicts lead to burning of effigies/ jack straws, houses, cottages, shops, vehicles, banners, tyres etc. out of jealousy and covetousness, which also creates huge amount of CO_2 and CO gases. These gases generally disturb the harmony and synchronization of the atmosphere. Ozonosphere protects the earth and it's creatures from the harmful effect of Ultra Violet rays. However, the pollutants generated from such envious political activities deplete the ozone layer. It increases the global temperature and accelerates the green house effect leading to Global warming. CO_2 is easily soluble in water and the ocean contains enormous amount of it.

Table 7.1: Automobile Parts and Related Pollutants

Part	Causes Emission of
Battery	Lead and HCl
Bumper	Wastes including cyanide, chromic and other heavy metals
Break shoes	Asbestos
Engine	Slag with toxic contaminants
Seat textiles	Dyes, acids, solvents, greases and waxes
Gasoline tank	Benzene and hydrocarbon during fuelling
Plastic compounds	Vinyl chloride, formaldehyde, phenols
Tyres	Amines, nitrosamines and solvents

The increase of temperature reduces its water solubility and contaminates the air. These pollutant gases are polluting the air, water, soil in particular and the whole environment in general. The government should take a number of measures to abate air pollution during election such as strict legislation, vehicular pollution control measures and promotion of environmental awareness.

Colour Pollution

Colours brighten our world. They are also ubiquities and pervasive. We are not talking about natural colours of nature, but of synthetic colours which are used in various ways during elections. Different materials like pigments, acids, paints, even colours used in plastics and printing inks used in making posters, banners and walling during election cause colour pollution. Before the election, advertisement of political parties and leaders are stuck on almost every tree, building walls, light post, vehicles, hoarding and at several other places. Besides sticking banners or posters, colour oil paints are also used for advertisement. After the election, the banners and posters are thrown here and there in road side. Temporary stages and daises/podiums for election rally, meeting are decorated with painted synthetic plastic flowers, cloth, paper, wood, bamboo and thermocole. Even vehicles deployed for election campaign are decorated with all these painted materials. The paper is degradable but plastics, inks, colours, paints, dyes etc. are non-degradable substances and most of them are toxic chemicals (Pattanaik and Goswami, 2008). These papers, plastics are dumped, thrown to water bodies or burnt or left behind as aftermath of an election. As a result, election causes soil, water and air pollution simultaneously.

The colour paper used for advertisements is obtained by dyeing the paper stock or the paper surface (size press, paper coating). Both inorganic and organic pigments (for instance azo and phthalocyanine types) and carbon black are used for paper dyeing. For paper printing lead is also used. High levels of lead ingestion can damage the heart, kidneys, liver, circulatory and central nervous systems. The most common form of lead poisoning seen today is the disturbance of the gastro-intestinal system known as lead colic. Children are the worst sufferers of lead poisoning (Pattanaik and Goswami, 2008).

Synthetic colour impacts the environment, when it is released into water and soil. The contaminated water inhibits photosynthetic activity of aquatic biota due to reduction in the penetration of sunlight. Besides, toxic chemicals directly affect the aquatic organism. The toxic chemicals enter into the water bodies and then to living aquatic organisms (especially fishes and weeds) and finally into the human body, which cause serious health effect. The colour compounds also contain heavy metals which pollute the surface and ground water. Research has revealed different extreme toxic effect of dyes, pigments, colours, paints etc. on people and the environment. Coloured products, papers, paints contain hazardous metals like lead, mercury and chromium. Dyes contain metals such as copper, nickel, chromium, mercury and cadmium (Das, 2004; Santra, 2004; Sharma, 2005). Particularly, red, blue, orange and green colour paints contain mercury, zinc oxide, chromium and lead. Blue colour in particular is generally used for walling during election campaign in large scale[1]. The synthetic colours and ways these are manufactured and their mode of uses in various ways during election are detrimental. It is clearly evident that election causes acute colour pollution and in turn pollutes surrounding atmosphere, soil and water bodies.

The synthetic colour containing hexavalent chromium causes cancer when ingested. Hexavalent chromium causes lung cancer in humans. It is very irritating to the skin and eye. Prolonged contact can cause ulcers to form in skin and partial to permanent damage in eye[2,3].

Synthetic colour containing Mercury may cause pharynx, abdominal pain, vomiting, corrosive ulceration, bloody diarrhea and renal failure. It also causes skin allergy and blurred vision. United States Environment Protection Agency (USEPA) considers organic compounds of mercury, for example, methyl mercury is human carcinogen. When it enters the human body, concentrates in the brain and destroys the brain cells, damaging the central nervous system, and also causes corrosion and ulceration of the digestive tract[1,4].

Other important constituent of synthetic colour such as Zinc oxide may cause abdominal pain, nausea, vomiting, diarrhoea, liver and kidney failure, metal fume fever, papular-pustular skin eruptions in the axilla, inner thigh, inner arm and scrotum etc[5-7].

Ingestion of cadmium contaminated water also causes metal fume fever, acute pulmonary, anemia and teeth discoloration. Chronic cadmium poisoning causes lung and prostate cancer. The first observed chronic effect is generally kidney damage, manifested by excretion of excessive (low molecular weight) protein in the urine. Cadmium is also believed to cause pulmonary emphysema and bone disease (osteomalcia and osteoporosis)[8].

Excess copper ingestion results in copper imbalance. It may cause arthritis, fatigue, adrenal burnout, insomnia, scoliosis, osteoporosis, heart disease, cancer, migraine headaches, seizures, fungal and bacterial infections including yeast infection, gum disease, tooth decay, skin problem and uterine fibroids, endometriosis in case of females. Copper imbalance also depletes the adrenal glands and lowers the necessary zinc level in the body[9].

Therefore, it is clearly evident that the election is practically causes water and soil pollution and is responsible for different health hazards.

Paper Pollution

The packets, posters, banners, decorative articles made up of paper, polyethylene, plastics used in election meeting/ assembly/ procession/ rally etc. are scattered here and there after such activities. The polyethylene and plastics are non-degradable and are germ carriers. The ink used in leaflets and posters are mainly carbon black and lead. These papers are dumped in a place or burnt. After burning and degradation of leaflets and posters; lead is released into the soil, water and air. As a result, lead could possibly enter the food chains and has detrimental effects far from the source of pollution. The lead enters into the body through food or water or by breathing. The most common form of lead poisoning seen today is the disturbance of the gastro-intestinal system known as lead colic. Its symptoms are excessive tiredness, continued headaches, loss of appetite, muscular pains and nausea. These symptoms are produced only when the lead content in the blood increases above 80mg in 100ml of blood. Children are the worst sufferers of lead poisoning. The dust also receives lead from these materials. The lead usually sticks to soil particles. Lead compound moves from soil to ground water. Lead also causes cancer. Therefore election causes paper pollution which in turn leads lead pollution having detrimental health risk (Pattanaik and Goswami, 2008).

Noise Pollution

The political parties arrange meeting, faction, assembly and procession for political campaigning, which cause the noise pollution. The unlimited use of loudspeakers, megaphones, mikes, massive deployment of vehicles and frequent noisy gatherings of people in meetings or processions or rallies are the source of acute noise pollution, which causes different problems to the living world. Such noise causes several social and health problems and mainly causes' auditory and non auditory effects on human health (Pattanaik and Goswami, 2008). Though noise pollution is a slow and subtle killer, yet very little efforts have been made to ameliorate the same.

During election, the sound generally crosses its threshold level. It may cause hypertension, disrupt sleep and/or hinder cognitive development in children. The effects of excessive noise could be so severe that either there is a permanent loss of memory or a psychiatric disorder. Excessive noise during election can lead to mental and physical health problems such as headache, bad temper, hearing problem, loss of concentration, aural communication disturbances etc. (Lam et al., 2009). Non-auditory physical health effects in general and annoyance from noise exposure in particular include changes in blood pressure, heart rate, and levels of stress hormones (Babisch, 2005). The biological mechanism linking noise to hypertension is thought to be mediated through sympathetic and endocrine stress response with subsequent acute changes in vascular tension. The hypothesis is that long-time exposure to noise could result in lasting cardiovascular changes such as atherosclerosis, and increase cardiovascular risk as well as hypertension (Belojevic et al., 2008; Bodin et al., 2009). Excessive traffic noise during election seemed to moderately increase mean blood pressure in children, and possibly in adults.

Health Hazard

Each and every unplanned activity of man not only pollutes the environment but also creates health hazard. Some activities during election make life of common and ignorant people peril. During election, vehicular pollution, water pollution, paper and colour pollution cause harmful effects on health. Injurious effects of these respective pollutions are already discussed earlier.

The political parties motivate people in various ways and virtually in other words they try to buy votes in various means. They motivate the poor, illiterate people to drink wine and other local cheap alcohols for votes. The tribal peoples are worstly affected. Over drinking of Mohua, Handia etc. damages liver and stomach. In the time of election and after winning the election, people becomes addicted to narcotics like-raw tobacco, gutkha, opium, chewing tobacco etc., which are carcinogenic. These narcotics effects lungs, heart and nervous system and cause various fatal diseases such as cancer.

The political parties create nuisance here and there in which many people become injured or killed. They encouraged and tempted people to do social evils. During this period illegal sexual relationship also occurs widely. As a result AIDS like uncured fatal diseases are spreading out day by day. Thus, the life of general public is in peril without any cause and they are suffering from many deadly diseases.

Socio-economic Hazard

The lack of homogeneity in the Indian population causes division between different sections of the people based on religion, region, language, caste and race. Many political parties are involved in caste-, religion- or language-based politics, which effects India's growth and progress. This has led to the rise of political parties with agendas catering to one or a mix of these groups. The narrow focus and vote bank politics of most parties, even in the central government and central legislature, sidelines national issues such as economic welfare and national security. Moreover, internal security is also threatened as incidences of political parties instigating and leading violence between two opposing groups of people is a frequent occurrence herein India. Economic issues like poverty, unemployment, development are main issues that influence politics and are not addressed properly by the ruling parties. The economic policies of most of the parties do not go much further than providing populist subsidies and reservations. Naxalism, religious violence and caste-related violence are important issues that affect the political environment of the nation especially during election.

Billions of black money is spent during the election campaign in a developing country like India, where more than 300 millions of people are below poverty line and 650 million people living in poverty. The evils done by the people during election not only create environmental pollution or health hazard, but also affect the social and economic structure of the state. Various types of social crimes like committing frauds, cheating, robbing/looting, rape and murder increase during the election. The life of general public becomes peril without any cause. Political strikes and nuisance, malicious political beliefs and malevolent political affairs not only create social hazard but also misbalance the economic structure and harmony of the society. Many often various genuine environmental issues are raised by the NGOs and social workers. After unnecessary political interferences the general public is gradually forgetting those issues. Actually we are just wounding our own legs in our own axe. Ultimately, the poor people and the environment suffer for these illegal activities.

Conclusion

Unfortunately, attempts to manipulate and corrupt the polls are very common phenomenon. We must pay for the evil we do. We are digging our own grave. We deserve punishment from the nature for our selfish and unplanned behaviours. The political leaders irrespective of parties forget that they all belong to the same environment and society, where they are doing evils and corruptions, and in turn creating pollution. However, in a democratic country, the election is the only way to form the Government. Hence, it cannot be stopped or banned. The present ways and means of promoting and publicizing own political parties in the election should be restrained. Though a single solution can not handle all the problems arose due to election, a variety of practices should definitely be attempted and implemented. So, to save future generation and to elect a right leader of the nation, we have to wake up to make a greener and cleaner sustainable society of wholesome oxygen, light and water.

The spread of genuine democracy and free election around the world will certainly create a new generation of political leaders who realize the painful truth of sixth extinction before hand. Humankind is rapidly bringing about the extinction of life worldwide, irreversibly destroying the natural beauty and diversity of our Earth, impotently converting our planet to a sad, sullen slum. We are forging the Sixth Global Extinction: the fifth was that caused, we believe, by a massive asteroid 65 million years ago that brought the reign of the dinosaurs to an abrupt close. We must act now to stop sixth extinction. In ten years time we will have lost the opportunity[3]. We cannot shift the blame and responsibility-neither to any politicians or to coming generations. This article takes up this challenge with a three-fronted approach— assembling and spreading the relevant knowledge on "Election Pollution"; canvassing a critical mass of concerned opinion; sustaining action through coming decades. Through this article, an effort is also made to warn about the erroneous way we conduct and participate in the election here in India and this effort will certainly create the ways and means of the environmental awareness to the society.

Acknowledgements

Author is thankful to Dr. J.M. Anderson, Specialist Scientist, South African National Biodiversity Institute, Pretoria, South Africa; Prof. M. Das and Prof. B.C. Guru, Utkal University, Bhubaneswar for encouraging me to write this article and for critically going through my manuscript.

REFERENCES

Goswami, S., Das, M. and Guru, B.C. (2007): Need of Environmental Education in school level. Jour. Soc. Geoscientist and Allied Technol., **8** (2): 27-35, 2007.

Bapat, M.N. and Rao, N.R.N. (2004): Environmental Education at Primary Level-Why and How? 10-20, The Primary Teacher, 2004 (April issue)

Anderson J.M. (2001): Towards Gondwana Alive: promoting biodiversity and stemming the Sixth Extinction, Gondwana Alive Society, Pretoria, pp: 1-140.

Pattanaik, S. and Goswami, S. (2008): Election Pollution. Science Reporter, **45** (2): 30-31.

Das, M.C. (2004): Ecology, Chemistry and Management of Environmental pollution, McMillan India Limited, pp.: 1-322.

Santra, S.C. (2004): Environmental science, New Central Book Agency (p) LTD, Kolkata.

Sharma, B.K. (2005): Environmental Chemistry. Goel publishing house, Eight Revised and Enlarged Edition, Meerut, India.

Babisch, W. (2005): Noise and health. Environ Health Perspect, **113**(1):A14-15.

Belojevic, G.A., Jakovljevic, B.D., Stojanov, V.J., Slepcevic, V.Z. and Paunovic, K.Z. (2008): Nighttime road-traffic noise and arterial hypertension in an urban population. Hypertens Res, **31**(4):775-781.

Bodin, T., Albin, M., Ardö, J., Stroh, E., Östergren, P. and Björk, J. (2009): Road traffic noise and hypertension: results from a cross-sectional public health survey in southern Sweden. Environmental Health, **8:** 38-44.

Lam, K.C., Chan, P.K., Chan, T.C., Au, W.H. and Hui, W.C. (2009): Annoyance response to mixed transportation noise in Hong Kong. App. Acou., **70**: 1-10.

Useful web references

1. http://www.gobartimes.org/20060831/festivals_you.htm
2. http://cancer.about.com/b/2007/05/17/chromium-in-drinking-water-causes-cancer.htm
3. http://www.dhs.ca.gov/ohb/hesis/cr6.htm
4. http://www.tdcenvironmental.com/MercuryIssues.html
5. http://pesticideinfo.org/Detail_Chemical.jsp?Rec_Id=PC35158
6. http://www.marvistavet.com/html/body_zinc_poisoning.html
7. http://www.osha.gov/SLTC/healthguidelines/zincoxide/recognition.html
8. http://www.osha.gov/SLTC/cadmium/recognition.html
9. http://www.drlwilson.com/articles/copper_toxicity_syndrome.htm

8

Adsorption of dyes by Non-Conventional Adsorbents

—*Rais Ahmad, India*

ABSTRACT

The effective removal of dyes from aqueous wastes is an important issue for many industrialized countries. The traditional treatment methods used to remove dyes from wastewater have certain disadvantages such as incomplete dye removal, high reagent and energy requirements, generation of toxic sludge or other waste products that require further disposal. The search for alternative and innovative treatment techniques has focused attention on the use of non conventional adsorbents for dye removal and recovery technologies. In this respect, adsorption has gained an important credibility during recent years because of its good performance and low cost as a pollutant removal technology. Adsorption techniques are widely used to remove certain classes of pollutants from waters, especially those that are not easily biodegradable. Dyes represent one of the problematic groups. Currently, a combination of biological treatment and adsorption on activated carbon is becoming more common for removal of dyes from wastewater. Although commercial activated carbon is a preferred sorbent for color removal, its widespread use is restricted due to high cost regeneration. As a result, other alternative non-conventional sorbents have been investigated. It is well-known that natural materials, waste materials from industry and agriculture and bio-sorbents can be obtained and employed as inexpensive sorbents. In this chapter, an extensive list of sorbent literature has been compiled. It is evident from a literature survey of about 215 recent papers that low-cost sorbents have demonstrated outstanding removal capabilities for certain dyes. In particular, agricultural waste materials might be a promising adsorbent for environmental and purification purposes.

Keywords: *Adsorption, dye, non conventional adsorbent, activated carbon, isotherms.*

INTRODUCTION

Dyes and pigments are widely used as colouring agents. The total dye consumption in textile industry worldwide is more than 10,000 tonnes/year and approximately 100 tonnes/ year of dyes discharged into waste streams. Dye effluents are aesthetic pollutants that contain chemicals which exhibit toxic effect towards microbial populations and can be toxic and carcinogenic to organisms and mammals (Dizge et al, 2008; Iqbal et al, 2007). The textile industries are major consumer of synthetic dyestuffs and utilize large volumes of water in wet processing operations. Dyes in wastewaters affect the nature of water by inhibiting the sunlight penetration into the stream thereby reducing the photosynthesis reaction. Some synthetic dyes such as azo dyes may be carcinogenic or mutagenic and under anaerobic conditions, can be transformed into aryl amines which are potentially more toxic than the parent compounds (Iqbal et al, 2007; Ramsay et al, 2006). Amaranth is an azo dye and its toxicity has been reported for some animals for eg. carcinogenic to rat fetus. The amaranth dye is degraded by intestinal microorganisms in vivo and is possible that the toxic or carcinogenic effects may be due to their degradation products (Chuung et al, 1978).

Numerous advanced technologies such as adsorption, membrane separation, flocculation-coagulation, aerobic or anaerobic treatment have been developed and applied worldwide for the scavenging of dyes (Binupriya et al, 2007). Among these processes, adsorption techniques for wastewater treatment have become more popular in recent years owing to their efficiency in the removal of pollutants than other conventional methods. Although activated carbons are used abundantly throughout the water and wastewater treatment industries. Carbon adsorption is an expensive process because of high cost of producing activated carbons. Over recent years, this has attracted considerable research into low-cost alternative materials for the production of carbon from agricultural wastes for dye removal, such as agricultural waste (Chowdhury et al, 2009), polymers (Huttermann et al, 2009; Xu et al, 2003; Crini et al, 2008), carbon materials (Ahmad et al, 2010; Wu et al, 2010; Gupta et al, 2008), clay minerals (Iyim et al, 2009; Vijayakumar et al, 2009; Ozcan et al, 2005; Tabak et al, 2009), and other solid materials (Kannan et al, 2008; Ahmad et al, 2010; Gupta et al, 2009; Mittal et al, 2005) have been investigated as adsorbents for the removal of dyes.

Since this chapter deals with the removal of dyes which falls under the category of organic pollutant, the following section is devoted to the brief description of dyes.

DYES

A coloured substance can act as a dye only when it fulfills the following conditions:

- It must have suitable colour.

- It must be able to attach itself permanently to the fabric.
- The fixed dye must have fastness properties. Its colour should not fade in light. It should be rasistant to the action of water, dilute acid, alkalies, detergents and organic solvents used in dry cleaning.

Mauveine, was the first synthetic organic dye containing N-phenyl phenosafranine, produced by **William Henry Perkin** in 1856. Thousands of synthetic dyes have since been prepared. At present, almost all the dyes are synthetic and are prepared from very few starting materials, such as benzene, phenol, aniline, etc. These starting materials are obtained from coal tar and hence synthetic dyes are also known as coal tar dyes (Shrivastava 2001).

According to Otto N. Witt (1876), the colour of the organic compounds is associated with the presence of certain groups in the molecules called "chromophores" and the colour is augmented by the presence of certain groups called "auxochromes".

Dye = Chromogen + Auxochrome

The important chromophores are nitroso, nitro, azo, azoxy, azomethine, ethynyl, azo amine, carbonyl, o-quinonoid, p-quinonoid etc. Auxochromes are unable to produce colour itself, but can deepen the colour produced by chromophore. Auxochromes are certain acidic or basic groups eg. "COOH, "SO_3H, "OH, "NH_2, "NHR, "NH_2 etc.

Nomenclature and Classification of Dyes

The commercial names of dyes are frequently followed by letters, some of which have special designation. For example, B stand for blue, BB or 2B stand for more bluish and the numbers (2, 3, 4 etc.) indicate the intensity of shade. G stands for yellow and occasionally for greenish. R stands for reddish (Sharma 1994).

Most of the commercial dyes are classified in terms of colour, structure or method of application in the Colour Index (C.I.), which is edited every three months since 1924 by the "Society of Dyers and Colourists" and the "American Association of Textile Chemists and Colourists". The last edition of the Colour Index lists about 13000 different dyes. Each dye is assigned to a C.I. generic name determined by its application and colour. Dyes may be classified in two ways

- According to the methods of application
- According to their chemical constitution

Classification According to Methods of Application

Direct or Substantive Dyes

These can be directly applied to the fiber. These dyes are two types.

(*i*) **Acid Dyes:** These are the sodium salts of the colour acids containing sulfonic and phenolic groups. These are always used in an acidic solution.

They dye silk and wool (animal fiber) directly. For example- Maritus yellow, orange II, naphthol yellow etc.

(*ii*) Basic Dyes: These are either hydrochloride or zinc chloride complexes of colour bases which are directly used for silk or wool in basic medium. Azo dyes and triphenyl methane dyes are the typical example of this class.

Mordent Dyes

These are unable to attach themselves to the fiber. Therefore, they require a pretreatment of fiber with the certain substance called "mordent" like tannin or tannic acid. The mordent gets itself attached to the fiber and then combines with the dye to form an insoluble coloured complex. Alizarin, anthraquinone and azo dyes belong to this class.

Vat Dyes

These dyes are insoluble in water, but their reduced form is soluble in an alkali solution whereby leuco vat is obtained. The leuco compound is adsorbed on fiber and upon exposure to the air, is oxidized to the dye which remains fixed to the cloth. Indigo and anthraquinone vat dyes are the good example of this class.

Ingrain Dyes

These are synthesized within the fiber and may be applied to both animal and vegetable fibers by diazotization and coupling process. The colour obtained in this type of dyeing are also called ice colour because diazotization and coupling process are carried out at low temperature. Para red is an example of ingrain dyes.

Sulphur Dyes

These are similar to vat dyes and are sulphur containing complex, which are insoluble in water, but soluble in cold alkaline solution of sodium sulphide. These also form leuco complex. These dyes are dark in colour, inexpensive and have good fastness propertis. Sulphur black is an example of this class and are used for dyeing cotton.

Disperse Dyes

These dyes are used to dye acetate rayons, dacron, nylon and other synthetic fiber. The fiber to be dyed is dipped in a dispersion of finely divided dye in a soap solution in the presence of some solubilising agent such as phenol, cresol or benzoic acid. The adsorption onto the fiber is carried out at high temperature and pressure. Important example of this class is fast pink B and celliton fast blue.

Pigment Dyes

These dyes form insoluble compounds or lakes with salts of Ca, Cr, Ba, Al or phosphomolybdic acid. These dye molecules contains "OH and "SO_3H groups.

Due to their fastness to light, heat, acids and bases, they are valuable for paints, printing ink, synthetic plastic, fibers, rubbers etc. Lithol red, pigment red and acid red are the member of pigment dyes.

Solvent or Sprit Soluble Dyes

These are simple azo or triarylmethane bases or anthraquinone which are used to colour oils, waxes, varnishes, lipsticks, dressings and gasoline.

Food Dyes

These are harmless and used in colouring food, candles, confectionaries and cosmetics.

Classification According to Their Chemical Constitution

This classification is useful for the chemists who are interested in the synthesis and chemical constitution of dyes. Table 1 represents the classification of dyes based on their chemical constitution.

Table 8.1: Classification of Dyes based on their Chemical Constitution

Sl.No.	Class of Dyes	Remark	Example
1.	Nitroso	Nitro group as chromophores, phenolic as auxochrome in o-postion	Fast green, Napthol green Y
2.	Nitro	Nitro group as chromophore	Martius yellow, Napthol yellow S
3.	Anthraquinone	Presence of chromophore = C=O and =C=C arranged in anthraquinone complex	Alizarin red S, Alizarin blue
4.	Triphenylmethane	Quinonoid group as chromophore and acidic –OH and basic $-NH_{2,}$ –NHR, etc group as auxochrome	Malachite green, Methyl violet
5.	Diphenylmethane	NH=C= group as chromophore, also contains a diphenylmethane nucleus	Auraine–O
6.	Phthaleins	Regarded as derivative of triphenylmethane	Phenolphthalein
7.	Xanthene	=C=O or =C=N–as chromophore	Eosin
8.	Thiazole	>C=O, S–C, etc as chromophore	Premuline
9.	Azo dye (*i*) Acid azo (*ii*) Basic azo	–N=N– as chromophore Acidic group as –COOH, $-SO_3H$, –OH as auxochromeAmino or substituted amino group as auxochrome	Methyl orange Aniline yellow

Source of Dye Pollution and Hazardous Effects

Dyes are extensively used in textiles, paper, rubber, plastics, leather, cosmetics, pharmaceuticals and food industries, resulting in a steadily growing demand and production. Today there are more than 10,000 synthetic dyes available commercially and more than 7×10^5 tonnes are produced annually (McMullan et al, 2001; Pearce et al, 2003). Synthetic dyes usually have a complex aromatic molecular structure which possibly comes from coal tar based hydrocarbons such as benzene, naphthalene, anthracene, toluene, xylene, etc (Ramakrishna et al, 1997). From an environmental point of view, the disposal of synthetic dyes is of great concern (Gong et al, 2005). Dyes are known pollutants that not only affect aesthetic merit but also reduce the sun light penetration and photosynthesis thereby increasing the biological oxygen demand and causing lack of dissolved oxygen that sustains aquatic life and some are considered toxic, even carcinogenic for human (Wang et al, 2005; Al-Qodah et al, 2007). The harmful effects of the few important dyes are presented in Table 2.

Table 8.2: Some important dyes and their Hazardous Effects

Dye	Hazardous Effects
Methylene blue	Toxic to blood, reproductive system, liver, upper respiratory tract, skin and eye contact (irritant), central nervous system
Rhodamine B	Causes respiratory tract irritation, eye and skin irritation, digestive tract irritation, adverse reproductive and fetal effects in animals, vomiting and diarrhea
Fast green	Tumors of the liver, testes, or thyroid.
Fast ponceau disazo dye	Mutagen and a potential carcinogen; highly toxic, skin and eye irritant, must never be handled during pregnancy
Fast red salt B	Potential carcinogen, irritant to eyes and the respiratory tract, very toxic
Malachite green	Accumulates in the tissues, liver, thyroid gland and bladder
Crystal violet	Mutagen and mitotic poison
Eosin	Carcinogenic, estrogenic and clastogenic properties
Congo red	Mutagenic, hazardous in case of skin contact, eye irritant
Diamond black	Thyroid cancers, mutagenic effects, DNA-damaging

Dye production and textile industries are the major source of colour pollution. Easton, (Easton et al, 1995) estimated the degree of fixation for different dye/fibre combinations which is indicated in Table 3.

Choy et al., 2004 reported that 10–20% of dyes in the textile sector are lost in residual liquors through incomplete exhaustion and washing operations. These coloured effluents pollute surface water and ground water system. Due to the large degree of organics present in these molecules, the effluents of textile and related industry have to be treated carefully before discharge. This has resulted in a demand for environment friendly technologies to remove the dyes from effluents.

Table 8.3: Estimated degree of fixation for different dye/fiber combinations

Dye class	Fiber	Degree of fixation (%)	Lost to effluent (%)
Acid	Polyamide	80-95	5-20
Basic	Acrylic	95-100	0-5
Direct	Cellulose	70-95	5-30
Disperse	Polyester	90-100	0-10
Metal-complex	Wool	90-98	2-10
Reactive	Cellulose	50-90	10-50
Sulphur	Cellulose	60-90	10-40
Vat	Cellulose	80-95	5-20

Wastewater Treatment

Various treatment methods used in sewage and industrial wastewater treatment are as follows

Preliminary Treatment

The aim of preliminary treatment is the removal of gross solids such as large floating and suspended solid matter, grit, oil and grease if present in considerable quantities. Large quantities of floating rubbish such as cans, cloth, wood and other objects present in wastewater are usually removed under preliminary treatment.

Primary Treatment

Primary treatment involves the removal of gross solids, gritty materials and excessive quantities of oil and grease, followed by the removal of the remaining suspended solids as much as possible. This is aimed at reducing the strength of the wastewater and also to facilitate secondary treatment.

Secondary Treatment

Biological processes involve bacteria and other microorganisms to remove the dissolved and colloidal organic matter present in wastewaters. These processes may be aerobic or anaerobic. Secondary treatment reduces BOD, it also removes appreciable amounts of oil and phenol. However, commissioning and maintenance of secondary treatment systems is expensive.

Tertiary Treatment

It is the final treatment, meant for "polishing" the effluent from the secondary treatment processes and to improve the quality further. The main objectives of tertiary treatment are the removal of fine suspended solids, bacteria, dissolved inorganic solids and final traces of organics.

Depending upon the required quality of the final effluent and the cost of treatment that can be afforded in a given situation, the major methods for coloured wastewater treatment can be divided into three classes:

- Biological treatment
- Chemical treatment
- Physical treatment

Biological Treatments

Biological treatment processes are very useful and remove all types of dissolved degradable substances. Biodegradation is the process by which organic substances are broken down by other living organisms. Organic material can be degraded aerobically with oxygen, or anaerobically, without oxygen. A term related to biodegradation is biomineralisation, in which organic matter is converted into minerals. White-rot fungi are able to degrade dyes using enzymes, such as lignin peroxidases (LiP), manganese dependent peroxidases (MnP). Other enzymes used for this purpose include H_2O_2-producing enzymes, such as, glucose-1-oxidase and glucose-2-oxidase, along with lactase, and a phenoloxidase enzyme (Kirby et al, 1999; Archibald et al, 1992).

The ability of bacteria to decolorize the wastewater has been investigated by a number of research groups under the anaerobic and aerobic condition (Thurston et al, 1994; Kirby 1999; Knapp et al, 1995; Nigam et al, 1995). These microbial systems have the drawback of requiring a fermentation process and are therefore unable to cope with larger volumes of textile effluents. This process is time taking, may require nutrients, very large aeration tanks, lagoons, land areas and many toxic compounds are not removed.

Dead bacteria, yeast and fungi have also been used for the purpose of decolorizing dye-containing effluents. Textile dyes vary greatly in their chemistry and therefore their interactions with micro-organisms depend on the chemistry of a particular dye and the specific chemistry of the microbial biomass (Ong et al, 2010). The use of biomass has its advantages, especially if the dye-containing effluent is very toxic. Biomass adsorption is effective when conditions are not always favorable for the growth and maintenance of the microbial population. Adsorption by biomass occurs by ion exchange (Kulla 1981).

Chemical Treatment

Ozone Treatment

Ozone wastewater treatment is a thorough and effective oxidation process and is a suitable disinfectant for the organic matter found in wastewater. Ozone is a very good oxidizing agent due to its high instability (oxidation potential - 2.07) compared to chlorine, another oxidizing agent (1.36) and H_2O_2 (1.78). The dosage applied to the dye-containing effluent is dependent on the total colour and residual COD to be removed with no residue or sludge formation (Polman etal, 1996). After ozone treatment, chromophore groups in the dyes are generally organic compounds with conjugated double bonds that can be broken down forming smaller molecules, resulting in reduced colouration (Robinson et al, 2001). These smaller molecules may have increased carcinogenic or toxic properties, and so ozonation may be used alongside a physical method to prevent this. Decolouration occurs in a relatively short time.

Ozone for the treat wastewater has many benefits

- Kills bacteria effectively.
- Oxidizes substances such as iron and sulphur so that they can be filtered out of the solution.
- There are no nasty odours or residues produced from the treatment.
- Ozone converts into oxygen quickly and leaves no trace once it has been used.

The disadvantages of using ozone as a treatment for wastewater are

- The treatment requires energy in the form of electricity, which is costly and cannot work when the power is lost.
- The treatment cannot remove dissolved minerals and salts.
- Ozone treatment can sometimes produce by-products such as bromate that can harm human health if not controlled.
- A major disadvantage of ozonation is its short half-life (20 min).

Photochemical Treatment

Photochemical treatment is degradation of a photodegradable molecule caused by the absorption of photons, particularly those wavelengths found in sunlight, such as infrared radiation, visible light and ultraviolet light. Various processes like UV/H_2O_2, UV/Fenton's reagent, UV/O_3 etc are photochemical methods based on the formation of free radicals due to UV irradiation. The UV-based methods in the presence of a catalyst, e.g. a semiconductive material such as TiO_2 and ZnO have also shown to distinctly enhance colour removal (Ince et al, 1997; Zamora et al, 1999). Thus, different combinations such as ozone/TiO_2, ozone/TiO_2/H_2O_2 and TiO_2/ H_2O_2 have been investigated, but they are enormously influenced by the type of dye, dye concentration and pH (So et al, 2002). Degradation is caused by the production of high concentrations of hydroxyl radicals. The rate of dye removal is influenced by the intensity of the UV radiation, pH, dye structure and the dye bath composition (Byrappa et al, 2006). There are some advantages of photochemical treatment of dye-containing effluent i.e. no sludge is produced and foul odours are greatly reduced. The main disadvantage of this method is production of secondary pollutant.

Electrochemical Destruction

This is a relatively new technique, which was developed in the mid 1990s. It has some significant advantages for use as an effective method for dye removal by oxidation reactions using electricity (Galindo et al, 2000). There is little or no consumption of chemicals and no sludge build up. The breakdown metabolites are generally not hazardous leaving it safe for treated wastewaters to be released back into water ways. It shows efficient and economical removal of dyes and a high efficiency for colour removal and degradation of recalcitrant pollutants (Slokar et al, 1997; Metcalf and Eddy 2003). Relatively high flow rates cause a direct decrease in dye removal and the high cost of electricity is the main disadvantage of this technology.

Physical Treatment

Coagulation/Flocculation

Coagulation/flocculation is a commonly used process in water and wastewater treatment in which compounds such as ferric chloride or polymer are added to wastewater in order to destabilize the colloidal materials which cause the small particles to agglomerate into larger settleable flocs (Ogutveren et al, 1994; Pelegrini et al, 1999). The first step, coagulation is the addition of a coagulant to the wastewater and mixing. This coagulant destabilizes the colloidal particles that exist in the suspension, allowing particle agglomeration. Flocculation is the physical process of bringing the destabilized particles in contact to form larger flocs that can be more easily removed from the solution. The main advantage of the conventional processes like coagulation and flocculation is decolourization of the waste stream due to the removal of dye molecules from the dye bath effluents and not due to a partial decomposition of dyes, which can lead to an even more potentially harmful and toxic aromatic compound. The major disadvantage of coagulation/ flocculation processes is the production of sludge (Riera-Torres et al, 2010; Joo et a, 2007).

Filtration Method

Filtration methods such as ultrafiltration, nanofiltration and reverse osmosis have been used for water reuse and chemical recovery. These methods has the ability to clarify, concentrate and most importantly, to separate dye continuously from effluent (Mishra et al, 1993; Golob et al, 2005). Membrane filtration has some special features unrivalled by other methods i.e. they are resistance to, temperature, an adverse chemical environment and microbial attack. The specific temperature and chemical composition of the wastewater determine the type and porosity of the filter to be applied (Visvanathan et al, 2000)[54]. The main drawbacks of membrane technology are the high investment costs, the potential membrane fouling and the production of a concentrated dye bath which needs to be treated (Kulla 1981). The recovery of concentrates from membranes, e.g. recovery of the sodium hydroxide used in the mercerizing step or sizing agents such as polyvinyl alcohol (PVA), can attenuate the treatment costs (Xu et al, 2000). Water reuse from dye bath effluents has been successfully achieved by using reverse osmosis. However, a coagulation and micro-filtration pre-treatment was necessary to avoid membrane fouling (Porter 1997). A very good option would be to consider an anaerobic pre-treatment followed by aerobic and membrane post-treatments, in order to recycle the water

Ion-Exchange

The use of ion exchangers for demineralization of water is well known. Ion exchange has not been widely used for the treatment of dye-containing effluents, mainly due to the opinion that ion exchangers cannot accommodate a wide range of dyes (Vandevivere et al, 1998; Dulman et al, 2009). Wastewater is passed over the ion exchange resin until the available exchange sites are saturated. Both cation and anion dyes can be removed from dye-containing effluent this way. Advantages of this method include no loss of adsorbent on regeneration, reclamation of solvent after use and the removal of soluble dyes. Despite the simplicity of its operation, a major disadvantage is the high cost of ion-exchanger, its regeneration process and its ineffectiveness for all kind of dyes treatments (Mohanty et al, 2006).

Adsorption

Adsorption is one of the most efficient methods for the removal of colour, odour, organic and inorganic pollutants from industrial effluents. Adsorption process is considered better in water treatment because of the convenience, ease operation and simplicity of design. Adsorption operations exploit the ability of certain solids preferentially to concentrate specific substances from solution onto their surfaces. Adsorption generally depends on the nature of adsorbate, adsorbent and solution conditions. Structural properties of the adsorbate molecule or ion have an influence on its adsorption. The solution conditions like pH, temperature, co-ions etc. may alter the adsorption of adsorbate. The adsorption also depends on the adsorbent characteristics such as size, shape, surface area, porosity, functional groups on the surface, surface charge etc. Therefore characterization of the adsorbent is very important to understand the mechanism of adsorption process. There are many techniques which are generally used to characterize the adsorbent. Some of them are:

- **The Brunauer-Emmett-Teller (BET) analysis** – to determine the surface area and pore structure of the adsorbent.
- **Zeta potential and Zero point charge analysis** – to determine the surface charge on the adsorbent.
- **Elemental analysis** – to study the elemental composition such as C, N, H, O etc of the adsorbent.

- **Boehm titration analysis** – to determine the concentration of oxygenated surface groups on the adsorbent.
- **Scanning electron microscopy** (SEM) – to examine the surface morphology of the adsorbent.
- **Transmission electron microscopy (TEM)** – to determine the shape and size of the adsorbent.
- **Fourier transform infrared spectroscopy (FTIR) analysis** – to determine the presence of functional groups on the adsorbent.
- **X-ray diffraction (XRD) analysis** – to determine the amorphous or crystalline nature of the adsorbent.
- **Thermal analysis** – to determine the thermal stability of the adsorbent.
- **Inductively coupled plasma-mass spectrometer (ICP-MS)** - The analysis of the impurities composition, namely, Al, Ca, Cu, Fe, Li, Mg, Mn, P, Ti, V, and Zn in the adsorbent.

Theoretical Aspects of Adsorption

Adsorption

The term adsorption was first used by "Kayser" in 1881 and it refers strictly to the existence of higher concentration of any particular component at the surface of the liquid or solid phase than in the bulk. The adsorption may be of two types namely physical and chemical. The physical adsorption occurs mainly due to weak forces like ion-dipole, dipole-dipole, polarization or induced dipole, Van der Waals force etc. The physical adsorption is reversible, temporary in character. It usually involves lesser heat exchange.While chemical adsorption is due to formation of chemical linkages between adsorbate and adsorbent. The chemical adsorption is non reversible and is carried out at high temperature. It is characterized by a large heat change during adsorption.

Mechanism of Adsorption

A solid surface in contact with a solution has the tendency to accumulate a layer of solute molecules at the interface due to imbalance of surface forces. This accumulation of molecules is a vectorial sum of the forces of the attraction and repulsion between the solution and the adsorbent. Majorities of the solute ions or molecules, accumulated at the interface are adsorbed onto the large surface area within the pores of adsorbent and relatively a few are adsorbed on the out side surface of the adsorbent. Adsorption from an aqueous solution is influenced largely by the competition between the solute and solvent molecules for adsorption sites. The tendency of a particular solute to get adsorbed is determined by the difference in the adsorption potential between the solute and the solvent when the solute-solvent affinity is large. The low adsorption capacity of polar adsorbents like zeolite for solute in a polar solvent like water is an example of this phenomenon. In general, the lower the affinity of adsorbent for the solvent, the higher will be adsorption capacity for solutes. A polar (or non polar) adsorbent will preferentially adsorb the more polar (or non polar) component of a non- polar (or polar) solute.

Many factors influence the rate of adsorption and extent to which a particular solute can be adsorbed. The general effects of some more important factors like nature of adsorbent and adsorbate, concentration, extent of agitation, pH, temperature, contact time, etc., are summarized in Table 4.

Table 8.4. Effects of various Operational Parameters on Adsorption

Parametrs	Effects
Agitation/relative velocity	At low agitation film diffusion is rate controlling. At high agitation pore diffusion is rate limiting.
Contact time	Adsorption increases with increase in contact time until equilibrium achieved.
Adsorbent characteristics	Adsorption is a surface phenomenon. Adsorption rate increases with decreasing particle size of adsorbent and presence of surface charges.
Size and shape of adsorbate	Adsorption usually decreases, as the size of the molecules becomes large due to steric effect.
Concentration	Rate of adsorption increases with increase in concentration. Rate constant is directly proportional to concentration.
pH	Strong influence on adsorption due to change in ionic concentrations of water and solutes.
Temperature	Affects rate and capacity of adsorption.

Adsorption Isotherm

The relation of dye concentration in the bulk and the adsorbed amount at the interface is a measure of the position of equilibrium in the adsorption process and can generally be expressed by one or more of a series of isotherm models. The accuracy of these isotherms to simulate experimental data varies and is greatly influenced by the specific interactions between the adsorbate and adsorbent.. The interpretation of adsorption data through theoretical or empirical equations is essential for the quantitative estimation of the adsorption capacity or amount of the adsorbent required to remove the unit mass of pollutant from wastewater. Different isotherms that are commonly used for the dyes adsorption process and the linear equations of the applied models are

Langmuir model: $(C_e/q_e) = (C_e/q_m) + (1/\, q_m b)$ (1)

Freundlich model: $\ln q_e = \ln K_F + (1/n) \ln C_e$ (2)

Temkin model: $q_e = B \ln A + B \ln C_e$ (3)

Dubinin-Radushkevich model:
$$\ln q_e = \ln q_m - B_1 \Sigma^2 \quad (4)$$

$$\Sigma = RT \ln\left(1 + \frac{1}{C_e}\right) \quad (5)$$

$$E = \frac{1}{\sqrt{2.B_1}} \quad (6)$$

where C_e is the equilibrium dye concentration in the solution (mg/l), *b* is the Langmuir adsorption constant (l/mg) and q_m is the theoretical maximum monolayer adsorption capacity (mg/g). K_F (mg/g) and *n* are Freundlich isotherm constants indicating the capacity and intensity of the adsorption, respectively. A is equilibrium binding constant (l/mg) and B is related to the heat of adsorption. B_1 is the D–R model constant ($mol^2\ kJ^{-2}$) related to the mean free energy of adsorption per mole of the adsorbate and Σ is the polanyi potential. E is mean free energy of adsorption (kJ/mol).

The Langmuir isotherm is generally more appropriate to a monolayer adsorption where all binding sites are energetically equivalent and there is neither interaction between adsorbed molecules nor the transmigration of adsorbate in the plane of the surface (Langmuir et al, 1916; Kapoor et al, 1998). Meanwhile, the Freundlich isotherm can be used for non-ideal sorption that involves heterogeneous sorption (Freundlich et al, 1906; Yu et al, 2001).

Temkin isotherm (Temkin 1940) contains a factor explicitly taking into account of the adsorbent–adsorbate interactions. By ignoring the extremely low and large value of concentrations, the model assumes that heat of adsorption (as a function of temperature) of all molecules in the layer would decrease linearly rather than logarithmic with coverage (Temkin 1940). As implied in the equation, its derivation is characterized by a uniform distribution of binding energies (Aharoni et al, 1977).

Dubinin–Radushkevich isotherm (Foo et al, 2010) is generally applied to express the adsorption mechanism with a Gaussian energy distribution onto a heterogeneous surface (Dubinin 1947). The model has often successfully fitted well to high solute activities and the intermediate range of concentrations data, but has unsatisfactory asymptotic properties and does not predict the Henry's law at low pressure (Dabrowski et al, 2001). The approach was usually applied to distinguish the physical and chemical adsorption.

Adsorption Kinetics

The study of adsorption kinetics is important in wastewater treatment because it provides valuable information on the reaction pathways and the mechanism of sorption. In addition, predicting the solute uptake rate is of utmost importance in designing an appropriate wastewater treatment plant because it can control the residence time of solute at the solid-solution interface.

Various kinetic models have been proposed by different research groups where the adsorption has been treated as a pseudo-first order (Lagergren et al, 1898), a pseudo-second order (Ho et al, 1999), Elovich (Elovich 1962) and intraparticle diffusion (Wėber 1963). The linear equations of kinetic model are

Pseudo-first order model: $\log (q_e - q_t) = \log q_e - (k_1 t/2.303)$ (7)

Pseudo-second order model: $t/q_t = (1/k_2 q_e^2) + (t/q_e)$ (8)

Elovich model: $q_t = (1/\beta) \ln (\alpha\beta) + (1/\beta) \ln t$ (9)

where q_e and q_t are the amount of adsorption at equilibrium and at time t in (mg/g). k_1 (1/min) and k_2 (min g/mg) are the rate constant for the pseudo-first and pseudo-second order adsorption kinetics. α is the initial adsorption rate in (mg/g min) and β is related to the extent of surface coverage and the activation energy for chemisorptions in (g/mg).

Intra-particle diffusion Model

The adsorption can be described by three consecutive steps:

- The transport of adsorbate from bulk solution to the outer surface of the adsorbent by molecular diffusion, known as external or film diffusion.
- Internal diffusion, i.e. the transport of adsorbate from the particle surface into interior sites.
- The adsorption of solute molecules from the active sites into the interior surfaces of pores.

To determine rate limiting step (either film diffusion or intraparticle diffusion) as well as the corresponding rate constants, Weber and Morris intra-particle diffusion model is widely used.

$$q_t = K_{id}\, t^{1/2} + C \quad (10)$$

where, K_{id} is the intra-particle diffusion rate constant. The adsorption rates for intra-particle diffusion (K_{id}) under different conditions were calculated from the slope of the linear portion of the respective plot with units of mg/g min$^{0.5}$.

Adsorption Thermodynamics

Thermodynamic parameters are evaluated to confirm the nature of the adsorption process. The thermodynamic constants, free energy change, enthalpy change and entropy change are calculated to evaluate the thermodynamic feasibility and the spontaneous nature of the process. Thermodynamic parameters such as standard free energy change (ΔG^o), enthalpy change (ΔH^o) and entropy change (ΔS^o) are calculated using the following equations:

$$K_c = C_{ac}/ C_e \quad (11)$$

where, K_c is the equilibrium constant. C_{ac} and C_e are the equilibrium constants (mg/l) of the dye on the adsorbent and in the solution respectively. ΔG^0 was calculated from the Gibb's equation:

$$\Delta G^o = - RT \ln Kc \quad (12)$$

where, T is the temperature in Kelvin and R is gas constant (8.314 J/mol K). ΔH^o and ΔS^o were obtained from the slope and intercept of Van't Hoff plot of ln K_c versus $1/T$.

$$\ln Kc = (\Delta S^o / R) - (\Delta H^o / RT) \quad (13)$$

On the basis of thermodynamic parameters following conclusion can be made for the adsorption process. If:

ΔH^o	+ve	Endothermic process
ΔH^o	–ve	Exothermic process
ΔG^o	+ve	Non-spontaneous process
ΔG^o	–ve	Spontaneous process
ΔS^o	+ve	Increase in randomness at solid/solution interface
ΔS^o	–ve	Decrease in randomness at solid/solution interface

COLOR REMOVAL USING COMMERCIAL ACTIVATED CARBONS

Adsorption techniques employing solid sorbents are widely used to remove certain classes of chemical pollutants from waters, especially those that are practically unaûected by conventional biological wastewater treatments. However, amongst all the sorbent materials proposed, activated carbon is the most popular for the removal of pollutants from wastewater (Babel et al, 2003; Derbyshire 2001). In particular, the eûectiveness of adsorption on commercial activated carbons (CAC) for removal of a wide variety of dyes from wastewaters has made it an ideal alternative to other expensive treatment options (Ramakrishna et al, 1997). Table 2 shows a non-exhaustive list of examples of CAC used in wastewater treatment. Because of their great capacity to adsorb dyes, CAC are the most eûective adsorbents. This capacity is mainly due to their structural characteristics and their porous texture which gives them a large surface area, and their chemical nature which can be easily modiûed by chemical treatment in order to increase their properties. However, activated carbon presents several disadvantages (Babel and Kurniawan, 2003). It is quite expensive, the higher the quality, the greater the cost, non-selective and ineûective against disperse and vat dyes. The regeneration of saturated carbon is also expensive, not straightforward, and results in loss of the adsorbent. The use of carbons based on relatively expensive starting materials is also unjustiûed for most pollution control applications (Streat et al, 1995). This has led many workers to search for more economic adsorbents.

Table 8.5: Recent Reported Adsorption Capacities qm (mg/g) for Commercial Activated Carbons

Supplier	Dye	q_m(mg/g)	Sources
Tapei Chemical Corp. (Taiwan)	Acid yellow	1179	Chern and Wu (2001)
Chemviron Carbon (UK)	Remazol yellow	1111	Al-Degs et al. (2000)
Chemviron Carbon (UK)	Basic yellow 21	860	Allen et al. (2003)
Chemviron Carbon (UK)	Basic red 22	720	Allen et al. (2003)
Filtrasorb Corporation (USA)	Reactive orange 107	714	Aksu and Tezer (2005)
Merck Co. (Taiwan)	Reactive red 2	712.3	Chiou et al. (2004)
Miloje Zakic (Macedonia)	Basic dye	309.2	Meshko et al. (2001)
E. Merck (India)	Basic blue 9	296.3	Kannan and Sundaram (2001)
Filtrasorb Corporation (USA)	Reactive red 5	278	Aksu and Tezer (2005)
Merck Co. (Taiwan)	Direct red 81	240.7	Chiou et al. (2004)
Filtrasorb Corporation (USA)	Acid yellow 117	155.8	Choy et al. (2000)
Chemviron Carbon (UK)	Acid blue 40	133.3	O¨zacar and Sengil (2002)
Filtrasorb Corporation (USA)	Acid blue 80	112.3	Choy et al. (2000)
Calgon Corporation (USA)	Acid red 88	109	Venkata Mohan et al. (1999)
Chemviron Carbon (UK)	Basic red 46	106	Martin et al. (2003)
Filtrasorb Corporation (USA)	Acid red 114	103.5	Choy et al. (2000)
Chemviron Carbon (UK)	Acid yellow 17	57.47	O¨zacar and Sengil (2002)
Calgon Corporation (USA)	Direct red 28	16.81	Fu and Viraraghavan (2002a)
Calgon Corporation (USA)	Direct brown 1	7.69	Venkata Mohan et al. (2002)
S.D.Fine Chem. Ltd,(India)	Eosin	571.40	Purkait et al. (2005)
Norit Inc(USA)	Acid yellow	11.7	Ozsoy et al. (2011)
Fluka (Tunisie)	Yellow 59	256.4	Guezguez et (2011)
Prolabo (Tunisie)	Yellow 59	27.1	Guezguez et (2011)

ADSORPTION OF DYES BY NON-CONVENTIONAL ADSORBENTS

Conventional and Non-conventional adsorbents are used in this approach. Activated carbon is the most widely used conventional adsorbent for this purpose because of its extensive surface area, microporous structure, high adsorption capacity and high degree of surface reactivity. However, its widespread use in wastewater treatment is sometimes restricted due to its high cost and poor regeneration capacity (Khare et al, 1987; Wang et al, 2009). During the last decades, a lot of studies on dye adsorption by various non-conventional adsorbents such as algae (Sadhasivam et al, 2007; Dogar et al, 2010; Srinivasan et al, 2010; Sathishkumar et al, 2007; Russo et al, 2010; Khataee et al, 2010), fungi (Atar et al, 2008; Binupriya et al, 2007; Bhatnagar et al, 2010; Sun et al, 2010), industrial wastes (Mittal et al, 2007; Hsu et al, 2008; Genc et al, 2010; Vinod et al, 2003; Akar et al, 2010), clays (Eren et al, 2010; Petrolekas et al, 2007; Chao et al, 2010; Kyzas et al, 2010; Ozdemir et al,

2009), polymers (Dhodapkar et al, 2007; Hu et al, 2010; Kannan et al, 2008; Mak et al, 2004), metal oxides (Pirillo et al, 2008; Salehi et al, 2010; Zhu et al, 2010; Wang et al, 2007; Kasgoz et al, 2008), composites (Yao et al, 2009; Shi et al, 1999; Khorramfar et al, 2010), agricultural wastes (Oladoja et al, 2008; Langmuir et al, 1916; Kapoor et al, 1998) etc. have been undertaken in order to find out an alternate to the costly conventional adsorbent. It has been found that various adsorbents developed from different origins show little or poor sorption potential for the removal of dyes as compared to commercial activated carbon. Therefore, the search to develop efficient adsorbents is still going on.

Recent reported adsorption capacities qm (mg/g) for carbon materials made from solid wastes and coal-based sorbents are:

Table 8.6

Raw material	Dye	q_m(mg/g)	Sources
1	2	3	4
Tapei Chemical Corp. (Taiwan)	Acid yellow	1179	Chern and Wu (2001)
Sugarcane baggase	methylene blue	478.5	Karla et al. (2012)
Suc Sugarcane bagasse	Gentian Violet	1273.2	Karla et al. (2012)
Macauba palm cake	methylene blue	25.8	Sara et al. (2012)
Macauba palm cake	congo red	32	Sara et al. (2012)
Chitosan/poly(Vinyl alcohol)	congo red	470.1	Zhu et al. (2012)
Grafted carbon nanotube	methylene blue	61.92	Yan et al. (2012)
Grafted carbon nanotube	Neutral red	89.85	Yan et al. (2012)
Activated carbon loaded C.H	Bromocresol Green	108.7	Ghaedi et al. (2012)
Fe3O4@PAA nanoparticle	Rhodamine GG	55.8	Chen et al. (2012)
Polymeric sorbent	methylene blue	343.23	Ma et al. (2012)
Peanur hull (AC)	Remazol Brilliant Blue R	149.25	Zhong et al. (2012)
Magnetic Chitosan	alizarin red	43.08	Fan et al. (2012)
AC-PG	Congo red	19.23	Ghaedi et al. (2012)
AC-MC	Congo red	10	Ghaedi et al. (2012)
Clay composite	brilliant green	122.0	Xing et al. (2012)
Sugarcane baggase/TEP	eosin Y	399.04	Jiang et al. (2012)
Orange peel	methylene blue	382.75	Foo et al. (2012)
Jack fruit peel	methylene blue	400.06	Foo et al. (2012)
Jack fruit leaf powder	crystal violet	43.39	Saha et al. (2012)
Jujuba seed	Congo red	55.56	Reddy et al. (2012)
Raw pine	Congo red	32.65	Dawood et al. (2012)
Acid treated pine	Congo red	40.19	Dawood et al. (2012)
Sugar beet pulp	Methylene blue	714.29	Vesna et al. (2012)
Annona squmosa seed (CAS)	Malachite green	25.91	Santhi et al. (2011)

1	2	3	4
Annona squmosa seed (CAS)	Methylene Blue	8.52	Santhi et al. (2011)
POME	Methylene Blue	66.23	Gobi et al. (2011)
Sesame hull	Mathylene Blue	359.88	Feng et al. (2011)
Polyacylamide	Methyl Violet	1136	Rahchamni et. al (2011)
cupuassu shell	Reactive Red 194	66	Cardoso et al. (2011)
cupuassu shell	Direct Blue 53	38.8	Cardoso et al. (2011)
AMP	Malachite Green	334.8	Lee et al. (2011)
Ethylenediamine chitosan	eosin Y	294.12	Huang et al. (2011)
CBN1	Congo red	199.98	Chatterjee et al. (2011)
CBN2	Congo red	191.15	Chatterjee et al. (2011)
CBN3	Congo red	124.97	Chatterjee et al. (2011)
CBN4	Congo red	370.37	Chatterjee et al. (2011)
Coir pith	Acid yellow 99	442.13	Khan et al. (2011)
Succinyl Chitosan	Methylene Blue	289.02	Huang et al. (2011)
Beet pulp carbon	Chemazol RR 195	58.0	Dursan et al. (2011)
Hydroxyapatite	Reactive Yellow 84	50.25	Barka et al. (2011)
Milled Sugarcane bagase	Congo red	38.2	Zhang et al. (2011)
PGA-MNPs	Methylene Blue	78.67	Inbaraj et al. (2011)
Lotus leaf	Methylene Blue	221.7	Han et al. (2011)
Rice Husk	Direct Red 31	57.88	Safa et al. (2011)
Rice Husk	Direct orange 26	36.14	Safa et al. (2011)
MNPs	Methyl Violet	416.7	Keyhanian et al. (2011)
Rejected Tea	Methylene blue	242.11	Nasuha et al. (2011)
Sunflower seed	Methylene blue	473.33	Foo et al. (2011)
Sunflower seed	Acid blue	430.37	Foo et al. (2011)
Native Potamogeton crispus	Reactive Red 198	14.3	Gulnaz et al. (2011)
Acid treated Potamogeton	Reactive Red	26.8	Gulnaz et al. (2011)
Alkali treated Potamogeton	Reactive Red	44.2	Gulnaz et al. (2011)
Modified wheat Residue	Reactive Red 24	200	Zhong et al. (2011)
Aspergillus oryzae	Acid Blue 25	89.80	Yang et al. (2011)
Aspergillus oryzae	Acid Red 337	128.98	Yang et al. (2011)
CDAB- Aspergillus oryzae	Acid Blue 25	138.83	Yang et al. (2011)
CDAB- Aspergillus oryzae	Acid Red 337	146.13	Yang et al. (2011)
Clay	Methyl Violet	625	Elass et al. (2011)
Cofee husk based AC	Remazol Orange 3R	66.76	Ahmad et al. (2011)
Oil palm fruit	Methylene Blue	344.83	Foo et al. (2011)
biomass of Nostoc lincki	Reactive Red 198	93.5	Mona et al. (2011)
beech sawdust	Malachite green	83.21	Anna (2011)
Capsicum seed	Reactive Blue 49	96.35	Akar et al. (2011)
biomass (A. filiculoides)	Basic Orange	833.33	Tan et al. (2011)

1	2	3	4
Pineapple leaf powder	Basic Green 4	54.64	Chowdhury (2011)
Spent AC	Methylene Blue	425.53	Zhang et al.(2010)
Cofee Bean	Methylene Blue	68.49	Franca et al. (2010)
MVM	Rhodamine B	24.39	Santhi et al. (2010)
CVM	Rhodamine B	22.37	Santhi et al. (2010)
SBA-3	Methy Orange	357.1	Anabia et al. (2010)
SBA-3	Oange G	434.7	Anabia et al. (2010)
SBA-3	Brilliant red X-3B	294.1	Anabia et al. (2010)
CMCD-MNP(P)	Methylene Blue	277.8	Badruzdoza et al (2010)
CMCD-MNP(C)	Methylene Blue	140.8	Badruzdoza et al. (2010)
Chitosan	Congo Red	450.4	Chatterjee et al. (2010)
Carbon Nanotube	Methylene Blue	35.4	Yao et al. (2010)
Rhizopus arrhizus	Yellow RI	625.0	Aksu et al. (2010)
Citrus cinensis	Reactive Yellow 42	36.36	Asgher et al. (2010)
Citrus cinensis	Reactive red 45	18.28	Asgher et al. (2010)
A. Filiculoides	Basic orange	833	Tan et al. (2010)
Bael Shell carbon	Congo red	98.03	Ahmad et al. (2010)
Paulownia leaf powder	Acid Orange 52	10.5	Deniz et al. (2010)
Mg-Al layer hydroxide	Benzopurpurine	153.88	Setti et al. (2010)
Natural Sepiolite	Methylene Blue	79.37	Kuncek et al. (2010)
Sonicated Sepiolite	Methylene Blue	105.26	Kuncek et al. (2010)
F-400	Reactive Black 5	175.81	Ip et al. (2009)
Bone Char	Reactive Black 5	156.51	Ip et al. (2009)
Peat	Reactive Black 5	7.0	Ip et al. (2009)
BACX2	Reactive Black 5	446.98	Ip et al. (2009)
BACX6	Reactive Black 5	545.22	Ip et al. (2009)
Loofa egiptiaca	Direct Blue 106	57.14	El Sayed et al. (2009)
Bottom ash/H2SO4	Reactive Red 141	29.9	Leechart et al. 92009)
Rice husk ash	Indigo carmine	29.27	Lakshami et al. (2009)
CS beads	Congo red	128.7	Chatterjee et al. (2009)
CS / CTAB beads	Congo red	385.9	Chatterjee et al. (2009)
Posidonia oceanica	Yellow 59	76.9	Guezguez et al. (2009)
Citosan p	Reactive yellow	373	Kyzas et al. (2009)
Chitosan p	BY	254	kyzas et al. (2009)
Treated ginger waste	Crystal vilet	64.93	Kumar et al. (2011)
Menthe waste	Alizarin Red S	94.59	Ahmad et al. (2008)
Menthe waste	Patent Blue VF	166.11	Ahmad et al. (2008)
Ginger waste	patent Blue VF	7.75	Ahmad et al. (2008)
Almond peel	Brilliant Green	123.41	Ahmad et al. (2009)
Water Nut	Malachite Green	47.69	Ahmad et al. (2010)

1	2	3	4
Water Nut	Congo red	38.8	Ahmad et al. (2010)
Treated water nut	Malachite green	40	Ahmad et al. (2009)
CPBP	Crystal Violet	32.78	Ahmad et al. (2009)
Treated Ginger waste	malachite green	188.6	Ahmad et al. (2010)
AC/Iron oxide	Brilliant green	64.1	Ahmad et al. (2010)
ARP	Amaranth	14.61	Ahmad et al. (2011)
PANI	Amido Black 10	147.05	Ahmad et al. (2010)

DISCUSSION

It is evident that natural materials, waste materials from industry and agriculture and biosorbents are an interesting alternative to replace activated carbons. Some promising results could be noted in the case of clays, peat and chitosan-based materials (Alkan et al., 2005). Several biosorption processes have also been developed, patented and introduced for application in removing contaminants from waters (Aksu, 2005). A comprehensive study of the application of biosorption for the removal of organic pollutants can be found in a recent review by Aksu (2005). However, despite the number of published laboratory data, non-conventional low-cost adsorbents have not been applied at an industrial scale. There are several reasons for this difficulty in transferring the process to industrial applications.

They can be summarized as follows:

- The variability in the material characteristics and the availability of the resource that is controlled by the demand at the commercial level can discourage industrial users (Guibal, 2004).
- The applicability of low-cost adsorbents such as chitosan, peat, zeolites, biomass, fly ashes and red mud for water treatment depends strongly on their origin (Wang et al., 2005).
- The adsorption process will provide an attractive technology if the low-cost sorbent is ready for use. However, physical and chemical processes such as drying, autoclaving, crosslinking reactions or contacting with organic or inorganic chemicals are proposed for improving the sorption capacity and the selectivity. For example, for the industrial application of biosorption, immobilization of biomass is necessary (Aksu, 2005). These pre-treatment methods are not cost effective at large scale. The production of chitosan also involves a chemical deacetylation process. Commercial production of chitosan by deacetylation of crustacean chitin with strong alkali appears to have limited potential for industrial acceptance because of difficulties in processing, particularly with the large amount of waste concentrated alkaline solution causing environmental pollution.

However, several yeasts and filamentous fungi have been recently reported as containing chitin and chitosan in their cell wall and septa. They can be readily cultured in simple nutrients and used as a source of chitosan. With advances in fermentation technology chitosan preparation from fungal cell walls could become an alternative route for the production of this biopolymer via an ecofriendly pathway.

- The effectiveness of treatment depends not only on the properties of the adsorbent and adsorbate, but also on the following environmental conditions and variables used for the adsorption process: pH, ionic strength, temperature, existence of competing organic or inorganic ligands in solution, contact time and adsorbent concentration. Despite the fact that industrial effluents contain several pollutants simultaneously, little attention has been given to adsorption of pollutants from mixtures (Aksu, 2005). The development of the adsorption process requires further investigation in the direction of testing low-cost sorbents with real industrial effluents.
- There is as yet little literature containing a full study of comparisons between sorbents. The comparison of sorption performance depend not only the parameters related to the experimental conditions and the effluent, but also on the analytical method used for decontamination tests (batch method, column, reactors, etc.). Thus, a direct comparison of data obtained using different low-cost sorbents is difficult because of inconsistencies in the data presentation (Babel and Kurniawan, 2003).
- There is a lack of data concerning the reproducibility of the adsorption properties and the equilibrium data, commonly known as adsorption isotherms. In view of industrial developments of the various kinds of sorbents described in the literature, the physical and chemical stability of the materials and the reproducibility of the sorption properties is of utmost importance. Unfortunately, there is little information on this subject. The design and efficient operation of adsorption processes also requires equilibrium adsorption data for use in kinetic and mass transfer models (Allen et al., 2004). These models play an important role in predictive modeling for analysis and design of adsorption systems. Additional work on this subject is needed.

CONCLUSIONS

In this chapter, a wide range of non-conventional low cost adsorbents has been presented. Inexpensive, locally available and effective materials could be used in place of commercial activated carbon for the removal of dyes from aqueous solution. Undoubtedly low-cost adsorbents offer a lot of promising benefits for commercial purposes in the future. In particular, from the recent literature reviewed, agriculture-based sorbents have demonstrated outstanding removal capabilities for certain dyes in comparison to activated carbon. However, despite a number of papers published on low-cost adsorbents, there is as yet little information containing a full study of comparison between sorbents. Although much has been accomplished in the area of low-cost sorbents, much work is necessary (i) to predict the performance of the adsorption processes for dye removal from real industrial effluents under a range of operating conditions, (ii) to better understand adsorption mechanisms and (iii) to demonstrate the use of inexpensive adsorbents at an industrial scale.

REFERENCES

A. A. Ahmad, B.H. Hameed (2010): Fixed-bed adsorption of reactive azo dye onto granular activated carbon prepared from waste. *J. Hazard. Mater.* 175: 298-303.

A. Bhatnagar, M. Sillanpaa (2010): Utilization of agro-industrial and municipal waste materials as potential adsorbents for water treatment—A review. *Chem. Eng. J.* 157: 277-297.

A. Dabrowski (2001): Adsorption from theory to practice. *Adv. Colloid Interf. Sci.* 93: 135-224.

A. Genc, A. Oguz (2010) : Sorption of acid dyes from aqueous solution by using non-ground ash and slag. *Desalination* 264 : 78-83.

A. Huttermann, L.J.B. Orikiriza, H. Agaba (2009): Application of superabsorbent polymers for improving the ecological chemistry of degraded or polluted lands. *Clean* 37: 517-526.

A. Kapoor, T. Viraraghavan (1998): Biosorption of heavy metals on *Aspergillus niger* Effect of pretreatment. *Biores. Technol.* 63: 109-113.

A. Kapoor, T. Viraraghavan (1998): Biosorption of heavy metals on Aspergillus niger Effect of pretreatment. *Biores. Technol.* 63: 109-113.

A. Mittal, L. Kurup, J. Mittal (2007): Freundlich and Langmuir adsorption isotherms and kinetics for the removal of Tartrazine from aqueous solutions using hen feathers. *J. Hazar. Mater.* 146: 243-248.

A. Mittal, L. Kurup, V.K. Gupta (2005): Use of waste materials-bottom ash and deoiled soya, as potential adsorbents for the removal of Amaranth from aqueous solutions. *J. Hazard. Mater.* 117: 171-178.

A. Oladoja, I.O. Asia, C.M.A. Ademoroti, O.A. Ogbewe (2008): Studies on the Sorption of Methylene Blue in a Fixed Bed of Rubber Seed Shell. *Asia-Pacific J. Chem. Eng.* 3: 320-332.

A. Polman, C.R. Brekenridge (1996): Biomass mediated binding and recovery of textile dyes from waste effluents.Tex. *Chem. Colour.* 28: 31-35.

A. R. Binupriya, M. Sathishkumar, K. Dhamodaran, R. Jayabalan, K. Swaminathan, S. E. Yun (2007): Liquid-phase separation of reactive dye by wood-rotting fungus: a biotechnological approach. *Biotech. J.* 2: 1014-1025.

A. R. Khataee, G. Dehghan, A. Ebadi, M. Zarei, M. Pourhassan (2010): Biological treatment of a dye solution by macroalgae Chara sp.: Effect of operational parameters, intermediates identification and artificial neural network modeling. *Biores. Technol.* 101: 2252-2258.

A. Rais, (2009): Studies on adsorption of crystal violet dye from aqueous solution onto Coniferous Pinus Bark Powder (CPBP). *J. of Hazard. Mater.* 171 : 767-773.

A. Rais, P. K Mondal (2010): Application of Modified Water Nut Carbon as a Sorbent in Congo red and Malachite-Green Dye Contaminated Wastewater Remediation. *Sep. Sci. and Technol.* 45: 394–403.

A. Rais, P. K. Mondal (2009): Application of Acid Treated Almond Peel for Removal and Recovery of Brilliant Green from Industrial Wastewater by Column Operation. *Sep. Sci. and Technol.* 44:1638-1655.

A. Rais, P. K. Mondal (2009): Application of Acid Treated water Nut Activated carbon for the removal of malachite green from industrial waste water by column operation. *J. of Environ. Res. and Develop.* 3: 807-816.

A. Rais, R. Kumar (2008): Adsorption study for Patent Blue VF using Ginger Waste Material. *J. of Iranian Chem. Res.* 1: 85-94.

A. Rais, R. Kumar (2008): Comparative adsorption study for the removal of Alizarin Red S and Patent Blue VF by using menthe wast. *J. of Current World Environ.* 3 (2): 261-268.

A. Rais, R. Kumar (2010): Adsorption studies of hazardous malachite green onto treated ginger waste. *J. of Environ. Manag.* 91: 1032-1038.

A. Rais, R. Kumar (2010): Conducting polyaniline/iron oxide composite: a novel adsorbent for the removal of Amido Black 10 B. *J. Chem. Eng. Data*, 55: 3489-3493.

A. Rais, R. Kumar (2010): Kinetic and thermodynamic studies of brilliant green adsorption onto activated carbon/ iron oxide nanocomposite. *J. of the Korean Chem. Soc.* 54: 125-130.

A. Rais, R. Kumar (2011): Adsorption of amaranth dyes onto alumina reinforced polystyrene. J. of Clean- Soil, Air, Water. 39: 74-82.

A. S. Franca, L. S. Oliveira, A. A. Nunes, C. C.O. Alves, (2010): Microwave assisted thermal treatment of defective coffee beans press cake for the production of adsorbents. *Biores. Technol.* 101: 1068-1074.

A. S. Ozcan, B. Erdem, A. Ozcan (2005): Adsorption of Acid Blue 193 from aqueous solutions onto BTMA-bentonite. *Coll. Surf. A: Physicochem. Eng. Asp.* 266: 73–81.

A. Srinivasan, T. Viraraghavan (2010): Decolorization of dye wastewaters by biosorbents: a review. *J. Environ. Manag.* 91: 1915-1929.

A. Tabak, E. Eren, B. Afsin, B. Caglar (2009): Determination of adsorptive properties of a Turkish Sepiolite for removal of Reactive Blue 15 anionic dye from aqueous solutions. *J. Hazard. Mater.* 161: 1087-1094.

A. W. M. Ip, J.P. Barford, G. McKay (2009): Reactive Black dye adsorption/desorption onto different adsorbents:Effect of salt, surface chemistry, pore size and surface area. *J. of Coll. and Interf. Sci.* 337: 32-38.

A. Witek-Krowiak (2011): Analysis of influence of process conditions on kinetics of malachite green biosorption onto beech sawdust. *Chem. Engg. J.* 171: 976-985.

A. Y. Dursun, O. Tepe (2011): Removal of Chemazol Reactive Red 195 from aqueous solution by dehydrated beet pulp carbon. *J. of Hazard. Mater.* 194: 303-311.

A.K. Chowdhury, A.D. Sarkar, A. Bandyopadhyay (2009): Rice Husk Ash as a Low Cost Adsorbent for the Removal of Methylene Blue and Congo Red in Aqueous Phases. *Clean* 37: 581-591.

A.R. Binupriya, M. Sathishkumar, D. Kavitha, K. Swaminathan, S.E. Yun, S.P. Mun (2007): Experimental and isothermal studies on sorption of congo red by modified mycelial biomass of wood rotting fungus. *Clean* 35: 143-150.

A.Z.M. Badruddoza, G. S. S. Hazel, K. Hidajat, M.S. Uddin, (2010): Synthesis of carboxymethyl—cyclodextrin conjugated magnetic nano-adsorbent for removal of methylene blue. *Colloid and Surfaces A: Physico. and Engg Asp.* 367: 85-95.

B. S. Inbaraj, B.H. Chen (2011): Dye adsorption characteristics of magnetite nanoparticles coated with a biopolymer poly(c-glutamic acid). *Biores. Technol.* 102: 868–887.

B. Yu, Y. Zhang, A. Shukla, S.S. Shukla, K.L. Dorris (2001): The removal of heavy metals from aqueous solutions by sawdust adsorption—removal of lead and comparison of its adsorption with copper. *J. Hazard. Mater.* 84: 83-94.

B.K. Sharma, Industrial Chemistry, Sixth Edition, Goel Publishing house Meerut, India, 1994.

C. Aharoni, M. Ungarish (1977): Kinetics of activated chemisorption Part 2. Theoretical models. *J. Chem. Soc. Faraday Trans.* 73: 456-464.

C. Dogar, A. Gurses, M. Acikyildiz, E. Ozkan (2010): Thermodynamics and kinetic studies of biosorption of a basic dye from aqueous solution using green algae Ulothrix sp. *Colloids Sur. B: Biointer.* 76: 279-285.

C. F. Thurston (1994): The structure and function of fungal laccases. Microbiology 140: 19-26.

C. Galindo, P. Jacques, A. Kalt (2000) : Photodegradation of the aminobenzene acid orange 52 by three AOPs: UV/H_2O_2, UV/TiO_2 and VIS/TiO_2. Comparative mechanistic and kinetic investigations. *J. Photochem. Photobiol. A: Chem.* 130: 35-47.

C. Kannan, T. Sundaram, T. Palvannan (2008): Environmentally stable adsorbent of tetrahedral silica and non-tetrahedral alumina for removal and recovery of malachite green dye from aqueous solution. *J. Hazard. Mater.* 157: 137-145.

C. Kannan, T. Sundaram, T. Palvannan (2008): Environmentally stale adsorbent of tetrahedral silica and non-tetrahedral alumina for removal and recovery of malachite green dye from aqueous solution. *J. Hazar. Mater.* 157: 137-145.

C. M. So, M.Y. Cheng, J.C. Yu, P.K. Wong (2002): Degradation of azo dye Procian red MX-5B by photocatalytic oxidation. *Chemosphere* 46: 905-912.

C. Ma, L. Cao, X. Wang, L. Zhang, M. Shi, J. Wan (2012): Characterization and adsorption capacity of a novel high-performance polymeric sorbent synthesized in supercritical carbon dioxide. *The J. of Super. Flu.* 62: 232-239.

C. Visvanathan, R.B. Aim, K. Parameshwaran (2000): Membrane separation bioreactors for wastewater treatment. *Cri. Rev. Environ. Sci. Tech.* 30: 1-48.

C.I. Pearce, J.R. Lloyd, J.T. Guthrie (2003): The Removal of Colour from Textile Wastewater using Whole Bacterial Cells: A Review. *Dyes Pigm.* 58: 179-196.

Cai-yun Tan, Min Li, Yu-Man Lin, Xiao-Qiao Lu, Zu-liang Chen (2011): Biosorption of Basic Orange from aqueous solution onto dried *A. filiculoides* biomass: Equilibrium, kinetic and FTIR studies. *Desalination*, 266: 56-62.

D. J. Joo, W.S. Shin, J.H. Choi, S.J. Choi, M.C. Kim, M.H. Han, T. W. Ha, Y.H. Kim (2007): Decolorization of reactive dyes using inorganic coagulants and synthetic polymer. Dyes Pigm. 73: 59-64.

D. Sun, X. Zhang, Y. Wu, X. Liu (2010): Adsorption of anionic dyes from aqueous solution on fly ash. *J. Hazar. Mater.* 181: 335-342.

E. Eren, O. Cubuk, H. Ciftci, B. Eren, B. Caglar (2010): Adsorption of basic dye from aqueous solutions by modified sepiolite: Equilibrium, kinetics and thermodynamics study. *Desalination* 252: 88-96.

E. Guibal (2004): Interactions of metal ions with chitosan-based sorbents: a review. *Sep. Purif. Technol.* 38, 43–74.

Easton, J.R, The dye marker's view. In: Coppr P. (Ed) Colours and Dye House Effluent, 1995, 19-27.

El Sayed Z. El Ashtoukhy (2009): Loofa egyptiaca as a novel adsorbent for removal of direct blue dye from aqueous solution. *J. of Environ. Manag.* 90: 2755-2761.

F. A. Ozdemir, B. Demirata, R. Apak (2009): Adsorption renoval of methylene blue from simulated dyeing wastewater with melamine-formaldehyde-urea resin. *J. App. Poly. Sci.* 112: 3442-3448.

F. Archibald, B. Roy (1992): Production of manganic chelates by laccase from the lignin-degrading fungus Trametes (Coriolus) versicolor. *Appl. Environ. Microbiol.* 58: 1496-1499.

F. C. Wu, P.H. Wu, R.L. Tseng, R.S. Juang (2010): Preparation of activated carbons from unburnt coal in bottom ash with KOH activation for liquid-phase adsorption. *J. Environ. Manag.* 91: 1097-1102.

F. Deniz, S. D. Saygidege (2010): Equilibrium, kinetic and thermodynamic studies of Acid Orange 52 dye biosorption by Paulownia tomentosa Steud. leaf powder as a low-cost natural biosorbent. *Biores. Technol.* 101: 5137-5143.

F. Derbyshire, M. Jagtoyen, R. Andrews, A. Rao, I. Martin-Gullon, E. Grulke (2001): Carbon materials in environmental applications. In: Radovic, L.R. (Ed.), Chemistry and Physics of Carbon,Vol. 27. Marcel Dekker, New York, pp. 1–66.

Fereshte Keyhanian, Shahab Shariati, Mohammad Faraji, Maryam Hesab (2011): Magnetite nanoparticles with surface modiûcation for removal of methyl violet from aqueous solutions, Arab J. Chem. doi:10.1016/j.arabjc.2011.04.01.

G. Crini, P.M. Badot (2008): Application of Chitosan, a Natural Aminopolysaccharide, for Dye Removal from Aqueous Solutions by Adsorption Processes Using Batch Studies: A Review of Recent Literature. *Prog. Poly. Sci.* 33: 399-447.

G. Jiang, Z. Lin, X. Huang, Y. Zheng, C. Ren, C. Huang, Z. Huang (2012): Potential biosorbent based on sugarcane bagasse modiûed with tetraethylenepentamine for removal of eosin Y. Int. J. Biol. Macro. 50: 707-712.

G. McMullan, C. Meehan, A. Conneely, N. Kirby, T. Robinson, P. Nigam, I.M. Banat, R. Marchant, W.F. Smyth (2001): Microbial decolourisation and degradation of textile dyes. *Appl. Microbiol. Biotechnol.* 56: 81-87.

G. Mishra, M. Tripathy (1993): A critical review of the treatments for decolourization of textile effluent. *Colourage* 40: 35-38.

G. Vijayakumar, M. Dharmendirakumar, S. Renganathan, S. Sivanesan, G. Baskar, K. P. Elango (2009): Renoval of congo red from aqueous solutions by perlite. *Clean* 37: 355-364.

G. Xing, S. Liu, Q. Xu, Q. Li (2012): Preparation and adsorption behavior for brilliant blue X-BR of the cost-effective cationic starch intercalated clay composite matrix. *Carbohy. Poly.* 87: 1447-1452.

G. Z. Kyzas, N. K. Lazaridi (2009): Reactive and basic dyes removal by sorption onto chitosan derivatives. *J. of Colloid and Interf. Sci.* 331: 32-39.

G.Z. Kyzas, M. Kostoglou, N.K. Lazaridis (2010): Relating interactions of dye molecules with chitosan to adsorption kinetic data. *Langmuir 26*: 9617-9626.

H. Chen, X. Chen, (2012): A simpliûed method for synthesis of Fe_3O_4@PAA nanoparticles and its application for the removal of basic dyes. *Appl. Surf. Sci.* 258: 3897-3902.

H. Duygu Ozsoy, J. Van Leeuwe (2011): Removal of color from fruit candy waste by activated carbon adsorption, *J. of Food Engg,* 101: 106-112.

H. Kasgoz, A. Durmus (2008): Dye Removal by a Novel Hydrogel-Clay Nanocomposite with Enhanced Swelling Properties. *Poly. Adv. Technol.* 19: 838-845.

H.C. Shrivastava, Comprehensive chemistry. Second Edition, Pragati Prakashan, Merrut, India, 2001.

H.M.F. Freundlich (1906): Uber die adsorption in losungen. *Z. Phys. Chem.* 57: 385-470.

H.Y. Zhu, R. Jiang, L. Xiao, W. Li (2010): A novel magnetically separable Fe2O3/crosslinked chitosan adsorbent: preparation, characterization and adsorption application of renoval of hazardous azo dyes. *J. Hazard.Mater.* 179: 251-257.

H.-Y. Zhu, Y.-Q. Fu, R. Jiang, J. Yao, L. Xiao, G.-M. Zeng (2012): Novel magnetic chitosan/ poly(vinyl alcohol) hydrogel beads: Preparation,characterization and application for adsorption of dye from aqueous solution. *Biores. Technol.* 102: 24-30.

I. Guezguez, S. Dridi-Dhaouadi, F. Mhenn (2009): Sorption of Yellow 59 on Posidonia oceanica, a non-conventional biosorbent: Comparison with activated carbons. *Indus. crops and Products*, 29: 197-204.

I. Guezguez, S. Dridi-Dhaouadi, F. Mhenni (2009): Sorption of Yellow 59 on Posidonia oceanica, a non-conventional biosorbent: Comparison with activated carbons, *Indus. Crops and product,* 29: 197-204.

I. Küncek, S. Sener (2010): Adsorption of methylene blue onto sonicated sepiolite from aqueous solutions. *Ultra. Sonochem.* 17: 250-257.

I. Langmuir (1916): The constitution and fundamental properties of solids and liquids. Part 1. solids. *J. Am. Chem. Soc.* 38: 2221-2295.

I. Langmuir (19916): Principles of Adsorption Chromatography. *J. Am. Chem. Soc.* 38: 2221-2295.

J. Hu, Z. Song, L. Chen, H. Yang, J. Li, R. Richards (2010): Adsorption properties of MGO (III) nanoplate for the dye pollutant from wastewater. *J. Chem. Eng. Data, 55:* 3742-3748.

J. J. Porter (1997): Filtration and recovery of dyes from textile wastewater. Treatment of Wastewaters from Textile Processing. Schriftenreihe Biologische Abwasserreinigung, Berlin, Germany.

J. K. Mohanty, T. Naidu, B.C. Meikap, M.N. Biswas (2006): Preparation and Charaterization of activated carbons from Terminalia Arjuna nut with Zinc Chloride activation for the removal of Phenol from waster. *Ind. Eng. Chem. Res.* 45: 5165-5171.

J. M. Chern, C. H. Wu (2001): Desorption of dye from activated carbon beds: effects of temperature, pH and alcohol. *Water Res.*35: 4159–4165.

J. Rahchamani, H. Zavvar Mousavi, M. Behzad (2011): Adsorption of methyl violet from aqueous solution by polyacrylamide as an adsorbent: Isotherm and kinetic studies, *Desalination*, 267: 256-260.

J. Ramsay, M. Shin, S. Wong, C. Goode (2006): Amaranth decoloration by Trametes versicolor in a rotating biological reactorJ. *Ind. Microbiol. Biotechnol.* 33: 791–795.

J. S. Knapp, P.S. Newby (1995): The microbiological decolorization of an industrial effluent containing a diazo-linked chromophore. *Water Res.* 7: 1807-1809.

K. A. G. Gusmao, L. V. A. Gurgel, T. M. S. Melo, L. F. Gil (2012): Application of succinilated sugarcane bagasse as adsorbent to remove methylene blue and gentian violet from aqueous solution- kinetic and equilibrium studies. *Dyes and Pigment*, 92: 967-974.

K. Byrappa, A.K. Subaramani, S. Ananda, K.M. Lokanath Rai, R. Dinesh, M. Yoshimra (2006): Photocatalytic degradation of rhodamine B dye using hydrothermally synthesized ZnO. *Bull. Mater. Sci.* 29: 433-438.

K. Elass , A. Laachach, A. Alaoui, M. Azzi (2011): Removal of methyl violet from aqueous solution using a stevensite-rich clay from Morocco. *Appl. Clay Sci.* 54: 90-96.

K. Gobi, M.D. Mashitah, V.M. Vadivelu (2011): Adsorptive removal of Methylene Blue using novel adsorbent from palm oil mill effluent waste activated sludge: Equilibrium, thermodynamics and kinetic studies. *Chem. Engg. J.* 17 3: 1246-1252.

K. R. Ramakrishna, T. Viraraghavan (1997): Dye removal using low cost adsorbents. *Water Sci. Technol.* 36: 189–196.

K.K.H. Choy, J. F. Porter, G. McKay (2000): Langmuir isotherm models applied to the multicomponent sorption of acid dyes from effluent onto activated carbon. *J. Chem. Eng. Data* 45: 575–584.

K.K.H. Choy, J. F.Porter, G. McKay (2000): Langmuir isotherm models applied to the multicomponent sorption of acid dyes from effluent onto activated carbon. *J. Chem. Eng. Data* 45: 575–584.

K.K.H. Choy, J.F. Porter, G. McKay (2004): Single and Multicomponent Equilibrium Studies for the adsorption of Acidic Dyes on Carbon from Effluents. *Langmuir* 20: 9646-9656.

K.R. Ramakrishna, T. Viraraghavan (1997): Dye removal using low cost adsorbents. *Water Sci. Technol.* 36: 189-196.

K.T. Chuung G (1978): Fulk,Reduction of azo dyes by intestinal anaerobes. *App. Enviro. Micro.* 35: 558-562

K.Y. Foo, B.H. Hameed (2010): Insight into modeling of adsorption isotherms system. *Chem. Eng. J.* 156: 2-10.

K.Y. Foo, B.H. Hameed (2012): Potential of jackfruit peel as precursor for activated carbon prepared by microwave induced NaOH activation, *Biores. Technol.* 10.1016/j.biortech.2012.01.17.

K.Y. Foo, B.H. Hameed (2012): Preparation, characterization and evaluation of adsorptive properties of orange peel based activated carbon via microwave induced K_2CO_3 activation. *Biores. Technol.* 104: 679-686.

K.Y. Foo, B.H. Hameed, (2011): Preparation and characterization of activated carbon from sunûower seed oil residue via microwave assisted K_2CO_3 activation. *Biores. Technol.* 102: 9794-9799.

K.Y. Foo, B.H. Hameed (2011): Preparation of oil palm (*Elaeis*) empty fruit bunch activated carbon by microwave-assisted KOH activation for the adsorption of methylene blue. *Desalination* 275: 302-305.

Kannan, N., Sundaram, M.M., (2001): Kinetics and mechanism of removal of methylene blue by adsorption on various carbons—a comparative study. *Dyes Pigments* 51: 25–40.

L. Chao, Z. Hong, Z. Li, Z. Gang (2010): Study on Adsorption Characteristic of Macroporou Resin to Phenol in Wastewater. *Canadian J. Chem. Eng.* 88: 417-424.

L. Fan, Y. Zhang, X. Li, C. Luo, F. Lu, H. Qi (2012): Removal of alizarin red from water environment using magnetic chitosan with Alizarin Red as imprinted molecules. *Colloid. and Surf. B: Biointerfaces*, 91: 250-257.

L. Wang, A. Wang (2007): Removal of Congo red from aqueous solution using a chitosan/organo-montmorillonite nanocomposite. *J. Chem.Tech. Biotechnol.* 82: 711-720.

Li Yan, P. R. Chang, P. Zheng, X. M, (2012): Characterization of magnetic guar gum-grafted carbon nanotubes and the adsorption of the dyes. *Carbohy. Poly.* 87: 1919-1924.

M. A. Ahmad, N. K. Rahman (2011): Equilibrium, kinetics and thermodynamic of Remazol Brilliant Orange 3R dye adsorption on coffee husk-based activated carbon. *Chem. Engg. J.* 170: 154-161.

M. Alkan, C. Apa, S. Demirbas, O¨. M. Dogan (2005): Removal of reactive blue 221 and acid blue 62 anionic dyes from aqueous solutions by sepiolite. *Dyes Pigments.* 65: 251–259.

M. Anbia, S. A. Hariri, S.N. Ashraûzade (2010): Adsorptive removal of anionic dyes by modiûed nanoporous silica SBA-3. *Appl. Surf. Sci.* 256: 3228-3233.

M. Asgher, H. N. Bhatti (2010): Mechanistic and kinetic evaluation of biosorption of reactive azo dyes by free, immobilized and chemically treated Citrus sinensis waste biomass. *Ecolo. Engg.* 36: 1660-1665.

M. E. Russo, F. Di Natale, V. Prigione, V. Tigini, A. Marzocchella, G.C. Varese (2010): Adsorption of acid dyes on fungal biomass: Equilibrium and kinetics characterization. *Chem. Eng. J.* 162: 537-545.

M. G. Kulla (1981): Aerobic bacterial degradation of azo dyes. Microbial degradation of xerobiotics and recalcitrant compounds. FEMS Symposium, 12. Academic Press, London.

M. Ghaedi, H. Khajeshariû, A. H. Yadkuri, M. Roosta, R. Sahraei, A. Daneshfa (2012): Cadmium hydroxide nanowire loaded on activated carbon as efûcient adsorbent for removal of Bromocresol Green. *Spectrochimica Acta Part A: Molecu. and Biomol. Spectro.* 86: 62-68.

M. Ghaedi, H. Tavallali, M. Shariû, S. Nasiri Kokhdan, A. Asghari (2012): Preparation of low cost activated carbon from Myrtus communis and pomegranate and their efûcient application for removal of Congo red from aqueous solution. *Spectrochimica Acta Part A: Mol. and Biomol. Spectro.* 86: 107-114.

M. J. Martin, A. Artola, M. Dolors Balaguer, M. Rigola (2003) Activated carbons developed from surplus sewage sludge for the removal of dyes from dilute aqueous solutions. *Chem. Eng. J.* 94: 231–239.

M. J. Temkin, V. Pyzhev (1940) : Recent modifications to Langmuir isotherms. *Acta Physiochim. USSR* 12: 217-222.

M. M. Dubinin (1947): L.V. Radushkevich, Equation of the Characteristic Curve of Activated Charcoal, in: *Proceedings of the Academy of Sciences*, 55. Physical Chemistry Section USSR.

M. Motiar, R. Khan, M. Ray, A. K. Guha (2011): Mechanistic studies on the binding of Acid Yellow 99 on coir pith, *Bioresour. Technol.* 102: 2394-2399.

M. O¨zacar, A. I.. Sengil (2002): Adsorption of acid dyes from aqueous solutions by calcined alunite and granular activated carbon. *Adsorption* 8: 301–308.

M. Riera-Torres, C. Gutierrez-Bouzan, M. Crespi (2010): Combination of coagulation-flocculation and nanofiltration techniques for dye removal and water reuse in textile effluents. *Desalination* 252: 53-59.

M. S. Chiou, P. Y. Ho, H. Y. Li (2004): Adsorption of anionic dyes in acid solutions using chemically cross-linked chitosan beads. *Dyes Pigments* 60: 69–84.

M. Sathishkumar, A.R. Binupriya, K. Vijayaraghavan, S. Yun (2007): Two and three-parameter isothermal modeling for liquid-phase sorption of procion blue H-B by inactive mycelial biomass of Panus fulvus. *J. Chem. Tech. Bio.* 82: 389-398.

M. Streat, J. W. Patrick, M. J. Pe´rez (1995): Sorption of phenol and para-chlorophenol from water using conventional and novel activated carbons. *Water Res.* 29: 467–472.

M. Vesna, N. Vuèuroviæ, N. R. Razmovski, M. N. Tekiæ (2012): Methylene blue (cationic dye) adsorption onto sugar beet pulp: Equilibrium isotherm and kinetic studies, *J. of Taiwan Inst. of Chem. Engg.* 43: 1, 108-111.

M.C. Somasekhara Reddy, L. Sivaramakrishna , A. Varada Reddy (2012): The use of an agricultural waste material, Jujuba seeds for the removal of anionic dye (Congo red) from aqueous medium. *J. of Hazard. Mater.* 92: 262.270.

M.J. Iqbal, M.N. Ashiq (2007): Adsorption of dyes from aqueous solutions on activated charcoal. *J. Hazard. Mater.* 139: 57-66.

M.K. Purkait, S. Das Gupta, S. De (2005): Adsorption of eosin dye on activated carbon and its surfactant based desorption, *Journal of Env. Manag.* 76: 135-142.

Metcalf and Eddy (2003): Wastewater Engineering: Treatment and Reuse, 4th ed. McGraw-Hill, New York, USA..

N. Atar, A. Olgun, F. Colak (2008): Thermodynamic, Equilibrium and Kinetic Study of the Biosorption of Basic Blue 41 using Bacillus macerans. *Eng. Life Sci.* 8: 499-506.

N. Barka, S. Qourzal, A. Assabbane, A. Nounah, Y. Ait-Icho, (2011): Removal of Reactive Yellow 84 from aqueous solution by adsorption onto hydroxyapatite. *J. of Saudi Chem. Soc.* 15: 263-267.

N. D. Setti, N. Jouini, Z. Derriche (2010): Sorption study of an anionic dye – benzopurpurine 4B – on calcined and uncalcined Mg–Al layered double hydroxides. *J. of Phys. and Chemis. of Solids.* 71: 556-559.

N. Dizge, C. Aydiner, E. Demirbas, M. Kobya, S. Kara (2008): Adsorption of reactive dyes from aqueous solutions by fly ash: kinetic and equilibrium studies. *J. Hazard. Mater.* 150: 737-746.

N. F. Cardoso, E. C. Lima, I. S. Pinto, C. V. Amavisca, B. Royer, R. B. Pinto, W. S. Alencar, S. F.P. Pereira (2011): Application of cupuassu shell as biosorbent for the removal of textile dyes from aqueous solution. *J. of Environ. Mang.* 92: 1237-1247.

N. H. Ince, D.T. Gonenc (1997) : Treatability of a textile azo dye by UV/H_2O_2. *Environ. Technol.* 18: 179-185.

N. Kirby (1999): Bioremediation of textile industry wastewater by white rot fungi. D. Phil Thesis, University of Ulster, Coleraine, UK.

N. Kirby, Bioremediation of textile industry wastewater by white rot fungi. D.Phil Thesis, University of Ulster, Coleraine, UK, 1999.

N. Nasuha, B.H. Hameed (2011): Adsorption of methylene blue from aqueous solution onto NaOH-modified rejected tea. *Chem. Engg. J.* 92: 1203-1212.

O. Gulnaz , A. Sahmurova, S. Kama (2011): Removal of Reactive Red 198 from aqueous solution by *Potamogeton crispus, Biores. Technol. 102: 9794-9799.*

P. C. Vandevivere, R. Bianchi, W. Verstraete (1998): Treatment and reuse of wastewater from the textile wet-processing industry: Review of emerging technologies. *J. Chem. Technol. Biotechnol.* 72: 289-302.

P. D. Petrolekas, G. Maggenakis (2007): Kinetic studies of the liquid-phase adsorption of a reactive dye onto activated lignite. *Ind. And Eng. Chem. Res. 46:* 1326-1332.

P. D. Saha, S. Chakraborty, S. Chowdhur (2012): Batch and continuous (ûxed-bed column) biosorption of crystal violet by Artocarpus heterophyllus (jackfruit) leaf powder. *Colloids and Surfaces B: Biointerfaces*, 92: 262-270.

P. Leechart, W. Nakbanpote, P. Thiravetyan (2009): Application of 'waste' wood-shaving bottom ash for adsorption of azo reactive dye. *J. of Environ. Manag.* 90: 912-920.

P. Nigam, R. Marchant (1995): Selection of a substratum for composing biofilm system of a textile-effluent decolorizing bacteria. *Biotechnol. Lett.* 17: 993-996.

P. Zamora, P. Kunz, S. Gomez de Morales, R. Pelegrini, P. de Capos Moleiro, J. Reyes, N. Duran (1999): Degradation of reactive dyes I. A comparative study of ozonation , enzymatic and photochemical processes. *Chemosphere* 38: 835-852.

Qian-Qian Zhong, Qin-Yan Yue, Qian Li, Xing Xu, Bao-Yu Gao (2011): Preparation, characterization of modified wheat residue and its utilization for the anionic dye removal. *Desalination*, 267: 193-200.

R. Ahmad, R. Kumar (2010): Adsorption studies of hazardous malachite green onto treated ginger waste. J. Environ. Manag. 91: 1032-1038.

R. Dhodapkar, N.N. Rao, S.P. Pande, T. Nandy, S. Devotta (2007): Adsorption of cationic dyes on super absorbent polymer and photocatalytic regeneration of the adsorbent. *React. Fun. Poly.* 67: 540-548.

R. Gong, M. Li, C. Yang, Y. Sun, J. Chen (2005): Removal of cationic dyes from aqueous solution by adsorption on peanut hull. *J. Hazard. Mater.* 121: 247-250.

R. Kumar, A. Rais (2011): Biosorption of hazardous crystal violet dye from aqueous solution onto treated ginger waste (TGW). *Desalination*, 265: 112-118.

R. Pelegrini, P. Peralto-Zamora, A.R. de Andrade, J. Reyers, N. Duran (2010): Electrochemically assisted photocatalytic degradation of reactive dyes. *App. Catal. B-Environ.* 22: 83-90.

R. Salehi, M. Arami, N.M. Mahmoodi, H. Bahrami, S. Khorramfar (2010): Novel biocompatible composite (Chitosan-zinc oxide nanoparticle): preparation, characterization and dye adsorption properties.Colloids Sur. B: Biointer. 80: 86-93.

Rais Ahmad, Rajeev Kumar (2010): Adsorptive removal of congo red dye from aqueous solution using bael shell carbon. Appl. Surf. Sci. 257: 1628-1633.

S. A. Ong, K. Uchiyama, D. Inadama, Y. Ishida, K.Yamagiwa (2010): Treatment of azo dye Acid Orange 7 containing wastewater using up-flow constructed wetland with and without supplementary aeration. Biores. Technol. 101: 9049-9057.

S. Babel, T. A. Kurniawan (2003): Low-cost adsorbents for heavy metals uptake from contaminated water: a review. *J. Hazardous Mater.* 97: 219–243.

S. Chatterjee, D. S. Lee, M. W. Lee, S. H. Wo (2009): Enhanced adsorption of congo red from aqueous solutions by chitosan hydrogel beads impregnated with cetyl trimethyl ammonium bromide. *Biores. Technol.* 100: 2803-2809.

S. Chatterjee, M. W. Lee, S. H. Wo (2010): Adsorption of congo red by chitosan hydrogel beads impregnated with carbon nanotubes. *Biores. Technol.* 101: 1800-1806.

S. Chatterjee, T. Chatterjee, S. Limb, S. H. Wo (2011): Effect of the addition mode of carbon nanotubes for the production of chitosan hydrogel core–shell beads on adsorption of Congo red from aqueous solution. *Biores. Technol.* 102: 4402-4409.

S. Chowdhury, S. Chakraborty, P. Sah (2011): Biosorption of Basic Green 4 from aqueous solution by Ananas comosus (pineapple) leaf powder. *Colloid. and Surfaces B: Biointerf.* 84: 520-527.

S. Dawood, T. K. Sen, (2012): Removal of anionic dye Congo red from aqueous solution by raw pine and acid-treated pine cone powder as adsorbent: Equilibrium, thermodynamic, kinetics, mechanism and process design. *Wat. Res.* http://dx.doi.org/10.1016/j.watres.2012.01.009

S. J. Allen, G. McKay, J. F. Porter (2004): Adsorption isotherm models for basic dye adsorption by peat in single and binary component systems. *J. Colloid Int. Sci.* 280: 322–333.

S. J. Allen, Q. Gan, R. Matthews, P.A. Johnson, (2003): Comparison of optimised isotherm models for basic dye adsorption by kudzu. *Bioresour. Technol.* 88: 143–152.

S. K. Khare, K.K. Panday, R.M. Srivastava, V.N. Singh (1987): Removal of victoria blue from aqueous solu- tion by fly ash. *J. Chem. Technol. Biotechnol.* 38: 99-104.

S. Khorramfar, N. M. Mahmoodi, M. Arami, K. Gharanjig (2010): Tamarind hull as a biosorbent for the removal of cationic dye from contaminated watercource. *Coloration Technol.* 126: 261-268.

S. Lagergren (1898): K., Zur Theorie der Sogenannten Adsorption Geloster Stoffe. Sven. *Ventenskapsakad. Handl.* 24: 1-39.

S. M. Venkata, N. R. Chandrasekhar, J. Karthikeyan (2002): Adsorptive removal of direct azo dye from aqueous phase onto coal based sorbents: a kinetic and mechanistic study. *J. Hazard. Mater. B* 90: 189–204.

S. M. Venkata., P. Sailaja, M. Srimurali, J. Karthikeyan (1999) Colour removal of monoazo acid dye from aqueous solution by adsorption and chemical coagulation. *Environ. Eng. Policy* 1: 149–154.

S. Mona, A. Kaushik, C.P. Kaushi (2011): Biosorption of reactive dye by waste biomass of Nostoc linckia. *Ecolo. Engg.* 37: 1589-1594.

S. Pirillo, L. Cornaglia, M.L. Ferreira, E.H. Rueda (2008): Removal of Fluorescein using different iron oxides as adsorbents: effect of pH. *Spectrochim. Acta Part A* 71: 636-643.

S. S. Vieira, Z. M. Magriotis, N. A. V. Santos, M. D. G. Cardoso, A. A. Saczk (2012): Macauba palm (Acrocomia Aculeata) cake from biodiesel processing: an efficient and low cost substrate for the adsorption of dyes. *Chem. Engg. J.* 183: 152-161.

S. Sadhasivam, S. Savitha, K. Swaminathan, Feasibility of using *Trichoderma harzianum* biomass for the removal of erioglaucine from aqueous solution World. *J. Microbiol. Biotechnol.* 23, 2007, 1075–1081.

S. T. Akar , A. Gorgulu, T. Akar, S. Celik, (2011): Decolorization of Reactive Blue 49 contaminated solutions by *Capsicum annuum* seeds: Batch and continuous mode biosorption applications. *Chem. Engg J.* 168: 125-133.

S. Wang, Y. Boyjoo, A. Choueib, Z. H. Zhu (2005): Removal of dyes from aqueous solution using fly ash and red mud. *Water Res.* 39: 129–138.

S. Wang, Y. Boyjoo, A. Choueib, Z.H. Zhu (2005): Removal of dyes from aqueous solution using fly ash and red mud. *Water Res.* 39: 129-138.

S.T. Akar, R. Uysal (2010): Untreated clay with high adsorption capacity for effective removal of C.I. Acid Red 88 from aqueous solutions: Batch and dynamic flow mode studies. *Chem. Eng. J.* 162: 591-598.

S.Y. Elovich, O.G. Larinov, Izv. Akad. Nauk (1962): Theory of adsorption from solutions of non electrolytes on solid (I) equation adsorption from solutions and the analysis of its simplest form, (II) veriûcation of the equation of adsorption isotherm from solutions. *SSSR, Otd. Khim. Nauk.* 2: 209-216.

S.Y. Mak, D.H. Chen (2004): Fast adsorption of methylene blue on polyacrylic acid-bound iron oxide magnetic nanoparticles. *Dyes Pigm.* 61: 93-98.

T. Robinson, G. McMullan, R. Marchant, P. Nigam (2001) : Remediation of dyes in textile effluent : a critical review on current treatment technologies with a proposed alternative. *Biores. Technol.* 77: 247-255.

T. Santhi, Ashly Leena Prasad, S. Manonmani (2011): A comparative study of microwave and chemically treated Acacia nilotica leaf as an eco friendly adsorbent for the removal of rhodamine B dye from aqueous solution. *Arab. J. of Chem.* doi:10.1016/ j.arabjc.2010.11.00

T. Santhi, S. Manonmani, V.S. Vasantha, Y.T. Chan (2011): A new alternative adsorbent for the removal of cationic dyes from aqueous solution. *Arab. J. of Chem.* doi:10.1016/ j.arabjc.2011.06.00.

T.B. Iyim, G. Guclu (2009): Removal of Basic Dyes from Aqueous Solutions Using. Natural Clay. *Desalination* 249 : 1377-1379.

T.C. Hsu (2008): Adsorption o fan acid dye onto coal fly ash. Fuel 87: 3040-3035.

U. B. Ogutveren, S. Kaparal (1994): Color removal from textile effluents by electrochemical destruction. *J. Environ. Sci. Health A* 29: 1-16.

U. R. Lakshmi, V. Chandra Srivastava, I. D. Mall, Dilip H. Latay, (2009): Rice husk ash as an effective adsorbent: Evaluation of adsorptive characteristics for Indigo Carmine dye. *J. of Environ. Manag.* 90: 710-720.

V. Dulman, C. Simion, A. Barsanescu, I. Bunia, V. Neagu (2009): Adsorption of Anionic Textile Dye Acid Green 9 from Aqueous Solution onto Weak or Strong Base Anion Exchangers. *J. App. Poly. Sci.* 113: 615-627.

V. Golob, A. Vinder, M. Simonic (2005): Efficiency of the coagulation/flocculation method for the treatment of dyebath Effluents. *Dyes Pigm.* 67: 93-97.

V. K. Gupta, Suhas (2009): Application of low-cost adsorbents for dye removal-a review. J. Envir. Manag. 90: 2313-2342.

V. Meshko, L. Markovska, M. Mincheva, A. E. Rodrigues (2001) Adsorption of basic dyes on granular activated carbon and natural zeolite. *Water Res.* 35: 3357–3366.

V. P. Vinod, T.S. Anirudhan (2003): Adsorption Behaviour of Basic Dyes on the Humic Acid Immobilized Pillared Clay. *Water Air Soil Poll.* 150: 193-217.

V.K. Gupta, I. Ali (2008) : Removal of endosulfan and methoxychlor from water on carbon slurry. *Environ. Sci. Technol.* 42 : 766-770

W. J. Weber, J.C. Morris (1963) : Kinetics of adsorption on carbon from solution. *J. Santi. Eng. Div. ASCE* 89 : 31-59.

W. Shi, X. Xu, G, Sun (1999): Chemically modified sunflower stalks as adsorbents for color removal from textile wastewater. *J. Appl. Poly. Sci.* 71: 1841-1850.

X. Han, Wei Wang, Xiaojian Ma (2011): Adsorption characteristics of methylene blue onto low cost biomass material lotus leaf, *Chem. Engg. J.* 171: 1-8.

X. Huang, H. Bu, G. Jiang, M. Zeng, (2011): Cross-linked succinyl chitosan as an adsorbent for the removal of Methylene Blue from aqueous solution, *Intern. J. of Biolog. Macromole.* 49: 643-651.

X. Huang, J. Bin, H. Bu, G. Jiang, M. Zeng (2011): Removal of anionic dye eosin Y from aqueous solution using ethylenediamine modiûed chitosan. *Carbohy Poly.* 84: 1350-1356.

X. S. Wang, J.P. Chen (2009): Removal of the Azo Dye Congo Red from Aqueous Solutions by the Marine Alga Porphyra yezoensis Ueda. *Clean* 37: 793-798.

Y. Al-Degs, M.A.M.. Khraisheh, S. J. Allen, M. N. Ahmad (2000): Effect of carbon surface chemistry on the removal of reactive dyes from textile effluent. *Water Res.* 34: 927–935.

Y. Feng, F. Yang, Y. Wang, L. Ma, Y. Wu, P. G. Kerr, L. Yang, (2011): Basic dye adsorption onto an agro-based waste material – Sesame hull (Sesamum indicum L.), *Biores. Technol.* 102: 10280-10285.

Y. Fu, T. Viraraghavan (2002a): Removal of Congo red from an aqueous solution by fungus Aspergillus niger. *Adv. Environ. Res.* 7: 239–247.

Y. Lee, E. J. Kim, J. Yang, H. Shin (2011): Removal of malachite green by adsorption and precipitation using aminopropyl functionalized magnesium phyllosilicate, *J. of Hazard. Mater.* 192: 62-70.

Y. M. Slokar, A.M.L. Marechal (1997): Methods of decoloration of textile wastewater. *Dyes Pigm.* 37: 335-356.

Y. S. Ho, G. McKay (1999): Pseudo-Second Order Model for Sorption Processes. *Pro. Biochem.* 34: 451-465.

Y. Xu, R.E. Lebrun (1999) : Treatment of textile dye plant effluent by nanofiltration membrane. *Sep. Sci. Technol.* 34 : 2501-2519.

Y. Yang, D. Jin, G. Wang, S. Wang, X. Jia, Y. Zha, (2011): Competitive biosorption of Acid Blue 25 and Acid Red 337 onto unmodiûed and CDAB-modiûed biomass of Aspergillus oryzae. *Biores. Technol.* 102: 7429-7436.

Y. Yao, F. Xu, M. Chen, Z. Xu, Z. Zhu (2010): Adsorption behavior of methylene blue on carbon nanotubes. *Biores. Technol.* 101: 3040-3046.

Yusra Safa, Haq Nawaz Bhatti, (2011): Biosorption of Direct Red-31 and Direct Orange-26 dyes by rice husk: Application of factorial design analysis. *Chem. Engg. Res. and Des.* 89: 2566-2574.

Z. Aksu, E. Balibe (2010): Effect of salinity on metal-complex dye biosorption by Rhizopus arrhizus. *J.l of Environ. Manag.* 91: 1546-1555.

Z. Aksu, S. Tezer (2005): Biosorption of reactive dyes on the green alga Chlorella vulgaris. *Proc. Biochem.* 40: 1347–1361.

Z. Aksu, S. Tezer (2005): Biosorption of reactive dyes on the green alga Chlorella vulgaris. *Proc. Biochem.* 40: 1347–1361.

Z. Al-Qodah, W. K. Lafi, Z. Al-Anber, M. Al-Shannag, A. Harahsheh 92007): Adsorption of methylene blue by acid and heat treated diatomaceous silica. *Desalination* 217: 212-224.

Z. Xu, Q. Zhang, H.H.P. Fang (2003): Application of porous resin. *Crit. Rev. Environ. Sci. Technol.* 33 : 363-389.

Z. Yao, L. Wang, J. Qi (2009): Biosorption of Methylene Blue from Aqueous Solution Using a Bioenergy Forest Waste: *Xanthoceras. Clean* 37: 642-648.

Z. Zhang, Z. Zhang, Y. Ferna´ndez, J.A. Mene´ndez, H. Niu, J. Pen, L. Zhang, S. Guo, (2010): Adsorption isotherms and kinetics of methylene blue on a low-cost adsorbent recovered from a spent catalyst of vinyl acetate synthesis. *Appl. Surf. Sci.* 256: 2569-2576.

Z. Zhang, L. Moghaddam, I. M. O'Hara, W.O.S. Doherty (2011): Congo Red adsorption by ball-milled sugarcane bagasse. *Chem.l Engg J.* 178: 122-128.

Z. Zhong, Q. Yang, X. Li, K. Luo, Y. Liu, G. Zen, (2012): Preparation of peanut hull-based activated carbon by microwave-induced phosphoric acid activation and its application in Remazol Brilliant Blue R adsorption. *Indus. Crops and Products*, 37: 175-185.

9

Study of Cropped based Physico-chemical Analysis of Salinity Areas through remote Sensing and GIS

—*Avadhesh Kumar Koshal, India*

ABSTRACT

Using IRS 1D images of March 2000 studies were conducted to assess the effects of secondary salinization on cereal crops. Plant samples collected consisted of roots, shoots, spikelets and grain of wheat (Triticum aestivum). Physico- chemical analysis that included chlorophyll estimation, leaf extract pH and ascorbic acid proved that 51 samples were normal, 44 samples of crop were affected by moderate salinity and 25 samples to severe salinity. Chlorophyll contents, leaf extract pH and ascorbic acid contents in the leaves showed inhibitory effects in wheat crop due to salinity.

It is important to take into consideration that remote sensing and GIS are an efficient and accurate source of information especially in the study of salt affected and waterlogged areas.

Keywords: *Chlorophyll, FCC, GIS, Image, IRS & LISS*

Introduction

Salt – affected soils are widespread over the world especially in arid, semi arid and some sub- humid regions. Salinity is one of the major causes of abiotic stress of where especially the soil salt content is naturally high. In India about 8.6 mha (Pathak, 2000) of land area is affected by soil salinity. Salt affected soils occur in the states of Uttar Pradesh, Gujarat, West Bengal, Rajasthan, Punjab, Maharashtra, Haryana, Orissa, Delhi, Kerala and Tamil nadu. Almost 2.8 million hectares of salt-affected soils are present within the Indo-Gangetic alluvial plain occupying parts of Punjab, Haryana, Uttar Pardesh, Delhi, Bihar and Rajasthan states (Abrol et al., 1971). Salinity affects any morphological, physiological and biochemical process, including plant growth and nutrient uptake (Willenborg et al., 2004) while conducting the survey it was observed that wheat crop look like burn and plant growth was stunted. Water and salt stresses are of particular significance to irrigated crops (Fowden et al., 1993). Salinity and sodicity stress bring about a general reduction in plant growth and yield of crops. Under both these conditions plants get stunted, exhibit poor tillering and branching and move over flowering and maturity being get delayed. Reduction in seed number and size occurs to varying in different plants. There was investigated effect of salinity on reproductive physiology of wheat **(Abdullah et al., 1978)**. Ray and Khaddar (1989) studied the influence of salinity, sodicity and their combinations on wheat (Triticum aestivum). It was reported that crop discrimination is a basic requirement for acreage estimation and yield prediction by satellite remote sensing (Sharma et al., 1994). The remote sensing, geographic information system (GIS) and global positioning system (GPS) have emerged powerful survey tools in the natural resource inventory and data handling. Application of remote sensing technology in mapping and monitoring degraded lands, especially salt – affected soils, has shown great promise of enhanced speed, accuracy and cost effectiveness (Dwivedi, 1996). Recent advances in remote sensing technology have opened new vistas in inventory, characterization and monitoring of degraded lands. Remote sensing by satellite offers tremendous possibilities for generating accurate spatial information over large geographical area. Punjab is a part of the vast alluvial expanse popularly known as Indo Gangetic plains. The districts of Bhatinda and Muktsar have been identified to the intensive area study site for this work.

Study area

The present study area lies between 30° 00′ to 30° 15′ N and 76° 30′ to 76° 45′ E and comprises parts of Bathinda and Muktsar districts (Punjab), The area

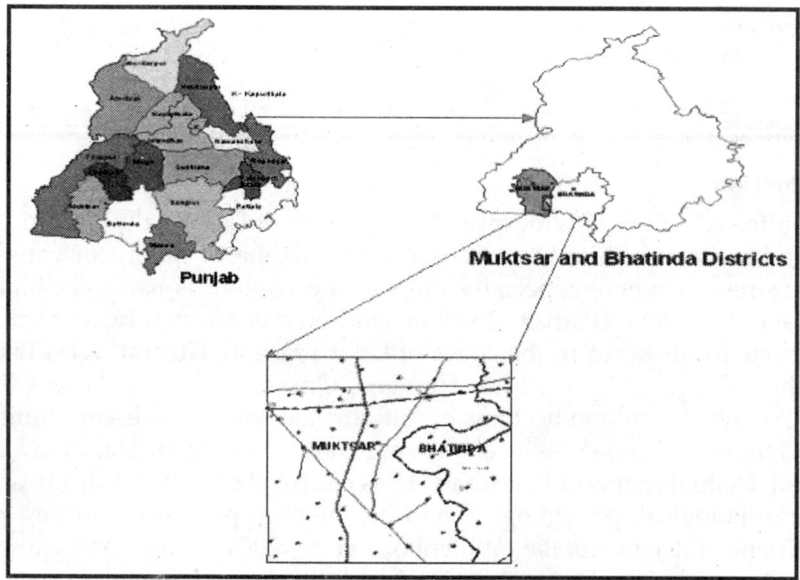

Fig. 9.1. Study area a part of Bhatinda and Muktsar Districts Area

is a part of the vast Trans-Gangetic Plain region of Indo-Gangetic alluvial plain (IGP), comprising of alternate bands of sands, silt and clay with pebbles (Fig.1). It is bounded by the state boundaries of Rajasthan and Haryana in the south whereas it is bordered by the district boundaries of Faridkot in the north, Ferozpur in the west and by Sangrur in the eas.

Material and Methods

Generation of False Colour Composite (FCC)

IRS ID LISS III geocoded March 2000 FCC data have four bands: blue (0.45-0.52mm), green (0.52-0.59mm), red (0.62- 0.68mm) and near infrared (0.77-0.86mm). The FCC was generated by combination with three bands: infrared, red and green bands projecting as red, green and blue image planes. The standard false colour composite was used. The vegetation was represented by red colour instead of green colour in the false colour composite.

Visual interpretation

During the month of March, wheat crop reaches maximum vegetative growth. Continuous upward flux of water from September to March brings salts from soil substratum on to the surface.

The satellite image for the month of March was most suitable for mapping crop affected by salinity (Fig.1a). The enhanced false colour composite image of March, 2000 month of the study area was displayed on 1:50,000 scale on monitor. The FCC (Fig.2) was visually interpreted for Normal crop, crop affected by moderate salinity and crop affected by severe salinity with the help of image elements like tone, texture, pattern and association etc. Crop affected by salinity was collated with soil salinity of soil samples taken during the field survey. The selection of the fields was based on "healthy" crop regions and crop affected by salinity (severe/ moderate salinity). The areas of healthy crops and crop affected by salinity (severe/ moderate salinity) were determined by the color spectrum of the LISS III image, Pseudo-natural

Crop affected by salinity **Crop affected by salinity and waterlogging**

Fig. 9.1a.

colour composite of RGB for bands (2, 3 and 4). After the fieldwork, the salinity measurements associated to those of expected area according to satellite image was established. Therefore, this observation strongly suggests that a relationship between the reflectance of the normal crop and crop affected by salinity, growing crops in the March month.

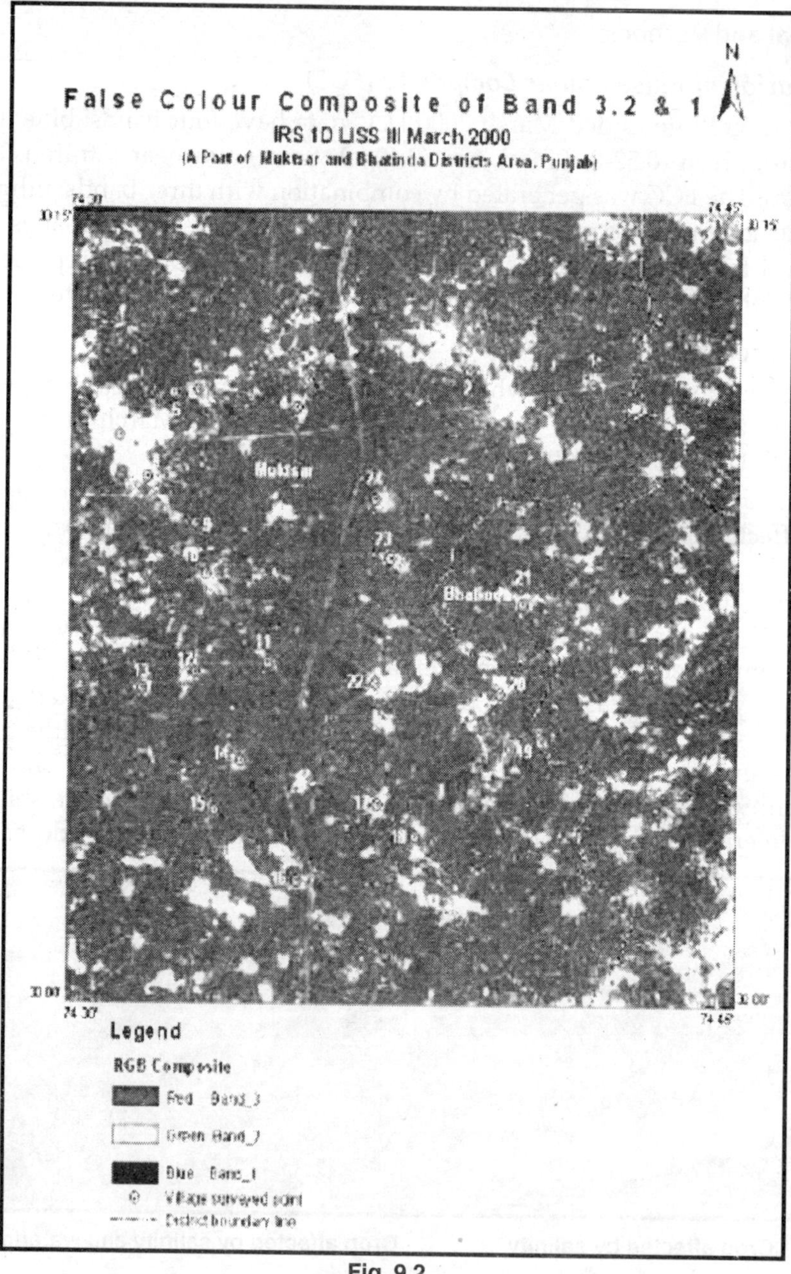

Fig. 9.2.

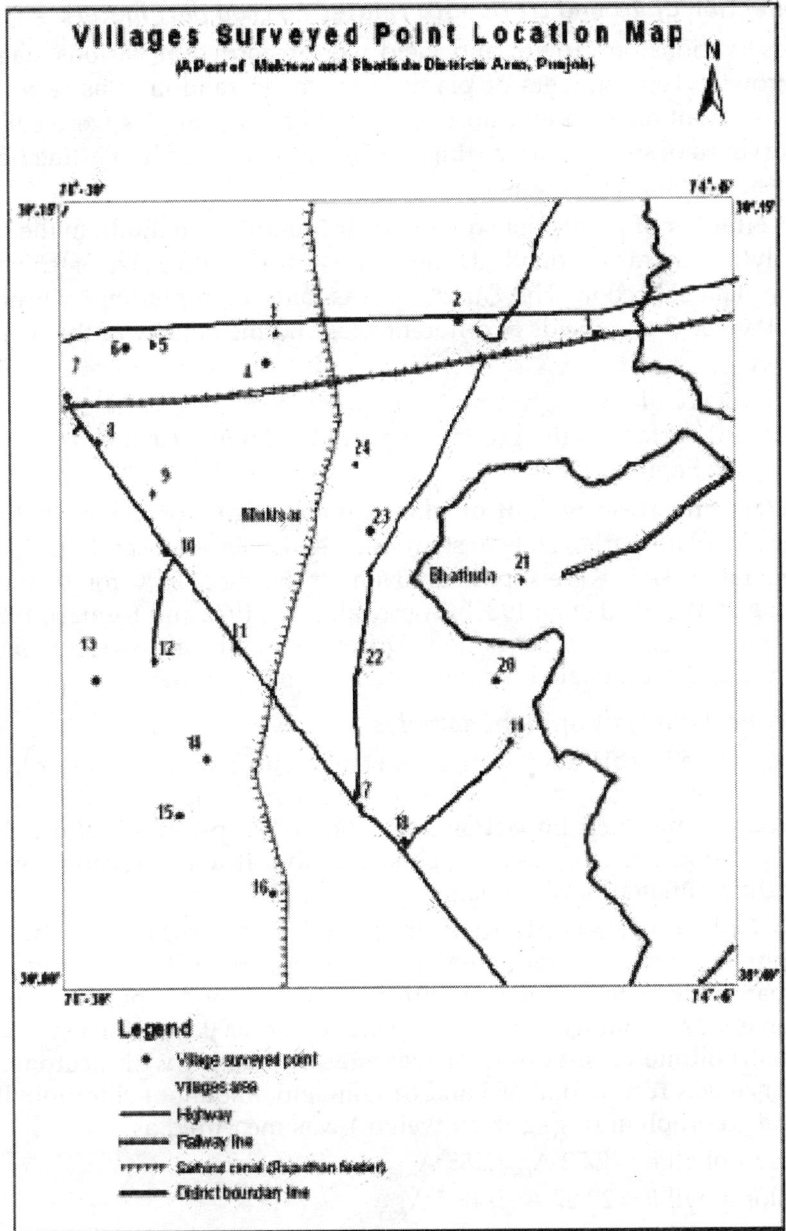

Fig. 9.2a.

Effect of salinity on Rabi crop (Wheat) physiology

In the study area, wheat crop was grown in the rabi season. The plant samples were collected from various categories of salt affected soils during December end and mid March. The geographic locations were obtained with the GPS (Global Positioning System).

(i) Collection of ground truth data related to crop parameters

The observations on growth and yield were recorded at various stages of crop growth. Ten numbers of plants were taken randomly as samples at locations of salt affected and normal cropped field. Samples were collected after surveyed of study area two times during growing and harvesting periods for physico-chemical analysis.

(*a*) **Number of plants per square meter (quadrate method):** In the study, the analytical characters quadrate method was used with a size of 0.5 × 0.5 m for crop data collection. The Quadrate was laid down randomly in normal and salt affected crop fields at different sites and the density of the crop was measured.

(*b*) **Average plant height (m):** Plants were measured for height (m) from their ground surface to the growing tip in March and at maturity of wheat crop in May. Sample size was ten.

(*c*) **Dry and fresh weight of plant biomass (g.):** For determination of biomass, all plant parts viz. leaf; stem, root, spike, spikelets and grains were first separated. They were kept in an oven for drying at 85°C for 48 hours as was done by Agrawal et al; 1981b, Agrawal, 1971, 1972 and Kumari, 1982 till the constant weight was obtained. Different plant parts were weighted separately and then totaled for their total weight of a plant.

(ii) Chemical analysis of plant samples

Chlorophyll, ascorbic acid, leaf extract pH, sulphur and some physical parameters of plant samples were worked out for identification of salt affected areas and their impact on vegetation or crops. In salt affected area wild vegetation growth was very good due to salt tolerance and could be clearly differentiated on the image.

(*a*) **Chlorophyll content:** Chlorophyll a, chlorophyll b and total chlorophyll content were measured according to Arnon (1949). For this 0.5 g plant material was homogenized with 80% acetone and a pinch of sodium bicarbonate. The homogenate was centrifuged at 3000 rpm for ten minutes and final volume of supernatant was made to 20 ml with acetone. The absorbance was recorded at 665 and 645 nm and amount of chlorophyll a, b and total chlorophyll (mg/g fresh weight) was measured as:

$$\text{Chlorophyll } a = 12.72\ A_{665} - 2.85\ A_{645}$$

$$\text{Chlorophyll } b = 22.87\ A_{645} - 4.67\ A_{665}$$

$$\textbf{Total chlorophyll} = 8.05\ A_{665} + 20.29\ A_{645}$$

(*b*) **Leaf extract pH:** It was measured with the help of digital electronic pH meter by homogenizing 5g fresh leaves with 25 ml double distilled water.

(*c*) **Ascorbic acid content:** The method was followed to measure the ascorbic acid content described (Keller and Schwager, 1977). Fresh leaves of 0.5 g were homogenized with 20 ml extracting solution prepared by dissolving 0.5 g oxalic acid and 0.075 g EDTA (Ethylene Di Amine Tetra Acetic Acid) in

100 ml distilled water kept in an ice bath. The homogenate was then centrifuged at 3000 rpm for 15 minutes. 1.0 ml of homogenate was mixed with 5.0 ml of 2-6 di chloro phenol indo phenol. After shaking it well, its optical density was measured at 520 nm wavelength on a spectronic –21 photometer. The ascorbic acid content in the sample was calculated by the following formula suggested (Keller and Schwager, 1977):

Ascorbic acid content (mg/g) = (Eo-Es-Et) × F (Factor)/w

Where,

W is weight of leaves, Eo, Es and Et are the respective optical densities of blank, plant sample and sample with one drop of 1% ascorbic acid, added to it. The calibration curve for the ascorbic acid was prepared by using chemically pure ascorbic acid (Figure).

Result & Discussion

Physico-chemical Characteristics of Crop Samples

The observations on plant growth and yield stage parameters were collected in March month during field survey. The impact of salinity was easily seen on the growing crop in the March month. In yield parameters, adverse impact was observed after maturation of the crop in May month. These months are very important for salinity point of view. The adverse effects were seen in the form of and physiological and biochemical parameters in the study area.

In physico- chemical analysis, 51 samples belongs to normal crop, 44 crop samples was crop affected by moderate salinity and 25 samples of crop affected by severe salinity. Out of 120 samples, the result obtained from wheat crop area is shown in Table (1&2) and Figures (3 to10).

Table 9.1: Physico-chemical Characteristics of Wheat Crop Samples

Crop characteristics	Crop classification		
	Normal crop	Crop affected by moderate salinity	Crop affected by severe salinity
No. of plants(m^{-2})	31.55+8.21	14.91+2.92	3.32+2.01
Plant height(m)	1.10+0.33	0.49+0.07	0.22+0.06
Fresh weight(g)	59.15+5.21	22.14+3.04	12.50+2.66
Dry weight (Biomass)(g)	28.39+2.64	10.54+1.06	6.11+1.16
Spike length(cm)	16.43+1.26	12.56+2.02	4.24+1.31
Spikelet weight(g)	6.47+0.43	5.34+0.23	4.39+0.19
Grain weight(g)	4.41+0.38	3.65+0.19	2.73+0.02

*Values are in mean based on total sample size, + Standard deviation

The quadrate methods for analysis of abundance of plants were also carried out. The numbers of plants were found maximum in the normal crop than the crop affected by moderate salinity. The number of plants in per sq meter was 31.55 in normal crop. However crop affected by severe salinity was 3.32 than in crop affected by moderate salinity were 14.91.

Table 9.2: Physico-chemical Characteristics of Wheat Crop Samples

Crop characteristics	Crop classification		
	Normal crop	Crop affected by moderate salinity	Crop affected by severe salinity
pH	7.35+0.15	8.12+0.26	8.62+0.08
Chlorophyll "a"(mg/g)	1.20+0.45	0.54+0.12	0.27+0.22
Chlorophyll "b"(mg/g)	0.62+0.24	0.31+0.09	0.51+0.46
Total chlorophyll(mg/g)	1.83+0.63	0.85+0.18	0.78+0.67
Ascorbic acid(mg/g)	3.15+0.61	2.96+0.57	2.91+0.56

Sample size for ascorbic acid test = 10, + Standard deviation

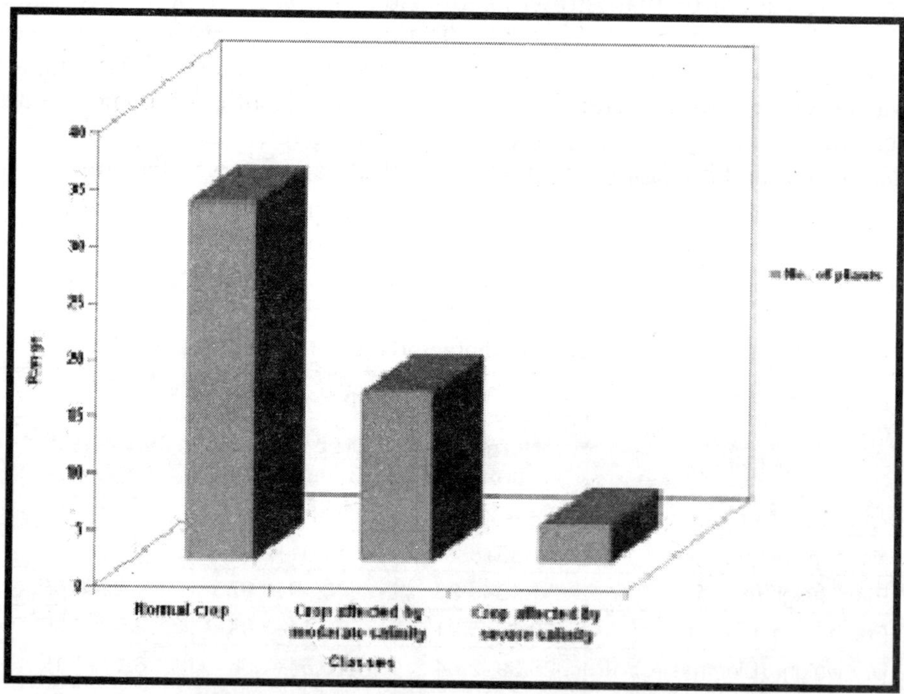

Fig. 9.3: Effect of Salinity on Abundance of Plant

During the course of experimental studies, different growth parameters associated with root, shoot and whole plant were carried out in three classes of crop. Crop affected by severe salinity showed the difference in their values, maximum reduction in total plant height 0.22 m as compare to crop affected by moderate salinity 0.49 m. Besides this, the maximum reduction in fresh weight and dry weight was also observed in crop affected by severe salinity

12.50 g and 6.11g respectively. The similar patterns were also observed in crop affected by moderate salinity 22.14g and 10.54g respectively.

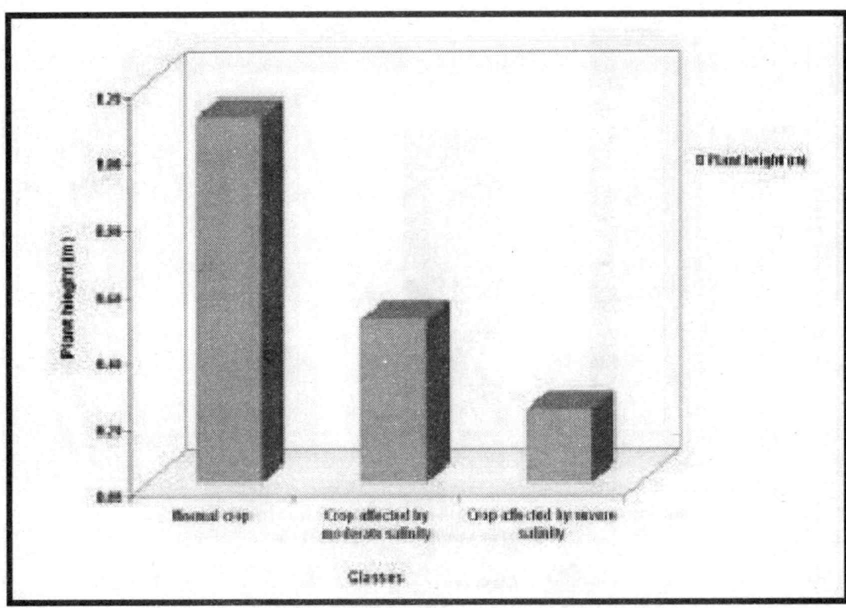

Fig. 9.4. Effect o Salinity on Plant Height (m)

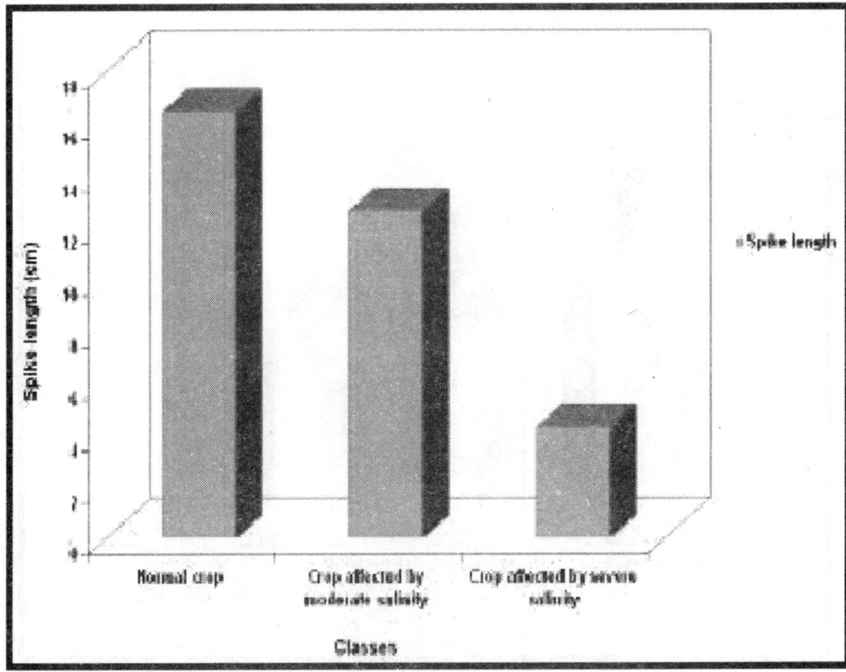

Fig. 9.5. Efect of Salnity on Spike length (cm)

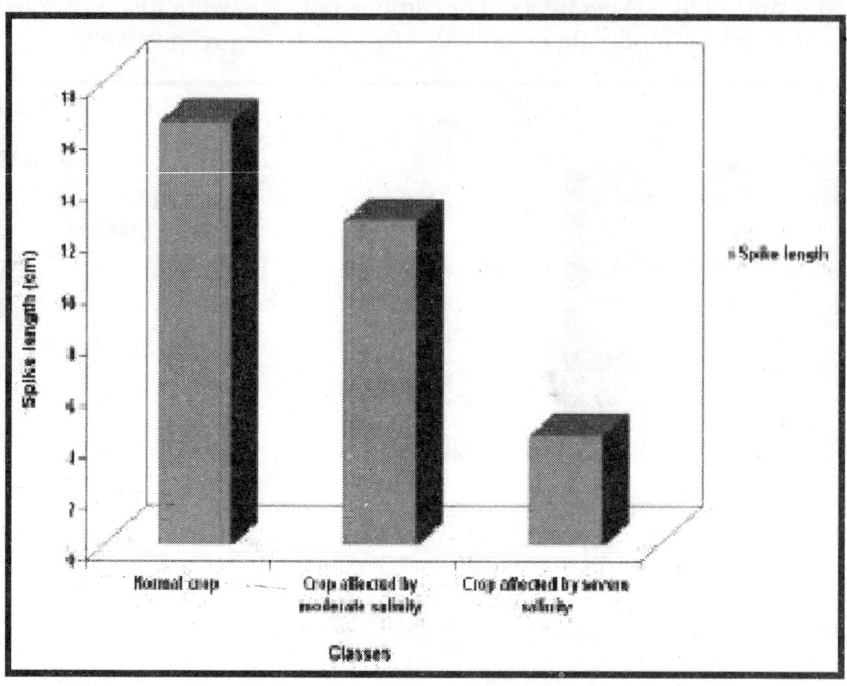

Fig. 9.6. Effect of salinity on Fresh weight & dry weight of Plant

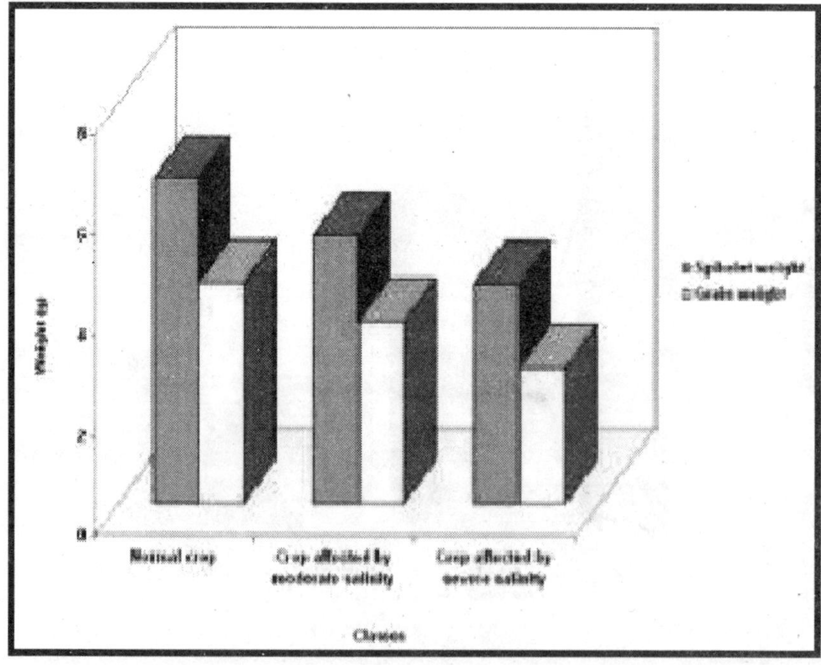

Fig. 9.7. Effect of Salinity on Yield Parameters

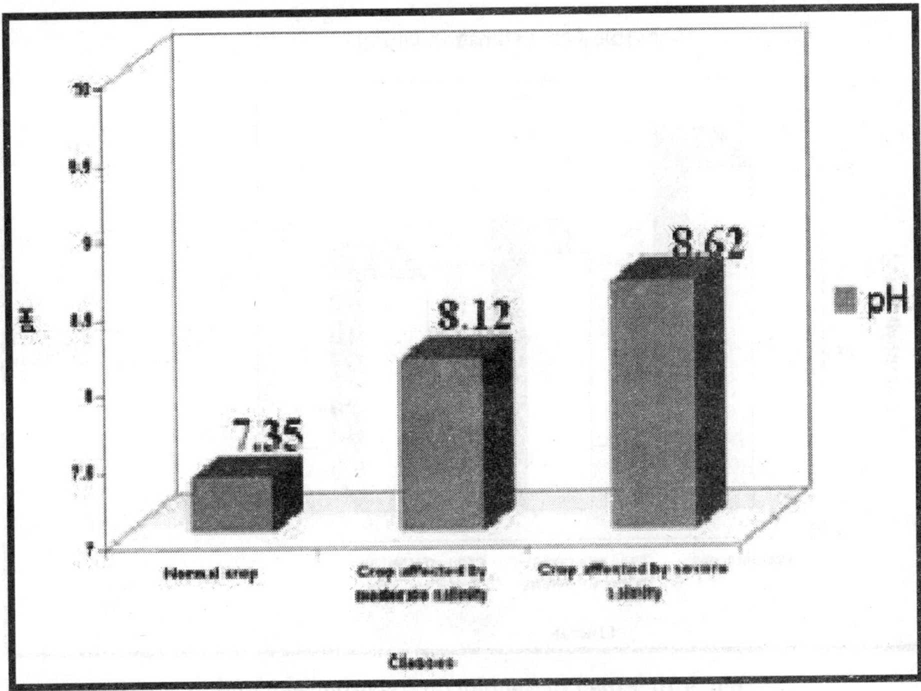

Fig. 9.8. Effect of salinity on leaf extract pH

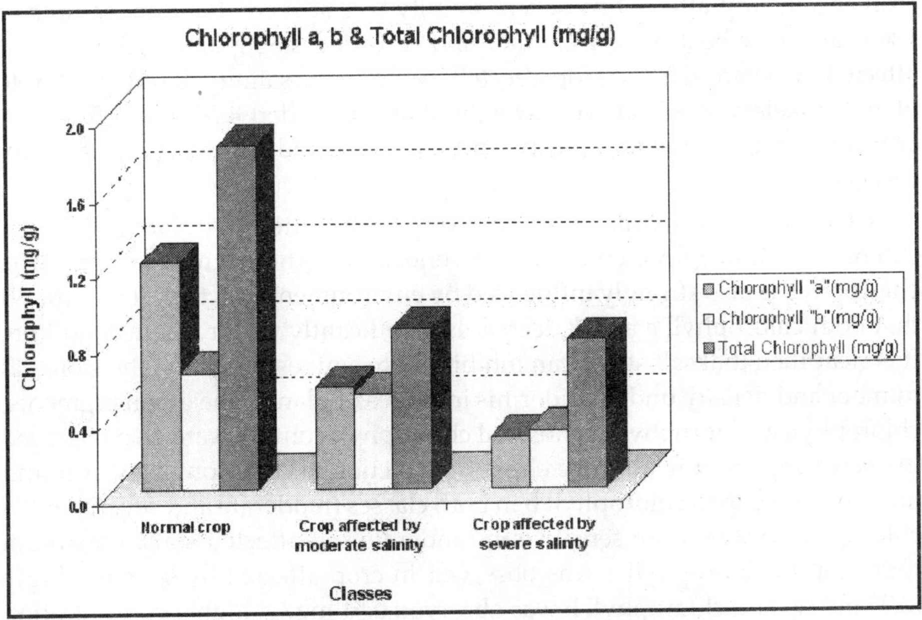

Fig. 9.9. Effect of Salinity onChlorophyll (mg/g)

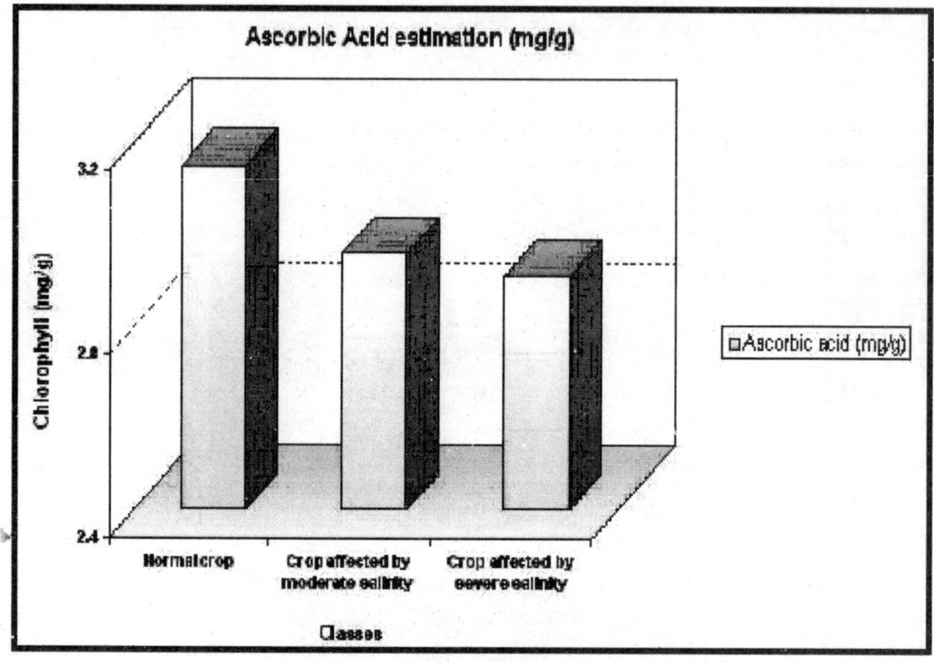

Fig. 9.10. Effect of Salinity on Ascorbic acid (mg/g)

Spike length recorded after maturation of the crop was 16.42cm in normal crop and in crop affected by severe salinity was 4.24 cm. Random sample of 100 grains of wheat were weighted and recorded 3.65 g and 2.73 g in crop affected by severe salt and crop affected by moderate salinity. Random sample of 100 spikelets of wheat were weighted and recorded 4.39 g and 5.34 g in crop affected by severe salinity and crop affected by moderate salinity respectively.

Chlorophyll is the main pigment of photosynthesis in plants. To some extent, the chlorophyll content also reflects the photosynthesis rate. It is chlorophyll is also strongly influenced by environmental factors. It was found that both chlorophyll *a* and *b* decreases significantly under saline condition. It is clear then that salt stress can inhibit photosynthesis activity, the stomatal number and density under epidermis in leaves of plants. The green pigments, chlorophyll a, chlorophyll b and total chlorophyll content were also observed in decreasing order in all three classes. Reduction in chlorophyll a was found more sensitive than chlorophyll b in both classes (moderate and severe) while chlorophyll b was more sensitive in moderate salt affected soils. Maximum reduction in chlorophyll a was observed in crop affected by severe salinity (0.27 mg/g) and chlorophyll b was observed 0.51 mg/g. higher concentration of salts showed inhibitory affect and maximum decrease in total chlorophyll was 0.78 mg/g in crop affected by severe salinity.

The biochemical analysis of crop samples showed significant effect of salinity. Alteration in the level of pH affects different pH development enzymatic activities of the plants, thereby influencing plant growth and development.

The maximum effect on leaf extract pH was recorded in the crop affected by severe salinity. The pH of leaf extract was recorded at 8.12 and 8.62 in the crop affected by severe and moderate salinity respectively. Maximum leaf extract pH 8.62 was observed in crop affected by sever salinity.

Ascorbic acid plays a crucial role in the physiology of plants during salt stress. In chloroplast ascorbic acid act as a powerful reductant responsible for the photo reduction of proto chlorophyll leading to several physiological complications in plants (Rudolph and Buckatsch, 1966). Ascorbic acid being a powerful reductant maintains the stability of cell membrane during pollution stress (Dhindsa et al.,1982). Ascorbate plays a diverse role in plant growth and metabolism. Ascorbic acid accumulation is essential for growth and development of both etiolated and combined stressed seedlings (Hamid et al., 2005). Ascorbate is required for the progression of the cell cycle, cell elongation (Metamoros et al., 2003) and expansion (Smirnoff and Wheeler, 2000). Ascorbate accumulates in all organs i.e. root, leaf and coleoptile, with increasing age of both etiolated and combined stressed wheat seedlings. The active biosynthesis and accumulation of ascorbic acid in different organs during early ontogenesis in wheat seedling is not unexpected, since it has been widely reported that both cell division and cell expansion require Ascorbate (De Tullio et al., 1999).

It has investigated the effect of ascorbic acid on consistency of hydrated wheat gluten (Zentner, 2006). Chlorophyll contents, leaf extract pH and ascorbic acid contents in the leaves showed inhibitory effects in the wheat crop. Losses incurred in chlorophyll b are far less in comparison to chlorophyll a. It was found that the plants affected by high levels of salinity ascorbic acid was had decreased in leaves. The cultivars with lower ascorbic acid tended to express enhanced sensitivity to salt as compared to cultivars with relatively higher concentrations of ascorbic acid.

It was reported ascorbic acid treatments exerted some favorable effects on growth and transpiration of wheat seedlings counteracting the inhibitory effects of relatively high salinity and drought stress (Hamad and Hamida, 2001). The ascorbic acid analysis were carried out in selected samples belonging to three classes. After analysis it was observed that amount of ascorbic acid was also affected by increasing salinity level. However the ascorbic acid content was observed to be substantially lower at higher concentration of the salt affected classes (Table-2). In the crop affected by moderate salinity ascorbic acid were 2.96 and 3.45 mg/g, respectively. The estimation of plant growth and other parameters (biochemical) variables improves significantly. The spectral parameters measured during maximum canopy coverage were found to be highly correlated with yield parameters.

After chemical analysis of plant samples, the ascorbic acid content in crop affected by moderate salinity and severe salinity were found 2.96 mg/g and 2.91 mg/g, respectively. It is clear from the results that with increased salinity the ascorbic acid content reduces significantly causing damage to the plant cell. The plants were affected adversely by the decreasing ascorbic acid content with increasing salinity.

Discussion

Soil salinity has been brought about by natural or human-induced processes and is a major environmental hazard. Crop growth reduction due to salinity is generally related to the soil in osmotic potential of the root zone. High soil salinity can also cause nutrient imbalances, resulting in the accumulation of toxic elements in plants. Using IRS 1D images of March 2000 studies were conducted to assess the effects of secondary salinization on cereal crops. In South-west Punjab areas affected by waterlogging due to seepage of water from canal and salinity due to salts on the surface appeared as a white salt encrustation. In the districts of Bhatinda and Muktsar salinity and waterlogging affect the low lying villages of Giddarbaha, Thiri, Fakarsar, Jandwala Chakatarsingh wala, Shekhu, Malaut, Danewala,Rathayan, Abulkharana, Mahuana, Tappakhera, Dewankhera, Adhnian, Sahnakhera, Kheowali, and Pajawa. Using the interpreted image as a base, soil and plant samples were collected with their geographic location using GPS. In total, ground truth was collected at 24 villages. 120 samples of soil and plants were collected from salt affected area and non-salt affected areas. Plant samples collected consisted of roots, shoots, spikelets and grain of wheat (Triticum aestivum). Due to irregular irrigation, seepage and high water requirement of crops the arid environment has turned into salt affected/secondary salinized and waterlogged area. In the salt affected lands, crops appear to wither away and there is a heavy loss of yield. Salt tolerant grasses and weeds cover the waterlogged areas. In the remotely sensed images of IRS 1D, LISS III, 1st March 2000, wheat appears at it's peak vegetative / crop growth stage.

Wheat is the only agricultural crop grown in the Rabi season. In March wheat attains its maximum growth and the adverse effect of salinity can be observed during this period as wheat grown in severely salt affected areas have a poor appearance and growth manifested in short plant height and pale brown leaves. The crop under normal soil on the other hand was of a good height, had dark green leaves with a dense canopy cover.

Plant growth and yield stage parameters were studied in March during field survey. The impact of salinity was easily seen on the growing crop in

March. In yield parameters the adverse impact was observed after maturation of the crop in May. Physico-chemical analysis that included chlorophyll estimation, leaf extract pH and ascorbic acid proved that 51 samples were normal, 44 samples of crop were affected by moderate salinity and 25 samples to severe salinity. The numbers of plants were observed in lesser numbers in land affected by salt. A gradual loss in number of plants was seen with an increase in salinity. The average plant height was 0.22 m in crop affected by severe salinity. The fresh weight and dry weight of plant was also affected by salinity. It was found that an increase in salinity inhibits the growth of the plant and the plant appears burnt and stunted in growth. Salinity causes a delayed flowering of plants and spike length of the plants is considerably reduced bringing about a decrease in plant yield. Increasing salinity showed adverse effect on spikelets and grain weight causing with maturity reduction.

The chlorophyll quantities decrease due to increase in the salinity in the soil. The green pigments chlorophyll a, chlorophyll b and total chlorophyll content were also observed in decreasing order in all three classes. Reductions in chlorophyll a were found more sensitive than chlorophyll b in both classes (moderate and severe). Maximum reduction in chlorophyll a was observed in crop affected by severe salinity (0.27 mg/g) and chlorophyll b was observed at 0.51 mg/g. Maximum leaf extract pH was 8.62 observed in crop affected by severe salinity. Ascorbic acid plays a crucial role in the physiology of plants especially during pollution/ salt stress. In chloroplast ascorbic acid acts as a powerful reductant, responsible for the photo-reduction of proto-chlorophyll leading to several physiological complications in plants. Ascorbate plays a diverse role in plant growth and metabolism. Ascorbic acid accumulation is essential for growth and development. Chlorophyll contents, leaf extract pH and ascorbic acid contents in the leaves showed inhibitory effects in wheat crop due to salinity. Losses incurred in chlorophyll b are far less in comparison to chlorophyll a. Ascorbic acid was found decreased in leaves of high salt affected plant.

It is important to take into consideration that remote sensing and GIS are an efficient and accurate source of information especially in the study of salt affected and waterlogged areas. Satellite remote sensing data provided real time information of these lands that proved an efficient analytical tool for estimating salt affected areas and crops affected by salinity. The present study has utilized satellite remote sensing data and GIS in characterization and mapping of salt affected and waterlogged area, the GIS (Geographic Information System) for generating the digital database (spatial and non-spatial) and in identifying and mapping the crop area affected by salinity and waterlogging. The image data and the GPS enabled accurate collection of soil and plant samples for the study of influences of salinity on plant parameters (physiological and chemical).

REFERENCES

Abdullah Z., R. Ahmed, and J. Ahmed (1978): Salinity induced changes in the reproductive physiology of wheat plants. *Plant and Cell Physiology*, 19 (1): 99-106.

Abrol, A.P. and D. R. Bhumbla (1971): Saline and alkali soils in India- their occurrence and management, *World Soil Resources Report,* 41-42.

Agrawal. P. K. (1971): Seed germination, seedling productivity, mineral status and energetics of *Acacia catechu* wild., *Butea monopserma* (Lam.) Taub. and *Buchanaria lanzanspreng.* Seedlings, *Ph.D. thesis* submitted to Banaras Hindu University, Varanasi India.

Agrawal.P.K. (1972): Rate of dry matter production in fruit tree seedlings with contrasting patterns of growth. *Proc. Symposium Biol., Land Plants,* 391.

Agrawal. P. K., V.P. Singh, and D. Kumar (1981b): Ecological aspects of *Oryza sativa* L. Var. IR 8 in relation to SO_2 gas. *Journal University Kuwait (Sci.),* 8:229.

Arnon, D. L. (1949): Copper enzymes in isolated chloroplasts polyphenol oxidase in *Beta vulgaris. Plant Physiology,* 24:1-15.

De-Tullio, M.C., C. Paciolla, V.F. Dalla, N. Rascio, S. Emerico, L. De-Gara, R. Liso and O. Arrigoni (1999): Changes in onion root development induced by the inhibition of petidyl-prolyl hydrolase and influence of the ascorbate system on cell division and elongation. *Planta*, 209: 424-434.

Dhindsa, R.S., P.L. Plumb- Dhinda, and D.M. Reid (1982): Leaf senescence and lipid per oxidation: effects of some phyto-hormones and free radical scavengers. *Plant Physiology,* 69 (suppl.) 10: Abstract no. 48.

Downton, W. J. S., B. R. Loveys, W. J. R. Grant (1990): Salinity effects on the stomatal behaviour of grapevine. New Phytologist, 116 (3): 499– 503.

Dwivedi, R. S. (1996): Monitoring of salt - affected soils of the Indo-Gangetic alluvial plains using principal component analysis. *International Journal of Remote Sensing,* 17(10): 1907-1914.

Fowden, L., T. Mansfield, and J. Stoddart (1993): Plant adaptation to environmental stress. Chapman & Hall. London.

Hamad, A.M.A., A.M. Hamada (2005): Grain soaking pre-sowing in ascorbic acid or thiamin versus the adverse effects of combined salinity and drought on wheat seedlings. S15-005. pp: 1-4.

Hameed, A., Iqbal, N., Malik, S.A., Syed, H. and M.A. Haq (2005): Age and organ specifiec accumulation of ascorbate in wheat (*Triticum aestivum* L.) seedlings grown under etiolation alone and in combination with oxidative stress. *Caderno de Pesquisa S'er. Bio,.* 17(1): 51-63.

Keller, T. and H. Schwager (1977): Air pollution and ascorbic acid. *European Journal Pathology,* 7: 338-350.

Kumari, S. (1982): Eco-physiological responses of vegetable crops to fluoride pollutant and its control by different doses of NPK nutrients. Ph.D. thesis submitted to *Meerut University, Meerut. India.*

Matamoros, M.A., A. David, J.R. Dalton, C.R. Maria and B. Manuel (2003): Biochemistry and molecular biology of antioxidants in the rhizobia- legume symbiosis. *Plant Physiology,* 133: 499-509.

Pathak P. S. (2000): Agro forestry: A tool for arresting land degradation. *Indian Farming,* 49 (11): 15-19.

Ray, N. and V. K. Khaddar (1989): Influence of salinity, sodicity and their combinations on wheat (*Triticum aestivum*). *Advance Plant Science,* 2(1): 216-223.

Rudolph, E. and F. Bukatsch (1966): Die proto chlorophyll (id) wandlung and ihre beziehung zur photo- oxidation der ascorbinsaure etiolirten kiemflanzen. *Planta.* 69: 124-134.

Sharma, R. K., K. S. Sarma, and D. K. Das (1994): Corp Discriminational in salt affected soils by Satellite Remote Sensing. *ACRS,* 1-8.

(http:// www.gisdevelopment .net /aarc/acrs/1994/ts/008pf.htm)

Smirnoff, N. and G.L. Wheeler (2000): Ascorbic acid in plants: biosynthesis and function. *Current Review in Plant Science,* 19: 267-290.

Willenborg, C.J., R.H. Gulden, E.N. Johnson, and S.J. Shirtliffe (2004): Germination characteristics of polymer – coated canola (*Brassica napus* L.) Seeds subjected to moisture stress at different temperatures. *Agronomy Journal,* 96: 786-791.

Zentner, H. (2006): Effect of ascorbic acid on wheat gluten. *Journal Science Food and Agriculture*, 19(8): 464-467.

Environment, Health and Safety Aspects in an Industrial Workzone

—Pawan Kumar, India
—Pawan K. Bharti, India

ABSTRACT

The present paper deals with the environmental, health and safety aspects in an industry. Now a days EHS management is global concern to maintain the health and safety of employees and making pleasuring working environment and to reduce and prevent environmental pollution in and around industry.

Introduction

Environmental Aspects

Environmental management system (EMS) refers to the management of an organization's environmental programs in a comprehensive, systematic, planned and documented manner. It includes the organisational structure, planning and resources for developing, implementing and maintaining policy for environmental protection. The term can also refer to software systems for organizational environmental management.

An Environmental Management System (EMS): works as a tool or technique to improve environmental performance

- Provides a systematic way of managing an organization's environmental management
- Is the aspect of the organization's overall management structure that addresses immediate and long-term impacts of its products, services and processes on the environment
- Gives order and consistency for organizations to address environmental concerns through the allocation of resources, assignment of responsibility and ongoing evaluation of practices, procedures and processes
- Focuses on continual improvement of the system of an organization

Water Pollution its Control

Water is one of the most abundantly available resources in nature. It is an essential constituent of living biomass and forms about 75% of the matter of earth's crust. Water is one of the widely distributed and abundant substance therefore, earth is sometimes called a **"water planet"** occurred in sea, river, ocean, pond, streams and even in the atmosphere in the form of humidity. The earth's atmosphere contains 0.02 to 4.0 percent water by volume, depending on the location. In addition to providing sources for precipitation, atmospheric water vapors intercept some of ultraviolet radiation and heat loss from the earth.

The word pollution is derived from the Latin word **"pollutionem"** meaning defilement (Haney, 1966). Water is said to be polluted if it has not been of sufficiently high quality to be useful for man in present or future (National Water Commission, 1975). Foreign substances, either from natural or anthropogenic sources, contaminated with water supplies, may be harmful to life because of their toxicity, reduction of normal oxygen level of water, aesthetically unsuitable or spread epidemic diseases (WHO, 2006). Pollution means the presence of any toxic substance in water that degrades the quality to constitute a hazard or impair its usefulness (USPHS, 1980).

During the past few decades Indian industries have registered a quantum jump, which has contributed to high economic growth but simultaneously it has also given rise to severe environmental pollution. Consequently, ambient air and water quality is seriously affected which is far lower in comparison to the international standards. The problem is worse in the case of water pollution. It is found that one-third of the total water pollution comes in the form of effluent discharge, solid wastes and other hazardous wastes (Gopal, 1994).

The industrial effluents and trade wastes play a significant role in pollution of water. The industries are pulp and paper, pharmaceuticals, distillery, fertilizer, electroplating, asbestos, silt, alcohol, detergents, steel, tannery, textile, cane sugar, oils, pesticides and herbicides, radioactive wastes, etc. The industries are beneficial increment of economy but they have some deleterious effect on environment also by way of pollution largely by water pollution. Metals such as arsenic, lead, cadmium, nickel, mercury, chromium, cobalt, zinc and selenium are highly toxic even in minor quantity. Increasing quantity of heavy metals in water resources is currently an area of greater concern especially since a large number of industries are discharging their metal containing effluents in to fresh water with out any adequate treatment (Canter, 1987).

Direct pollution effect implies generation of pollution per unit of output in a particular sector. Indirect effects are generated not in an industry in which production takes place directly but in those industries whose output is used as an input in the production process of a particular industry. These effects are important to consider because the overall quality of the environment greatly depends upon the total effect (direct plus indirect) (Nasrullah et al., 2006)

Most of the industries are discharging their effluent without any adequate treatment. But it is necessary, that primary (Physical), secondary (Biological) and tertiary treatment (chemical treatment), if necessary should be done before discharge outside. So it is important that all the discharge released from an industry should be treated properly before disposal in to any aquatic body or irrigation purposes.

Air Pollution

The air pollution is also known as the atmospheric pollution. The W.H.O defined it as the presence of materials in the air which are harmful to the living beings when they cross their threshold concentration levels. The foreign bodies, gases etc. act as an air pollutant. The chemical plants occur in the refineries, paper mills, ceramics, fertilizers, clay and in the glass manufacture. The important pollutants involved are the fluorides, vapors, sulphur dioxide and hydrogen sulphide. The crop spraying occurs in the pest and weed control. The important pollutants involved are the lead, arsenic, hydrocarbons and organophosphates. The fuel burning occurs in the domestic and power plants. The important pollutants involved are the sulphur and nitrogen oxides. The metallurgical plants and nuclear devise involves the refineries, steel plants and bomb explosions. The important pollutants involved are the lead and zinc fumes along with the radioactive fallout. The ore preparation and transportation occurs by the crushing, grinding, screening and car, trucks along with the railways. The important pollutants involved are the uranium, iodine, argon, CO, NO, lead and smoke. The waste recovery involves the scrap metals and rendering plants. The important pollutants involved are the smoke, soot, vapors and metal fumes. There are multiple causes of the air pollution. It involves the cosmetics, welding, crushing and grinding of stones and gems. The chemical processing play an important role in the air pollution. The processing of metals along with the combustion of fossil fuels also causes pollution. The pollutants which occur naturally are the pollen, spores, marsh and volcanic gas. In urban areas it is mostly caused by the automobiles. They account for more than 3/4th of the noise and air pollution. In some areas the industries are more in number as compared to the other areas which may lead to the air pollution. It occurs in many parts of the Gujarat. The sources of air pollution are multiple. They can be mobile, stationary or industrial. In the stationary combustion sources like the burning of fuels is involved. The mobile combustion sources involve the automobiles, locomotives and aircrafts. The industrial sources involve the crushing, mixing and grinding.

Sulfur oxides (SOx): especially sulphur dioxide, a chemical compound with the formula SO2. SO2 is produced by various industrial processes and volcanoes. Coal and petroleum often contain sulphur compounds, their combustion generates sulfur dioxide. Further oxidation of SO2, usually in the presence of a catalyst such as NO2, forms H2SO4, and thus acid rain. This is one of the causes for concern over the environmental impact of the use of these fuels as power sources. Nitrogen oxides (NOx): especially nitrogen dioxide is emitted from high temperature combustion and can be seen as the brown haze dome above or plume downwind of cities. Carbon dioxide is one of prominent pollutant in the several nitrogen oxides. This reddish-brown toxic gas has a characteristic sharp, biting odor.

Carbon monoxide (CO): is a colourless, odorless, non-irritating but very poisonous gas. It is a product by incomplete combustion of fuel such as natural gas, coal or wood. Vehicular exhaust is a major source of carbon monoxide. Carbon dioxide (CO2):- a colourless, odorless, non-toxic greenhouse gas associated with ocean acidification, emitted from sources such as combustion, cement production, and respiration. Volatile organic compounds (VOCs):- are an important outdoor air pollutant. In this field they are often divided into the separate categories of methane (CH4) and non-methane (NMVOCs). Methane is an extremely efficient greenhouse gas which contributes to enhance global warming. Other hydrocarbon VOCs are also significant greenhouse gases via their role in creating ozone and in prolonging the life of methane in the atmosphere, although the effect varies depending on local air quality. Within the NMVOCs, the aromatic compounds benzene, toluene and xylene are suspected carcinogens and may lead to leukemia through prolonged exposure. 1,3-butadiene is another dangerous compound which is often associated with industrial uses (Chauhan and Joshi, 2007).

Particulate Matter (PM): alternatively referred to as particulate matter or fine particles, are tiny particles of solid or liquid suspended in a gas. In contrast, aerosol refers to particles and the gas together. Sources of particulate matter can be man made or natural. Some particulates occur naturally, originating from volcanoes, dust storms, forest and grassland fires, living vegetation, and sea spray. Human activities, such as the burning of fossil fuels in vehicles, power plants and various industrial processes also generate significant amounts of aerosols. Averaged over the globe, anthropogenic aerosols, those made by human activities, currently account for about 10 percent of the total amount of aerosols in our atmosphere. Increased levels of fine particles in the air are linked to health hazards such as heart disease, altered lung function and lung cancer. Persistent free radicals connected to airborne fine particles could cause cardiopulmonary disease. Chlorofluorocarbons (CFCs) - harmful to the ozone layer emitted from products currently banned from use (Gupta et al., 2002).

Ammonia (NH_3): emitted from agricultural processes. Ammonia is normally encountered as a gas with a characteristic pungent odor. It contributes significantly to the nutritional needs of terrestrial organisms by serving as a precursor to foodstuffs and fertilizers. Ammonia, either directly or indirectly, is also a building block for the synthesis of many pharmaceuticals. Although in wide use, ammonia is both caustic and hazardous. Odors: like as from garbage, sewage, and industrial processes. Radioactive pollutants: produced by nuclear explosions, war explosives, and natural processes such as the radioactive decay of radon.

Secondary Pollutants

Particulate matter formed from gaseous primary pollutants and compounds in photochemical smog. Smog is a type of air pollution; the word "smog" is formed by smoke and fog. Classic smog results from large amounts of coal burning in an area caused by a mixture of smoke and sulfur dioxide. Modern smog does not usually come from coal but from vehicular and industrial emissions that are acted on in the atmosphere by ultraviolet light from the sun to form secondary pollutants that also combine with the primary emissions to form photochemical smog. Ground level ozone (O_3) formed from NOx and VOCs. Ozone (O_3) is a key constituent of the troposphere. It is also an important constituent of certain regions of the stratosphere commonly known as the Ozone layer. Photochemical and chemical reactions involving it drive many of the chemical processes that occur in the atmosphere by day and by night. At abnormally high concentrations brought about by human activities (largely the combustion of fossil fuel), it is a pollutant, and a constituent of smog. (Sharma et al., 2005)

Peroxyacetyl nitrate (PAN):- similarly formed from NOx and VOCs. Persistent organic pollutants (POPs) are organic compounds that are resistant to environmental degradation through chemical, biological, and photolytic processes. Because of this, they have been observed to persist in the environment, to be capable of long-range transport, bioaccumulation in human and animal tissue, bio-magnification in food chains, and to have potential significant impacts on human health and the environment.

Sources of air pollution refer to the various locations, activities or factors which are responsible for the releasing of pollutants into the atmosphere. These sources can be classified into two major categories which are: Anthropogenic sources, mostly related to burning different kinds of fuel. "Stationary Sources" include smoke stacks of power plants, manufacturing facilities and waste incinerators, as well as furnaces and other types of fuel-burning heating devices (Bhanarkar et al., 2002).

"Mobile Sources" include motor vehicles, marine vessels, aircraft and the effect of sound etc. Chemicals, dust and controlled burn practices in agriculture and forestry management. Controlled or prescribed burning is a technique sometimes used in forest management, farming, prairie restoration or greenhouse gas abatement. Fire is a natural part of both forest and grassland ecology and controlled fire can be a tool for foresters. Controlled burning stimulates the germination of some desirable forest trees, thus renewing the forest (Sharma, et al., 2005).

Air Emission Control

Necessary equipments as per requirement should be provided for measurement of pollutants and to its control. Height of stack should be as per the requirement to emit the pollutants at prescribed height. The quantity of SPM going to atmosphere is very much within the permissible limits.

Air Pollution control devices

These are the commonly used pollution control devices

Multicyclone with dust collector

Ambient air monitoring station-high volume samplers

Gas analyzer (CO, CO_2, CH_4 & other HC)

LEL vapor detector

Dust sampler

Portable oxygen meter

Gas chromatograph (lab)

Table 10.1: National Ambient Air Quality Standard (CPCB, 2009).

Sl. No.	Pollutant	Time Weighted Average	Concentration in Ambient Air		
			Industrial, Residential, Rural & Other Areas	Ecological Sensitive Area	Method of measurement
1	2	3	4	5	6
1.	Sulphur Dioxide (SO_2)	Annual Average* 24 hours**	50 μg/m^3 80 μg/m^3	20 μg/m^3 80 μg/m^3	- Improved west & Gaeke method - Ultraviolet fluorescence
2.	Nitrogen Dioxides (NO_2)	Annual Average* 24 hours**	40 μg/m^3 80 μg/m^3	30 μg/m^3 80 μg/m^3	- Modified Jacob & Hochheiser (Na-Arsenite) method - Chemiluminescence
3.	Particulate Matter less than 10 μm or PM_{10}	Annual Average* 24 hours**	60 μg/m^3 100 μg/m^3	60 μg/m^3 100 μg/m^3	- Gravimetric - TOEM - Beta attenuation
4.	Particulate Matter	Annual Average*	40 μg/m^3 60 μg/m^3	40 μg/m^3 60 μg/m^3	- Gravimetric - TOEM

1	2	3	4	5	6
	less than 2.5 µm or $PM_{2.5}$	24 hours**			- Beta attenuation
5.	Ozone (O_3)	8 hours** 1 hour**	100 µg/m³ 180 µg/m³	100 µg/m³ 180 µg/m³	- UV photometric - Chemiluminescence - Chemical method
6.	Lead (Pb)	Annual Average* 24 hours**	0.5 µg/m³ 1.0 µg/m³	0.5 µg/m³ 1.0 µg/m³	- AAS/ICP Method after sampling using EPM 2000 or equivalent filter paper - ED-XRF using Teflon filter
7.	Carbon Monoxide (CO)	8 hours** 1 hour**	2.0 mg/m³ 4.0 mg/m³	2.0 mg/m³ 4.0 mg/m³	- Non dispersive infrared (NDIR) spectroscopy
8.	Ammonia (NH_3)	Annual Average* 24 hours**	100 µg/m³ 400 µg/m³	100 µg/m³ 400 µg/m³	- Chemiluminescence - Indophenol blue method
9.	Benzene (C_6H_6)	Annual Average*	5 µg/m³	5 µg/m³	- Gas chromatography based continuous analyser - Adsorption & desorption followed by GC analysis
10.	Benzo (O) Pyrene (BaP)- particulate phase only	Annual Average*	01 ng/m³	01 ng/m³	- Gas chromatography based continuous analyser - Adsorption & desorption followed by GC analysis
11.	Arsenic (As)	Annual Average*	06 ng/m³	06 ng/m³	- AAS/ICP Method after sampling using EPM 2000 or equivalent filter paper
12.	Nickel (Ni)	Annual Average*	20 ng/m³	20 ng/m³	- AAS/ICP Method after sampling using EPM 2000 or equivalent filter paper

Soil Pollution

Soil pollution is defined or can be described as the contamination of soil of a particular region. Soil pollution mainly is a result of penetration of harmful pesticides and insecticides, which on one hand serve whatever their main purpose is, but on the other hand, bring about deterioration in the soil quality, thus making it contaminated and unfit for use. Insecticides and pesticides are not to be blamed alone for soil pollution, but there are many other leading causes of soil pollution too.

Soil pollution results from the build up of contaminants, toxic compounds, radioactive materials, salts, chemicals and cancer-causing agents. The most common soil pollutants are hydrocarbons, heavy metals (cadmium, lead, chromium, copper, zinc, mercury and arsenic), herbicides, pesticides, oils, tars, PCBs and dioxins (Kudesia, 1992).

Soil pollution is a result of many activities and experiments done by mankind and some of the leading soil pollution causes are discussed below:

- Industrial wastes, such as harmful gases and chemicals, agricultural pesticides, fertilizers and insecticides are the most important causes of soil pollution.
- Ignorance towards soil management and related systems.
- Unfavorable and harmful irrigation practices.
- Improper septic system and management and maintenance of the same.
- Leakages from sanitary sewage.
- Acid rains, when fumes released from industries get mixed with rains.
- Fuel leakages from automobiles, that gets washed away due to rain and seep into the nearby soil.
- Unhealthy waste management techniques, which are characterized by release of sewage into the large dumping grounds and nearby streams or rivers.

The intensity of all these causes on a local or regional level might appear very small and you may argue that soil is not harmed by above activities if done on a small scale! However, thinking globally, it is not your region or my place, which will be the only sufferer of soil pollution (Saxena, 1994).

Causes of Soil Pollution

Industry is to blame for some of the biggest soil-pollution disasters. Heavy metals come from iron, steel, power and chemical manufacturing plants that recklessly use the Earth as a dumping ground for their refuse. Plants that burn their waste on-site are guilty of releasing heavy metals into the atmosphere, which come to settle in the soil, thus leaving behind lasting effects for years to come. Even companies that try to dispose of their waste properly contribute to the problem when faulty landfills and bursting underground bins leach undesirable toxins into the soil (Malik and Bharti, 2007).

Noise Pollution

Noise pollution is excessive, displeasing human, animal or machine-created environmental noise that disrupts the activity or balance of human or animal life. The word noise comes from the Latin word nauseas, meaning seasickness. The source of most outdoor noise worldwide is mainly construction and transportation systems, including motor vehicle noise, aircraft noise and rail noise. Poor urban planning may give rise to noise pollution, since side-by-side industrial and residential buildings can result in noise pollution in the residential area.

Noise health effects are both health and behavioral in nature. The unwanted sound is called noise. This unwanted sound can damage physiological and psychological health. Noise pollution can cause annoyance and aggression, hypertension, high stress levels, tinnitus, hearing loss, sleep disturbances, and other harmful effects. Furthermore, stress and hypertension are the leading causes to health problems, whereas tinnitus can lead to forgetfulness, severe depression and at times panic attacks. Chronic exposure to noise may cause noise-induced hearing loss. Older males exposed to significant occupational noise demonstrate significantly reduced hearing sensitivity than their non-exposed peers, though differences in hearing sensitivity decrease with time and the two groups are indistinguishable by age 79. A comparison of Maaban tribesmen, who were insignificantly exposed to transportation or industrial noise, to a typical U.S. population showed that chronic exposure to moderately high levels of environmental noise contributes to hearing loss.

High noise levels can contribute to cardiovascular effects and exposure to moderately high levels during a single eight hour period causes a statistical rise in blood pressure of five to ten points and an increase in stress and vasoconstriction leading to the increased blood pressure noted above as well as to increased incidence of coronary artery disease. Noise pollution is also a cause of annoyance. A 2005 study by Spanish researchers found that in urban areas households are willing to pay approximately four Euros per decibel per year for noise reduction (Sangal, 2002).

Effect of Noise on Wildlife Health

Noise can have a detrimental effect on animals, increasing the risk of death by changing the delicate balance in predator or prey detection and avoidance, and interfering the use of the sounds in communication especially in relation to reproduction and in navigation. Acoustic overexposure can lead to temporary or permanent loss of hearing. An impact of noise on animal life is the reduction of usable habitat that noisy areas may cause, which in the case of endangered species may be part of the path to extinction. Noise pollution has caused the death of certain species of whales that beached themselves after being exposed to the loud sound of military sonar (Kumar, P. et al., 2008).

Noise also makes species communicate louder, which is called Lombard vocal response. Scientists and researchers have conducted experiments that show whales' song length is longer when submarine-detectors are on. If creatures do not "speak" loud enough, their voice will be masked by anthropogenic sounds. These unheard voices might be warnings, finding of prey, or preparations of net-bubbling. When one species begins speaking louder, it will mask other species' voice, causing the whole ecosystem to eventually speak louder (Singh and Davar, 2004). European Robins living in urban environments are more likely to sing at night in places with high levels of noise pollution during the day, suggesting that they sing at night because it is quieter, and their message can propagate through the environment more clearly. The same study showed that daytime noise was a stronger predictor of nocturnal singing than night-time light pollution, to which the phenomenon is often attributed. Zebra finches become less faithful to their partners when exposed to traffic noise. This could alter a population's evolutionary trajectory by selecting traits, sapping resources normally devoted to other activities and thus lead to profound genetic and evolutionary consequences.

Mitigation Measures for Noise Control

There are various strategies for mitigating roadway noise including: use of noise barriers, limitation of vehicle speeds, alteration of roadway surface texture, limitation of heavy vehicles, use of traffic controls that smooth vehicle flow to reduce braking and acceleration, and tire design. An important factor in applying these strategies is a computer model for roadway noise, which is capable of addressing local topography, meteorology, traffic operations and hypothetical mitigation. Costs of building-in mitigation can be modest, provided these solutions are sought in the planning stage of a roadway project.

Table 10.2: Standards for Noise Level in different Countries

Sl. No.	Country	Ind. Area Day/Night	Comm. Area, Day/Night	Residential Area Day/ Night	Silent Area Day/Night
1.	Australia	65/55	55/45	45/35	45/35
2.	India	75/70	65/55	55/45	50/40
3.	Japan	60/50	60/50	50/60	45/35
4.	U.S. (E.P.A.)	70/60	60/50	55/45	45/35
5.	WHO (E.C.)	65	55	55/45	45/35

Solid Waste Management

Assessment of industrial solid waste management problem greatly varies depending on the nature of the industry, their location and mode of disposal of waste. Further, for arriving at an appropriate solution for better management of industrial solid waste, assessment of nature of waste generated is also essential. Industries are required to collect and dispose of their waste at specific disposal sites and such collection, treatment and disposal is required to be monitored by the concerned State Pollution Control Board (SPCB) or Pollution Control Committee (PCC) in Union Territory. The following problems are generally encountered in cities and towns while dealing with industrial solid waste

- There are no specific disposal sites where industries can dispose their waste.
- Mostly industries generating solid waste in city and town limits are of small scale nature and even do not seek consents of SPCBs/PCCs.
- Industries are located in non-conforming areas and as a result they cause water and air pollution problems besides disposing solid waste.
- Industrial estates located in city limits do not have adequate facilities so that industries can organize their collection, treatment and disposal of liquid and solid waste.
- There is no regular interaction between urban local bodies and SPCBs/PCCs to deal such issues relating to treatment and disposal of waste and issuance of licenses in non-conforming areas.

Bio-composting

The term bio-compost means plant matter that has been decomposed and recycled as a fertilizer or manure. Bio-compost is considered as a key ingredient in organic farming

Bio-compost is very rich in nutrients. It is mainly used in gardens, landscaping, horticulture, and agriculture. The process bio-composting is done by simply piling up wastes in the garden or any outdoor place and then leave it undisturbed for a year or more. Bio-compost in the ecosystems is very useful for control of soil erosion, wetland construction, and as landfill cover.

Modern day bio-composting process has many steps like monitoring of the composting. It is usually done by shredding the plant matter, adding of sufficient water to maintain the proper moisture level and then regularly turning the mixture to provide better aeration. Worms and fungi added helps in the process of decomposition. They break up the complex compounds into simpler ones and during the process lots of heat, carbon dioxide and ammonium is produced. This ammonium is again utilized by the microbes which are made available to the plants as nitrites and nitrates.

Disposal of Bio-Medical Waste

- All Bio-medical waste shall be treated and disposal of accordance to statutory regulation.
- Bio-medical waste shall not be mixed with other waste.
- Bio-medical waste shall be segregated into containers/bags at the point of generation prior to its storage, Transportation, treatment and disposal. The containers shall be labeled and colored.
- A pit or trench should he dug about 2 meters deep.
- A pit should be half filled with, then covered with lime within 50cm of the surface, before filling the rest of pit with soil.

- It must be ensured that animals do not have any access to burial sites.
- Cover of galvanized iron/wire meshes may be used.
- On each occasion, when wastes are added to the pit, a layer of 10 mm of soil shall be added to cover the wastes.
- Burial must be performed under close and dedicated supervision.
- The deep burial site should be relatively impermeable and no shallow well should be close to the site.
- The pits should be distant from habitation, and sited so as to ensure that no contamination occurs of any surface water or ground water.
- The area should not be prone to flooding or erosion.
- The location of the deep burial site will authorize by the prescribed authority.
- The organization shall maintain a record of pits for deep burial.

Advantages of Biocomposting

1. Power consumption is almost nil.
2. Zero discharge to in land watercourse.
3. Free from river/ground water pollution problem and continuous fear of distillery shut down by the authorities.
4. Clean environment in around of the sugar mills/ distillery units
5. Organic manure produce will be rich in micronutrients with free organic and inorganic nutrients.
6. By using the organic manure, application of chemical fertilizer can be reduced, there by the soil fertility can be enhancing. It also will provided bacteria for Nitrogen fixing, Humus that keeps soil health and develop the self-reclamation cycle in the soil.
7. Bio composting is done at high temperature thus the manure is free from all pathogens and harmful bacteria.

Occupational Health and Safety

Implementation of Occupational Health and safety management safety system not only helps to improve health and safety of workers bur also helps the organizations improve the quality of their products and services as well as the environment conditions at workplace. To ensure compliance to the statutory requirements of the country in the field of OH & S, Indian industries are required to get certified their units as per IS 18000:2000.

It is this writer's opinion, however, that as differing opinions emerged in how to do that, the process became more competitive and complicated, losing the "pure" concept of helping people make the right choices in job performance. The perception is that behavior-based safety can only work if following specific outlines and programs and which one is chosen is based on what comes the closest to fitting the company culture. The frustration level builds, however, when what is chosen does not exactly fit and, therefore, does not produce the results expected. Company managers become discouraged and, based on poor results, move on to yet another type of injury reduction process. Often, this causes the "baby" to be thrown out with the bath water. There are fundamental principles within all the methods that are necessary and that do not change, regardless of HOW the process is followed, addressing individual performance. With over five years of focusing on total performance, not strictly employee "behavior," these principles have been proven to work with various management styles and different corporate cultures.

Identify & Assess Hazards

Hazard assessment should be an essential part of your organization's safety culture and safety management systems. Hazard assessment methods will help reduce injuries and illnesses in your workplace. Employers need to consider their practices relating to hazard assessment and continually review and improve these practices.

Hazard assessment is about identifying and assessing hazards. then dealing with them. That is, taking steps to eliminate the hazards in the first place, or, if they can't be eliminated, then controlling them to an acceptable degree.

Where the hazard assessment identifies an actual or potential hazard to workers, reasonable measures must be taken either to eliminate the hazard or, where elimination is not practicable, to control it.

Risk Assessment

We take five steps to complete risk assessment:

- Identify the hazards
- Decide who might be harm and how
- Evaluate the risk and decide on precaution
- Record your findings and implement them
- Review your assessment and update if necessary

Five Ess (5 S)

5s is a famous Japanese method of work place management. (term given by Hiroyuki Hirano)

- Seiri – sorting
- Seitori – setting in order/ straightening
- Seiso – shining/sweeping
- Seiketsu - standardizing
- Shitsuke – sustaining the discipline/ self-discipline

Industrialization and Accidents

There are constant dangers that surround workers and one mistake can lead to a fatal construction accidents.

The most common fatal construction accidents are:

- Falls from different levels or elevated heights such as roofs
- Struck by nail
- Explosion because of improper use and storage of explosive devices and chemicals
- Crashed by falling wall
- Struck by falling object
- Trench cave in
- Crushed by malfunctioning machinery and equipment
- Electrocution
- Asphyxiation

There are a number of reasons for these accidents to happen. But most of the time, it is a result of negligent actions by other people and sometimes even the employers. Here are some of the most common causes of fatal construction accidents:

- One of the most common cause of construction accidents are malfunctioning machines and equipment. This may be caused by a defective product, none or insufficient maintenance, and/or improper use.
- Another cause of construction accidents are unsafe working conditions. Employers have the responsibility to keep the working environment as safe as possible for workers. Lack of safety equipment like nets, harness, helmets or other gears could lead to death. Improperly constructed scaffoldings also contribute to hazardous conditions that can lead to more fatalities.
- Another cause of construction accidents is lack of training. Workers in the construction industry are operating potentially hazardous equipments and machineries like cranes, forklifts and tractors. Before operating such machineries, training should be provided to avoid accidents. The employer could also invest in safety trainings so as to avoid accidents and to inform employees on what to do in case an accident cannot be avoided.
- Last, as a result of employers trying to cut costs, some do not meet the standard set by the Occupational Safety and Health Administration (OSHA). They try to save money by not following the safety

regulations set by OSHA that could result to unsafe working conditions.

Employers and workers should work hand in hand to ensure that the working conditions are safe to avoid any accidents. Some of the most basic tips employers and employees can follow are the following:

- Employers and employees should observe and watch out for possible dangers in the workplace. If the dangers can be recognized, then proper measures can be taken. An example would be if you observed that chemicals are stored near explosive devices; once reported, the employer can take measures like storing the chemicals in much safer conditions that is far from the explosives.
- Invest in training. Train employees on the proper use of each equipment and machineries. Cranes, tractors and forklifts are special machines that need special instructions. Continuous safety trainings could also be provided to ensure that employees are informed and is always updated on what to do in case of an accident.
- Post the safety rules and regulations somewhere that is visible to everyone. Rules about proper clothes and gears inside the workplace should also be included.

Causation of Occurrence of Accidents

I prefer the phrase 'Accident causation' instead 'Accident Occurrence' because of our simple safety philosophy that accidents do not occur they are caused. Most of the accidents are caused by latent or patent, visible, or invisible, known or unknown, detectable or undetectable, intentional or unintentional unsafe acts, conditions and sequential events leading to injury or accident explain rather the causation and not just the occurrence. Therefore all safety people should analyze his causation to find the appropriate measures for prevention of accidents.

The word causation points out responsibility and suggests the positive preventive measures to remove unsafe conditions. The word occurrence points out occurring by itself of due to fate or something else and indicates others responsibility which is not the healthy or safe philosophy of safety. There are a number of reasons for these accidents to happen. But most of the time, it is a result of negligent actions by other people and sometimes even the employers.

Personal Protective Equipments

The PPE provides good defense against hazards of toxic exposure, dusting chemical splashes, steam, water and liquids, flying particles, hot substances, radiation, sharp edges, wielding, striking against and stopping over objects, glare, personal fall, and injuries due to falling bodies, noise, scrap cleaning, material handling, electric shocks, burns and fire fighting. Many fatal accidents are caused due to these reasons and use of appropriate PPE can prevent and lesson many of them (Kumar P., 2011).

When an engineering control fails or become ineffective, what is the protection? Then this line of defense i.e. PPE comes to help and protect in most of the cases. The employer is expected to implement a "hierarchy of controls," looking first at elimination, then at engineering controls and administrative controls, and finally at personal protective equipment (PPE). Implementation of control measures will involve documentation, creation of procedures and training.

The Personal Protective Equipment at Work Regulations as:

'All equipment (including clothing affording protection against the weather) which is intended to be worn or held by a person at work which protects them against one or more risks to their health and safety'.

PPE includes equipment such as safety footwear, hard hats, high visibility waistcoats, goggles, life jackets, respirators and safety harnesses. Waterproof, weatherproof, or insulated clothing is subject to the Regulations only if its use is necessary to protect employees against adverse climatic conditions that could otherwise affect their health and safety.

Employers are responsible for providing, replacing and paying for personal protective equipment. PPE should be used when all other measures are inadequate to control exposure. It protects only the wearer, while being worn by workers (Bharti, 2012).

If it fails, PPE offers no protection at all.

Types of PPE

Respirators

Protective gloves

Protective clothing

Protective footwear

Eye protection

Selection of PPE

All PPE clothing and equipment should be of safe design and construction, and should be maintained in a clean and reliable fashion. Employers should take the fit and comfort of PPE into consideration when selecting appropriate items for their workplace. PPE that fits well and is comfortable to wear will encourage employee use of PPE. Most protective devices are available in multiple sizes and care should be taken to select the PPE is defined in proper size for each employee. If several different types of PPE are worn together, make sure they are compatible. If PPE does not fit properly, it can make the difference between being safely covered or dangerously exposed. It may not provide the level of protection desired and may discourage employee use.

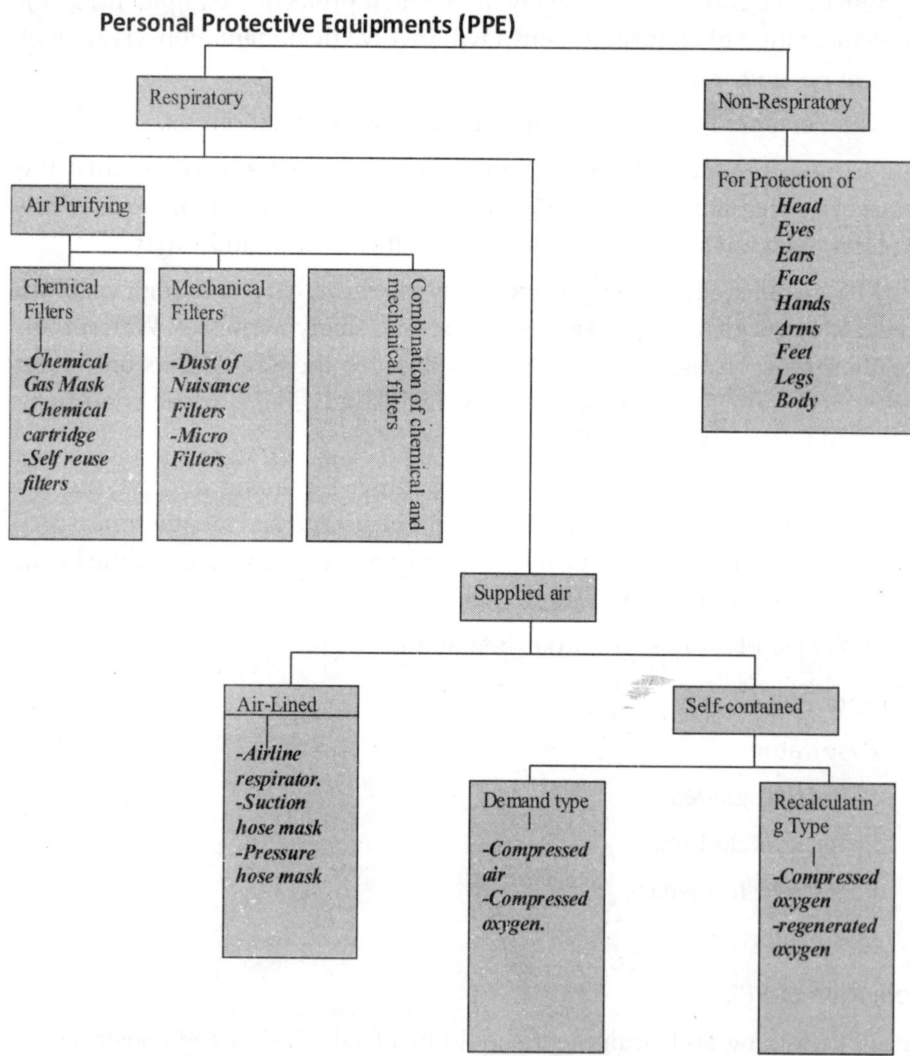

Flow Chart showing the selection process of PPE

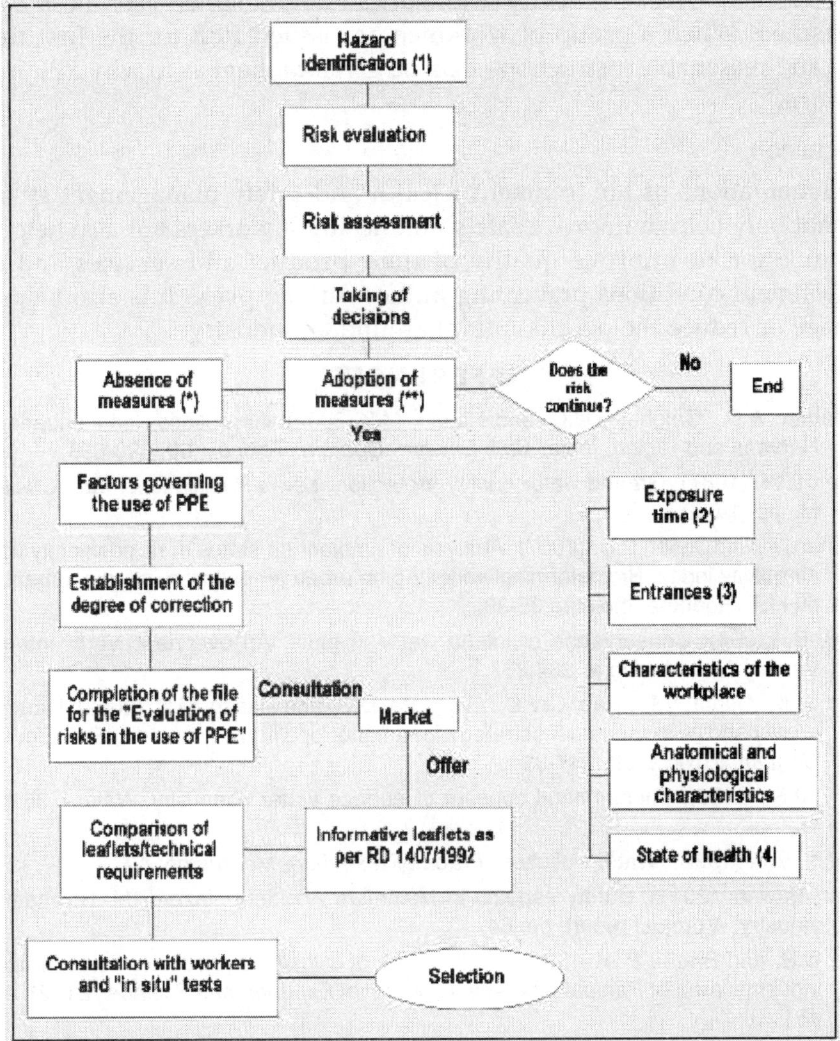

Proper Use of PPE

Having selected the proper type of PPE, it is essential that the workman wears it. Often the workman avoids using PPE. The following factors influence the solution to this problem:

- the extent to which the workman understands the necessity of using PPE,
- the ease and comfort with which PPE can be worn with least interference in normal work procedures, and
- the available economic, social and disciplinary sanctions which can be used to influence the attitude of the workman.

The best solution to this problem is to make 'wearing of PPE' mandatory for every employee. At other places, education and supervision need to be intensified. When a group of workmen are issued PPE for the first time, clear and reasonable instructions shall be given to them as to why PPE must be worn.

Conclusion

Implementations of Environment, Health and safety management system will not only help to improve safety and health of workers but also help the organization to improve quality of their product and services and the environment conditions preventing in the working place. It is also helps to manage or reduce the pollution level around an industry.

REFERENCES

Bhanarkar, A.D., Gajghate, D.G. and Hasan, M.Z.(2002): Air pollution concentration in Haryana sub region, India, *Bull. Environ. Contam. Toxicol.*, 69, 690-695.

Canter, L.W. (1987): Ground water quality protection. *Lewis Publications. Inc., Chelsea,* MI, pp: 1-650.

Chauhan, A. and Joshi, P.C. (2007): Analysis of ambient air status in Haridwar city using air quality index. Brainstorming workshop on urban air pollution in India. organized by I.I.T. Roorkee, India pp 35-39.

Gopal, B. (1994): Conservation of inland water in India: An overview. Verh. Internet. Verein. *Hydrobiologia,* 384:267.

Gupta, H.K., Gupta, V.B., Rao, C.V.C., Gajghate, D.G. and Hasan, M.Z. (2002): Urban air quality and its management strategy for am metropolitan city of India. *Bull. Environ. Contam. Toxicol.* 68, 347-354.

Haney, J.S. (1966): Fundamental concept of surface water chemistry. *Nature,* 36:176-182.

Kudesia, V.P. (1992): Water Pollution. *Pragati Prakashan, Meerut,* pp: 407.

Kumar, Pawan: (2011): Safety aspects in Maximum Accident Hazard (MAH) chemical industry, A project report, pp. 64.

Malik, D.S. and Bharti, P. K. (2007): Soil quality of irrigated agricultural fields in textile industrial area of Panipat city. *Asian Journal of Experimental Science.,* 21 (2): 445-451.

Nasrullah.; Naz, R.; Bibi, H.; Iqbal, M. and Durrani, M. I. (2006): Pollution load in industrial effluent and ground water of Gadoon Amazai Industrial Estate (GAIE) Swabi, NWFP. *Journal of Agriculture and Biological Science,* 1(3):18-24.

National Water Commission, (1975): Report on water budget and implication on human health. *Ministry of Health, India,* pp: 275.

Pratap Kumar Padhy and Bijaya Kumar Padhi (2008): Assessment of noise quality in bolpursantiniketan areas (India). *Journal of Environmental Research and Development,* 3(1), 301-306.

Sangal. P.P. (2002): Little noise about noise pollution, Financial Daily from THE HINDU group of publications, Oct. 08, 2002.

Saxena, M.M. (1994): Environmental analysis water, soil and air. *Agro Botanical Publishers,* pp: 1-180.

Sharma, R., Pervez, Y. and Pervez, S. (2005): Seasonal evaluation and spatial variability of suspended particulate matter in the vicinity of a large coal-fired power station in India-a case study. *Environmental Monitoring and Assessment*, 102, 1-13.

Singh, N. and Davar, S. C. (2004): Noise Pollution- Sources, Effects and Control. *J. Hum. Ecol.*, 16(3): 181-187.

USPHC, (1980): Comprehensive project report on status of drinking water quality and its impact assessment on human health, pp-430.

WHO, (2006): Guidelines for Drinking Water Quality. Vol.1-4, Geneva, pp. 515.

11

Environmental Monitoring and Assessment in Antarctica

—Pawan Kumar 'Bharti', India
—Khwairakpam Gajananda, Ethiopia

ABSTRACT

Being at a unique geographic location, Antarctica offers unique opportunities for Scientists to conduct number scientific research experiments. Antarctica is attracting world attention because of the tremendous biological species in surrounding seas and likelihood of vast hydrocarbons. Even though it is difficult to survive at Antarctica, still Scientists all around the worlds have been engaged in pursing the exciting scientific research investigations. The investigations are essential not for the exploitation of natural resources buried under the region but for the preservation of environment and ecology on earth; especially in the light of climate change.

The Larsemann Hills (Lat. 69°202 –69°302 S and Long. 75°552 –76°302 E) is an ice-free coastal oasis with exposed rock and low rolling hills. The Larsemann Hills contain hundreds of freshwater lakes of varying sizes, depth and biology. An environmental study is being conducted at Larsemann Hills in East Antarctica to evaluate the Ambient air quality, Lake and sea water quality, soil and sediment, Noise level monitoring, solid waste generation, handling and disposal practices. Geographically, the study area (Bharti Island) is situated on Latitude 69° 24' 00.0" S and 76° 10' 00.0" E on southern part of globe. The water, soil and sediment samples were collected from various locations of different Islands/Peninsulas like Bharti Island, Fisher Island, McLeod Island, Broknes peninsula and Stornes peninsula.

The aim of this study is to assess the general characteristics, metal content, pesticide, radiation contamination and bacteriological analysis of water, soil and sediment. Noise level, solid waste generation, fuel consumption studies were also performed. The present work is aimed towards developing base line data for the local environmental settings and to evaluate the impacts of various activities on the environmental components during the construction work of third Indian scientific station (Bharti) in Antarctica.

Introduction

Antarctica is the coldest, windiest, driest, whitest, highest (averagely) and least accessible continent on the earth. Ice is covered here continuously for the last 25 million years. Antarctica is the 5th largest continents on the earth. Antarctica has no government and is considered no mans-land. Antarctica is the most fragile, vulnerable and pristine environment on the earth.

The ice-free area consists of two major peninsulas (Stornes and Broknes), four minor peninsulas, and approximately 130 near shore islands at Larsemann Hills. Nella Fjord further divides the eastern-most peninsula, Broknes, into western and eastern components. The closest significant ice-free areas are the Bølingen Islands (69°31′58"S, 75°42′E) 25 km to the south-west and the Rauer Islands (68 °50′59"S, 77°49′58"E) 60 km to the north-east[1]. Broknes is one of very few coastal areas of Antarctica that remained partially ice-free through the glaciating period, and sediments deposited there contain continuous biological and palaeoclimate records dating back c. 130 000 years.

The Larsemann hills area was first discovered by a Norwegian expedition led by Christensen in 1935. Subsequently, visits were made by several nations during the last 50 years, but human activity of a significant or sustained nature did not occur until the mid-1980s[2].

However, from 1980 to 1990 saw rapid infrastructure development in the area: an Australian summer research base, a Chinese year-round research station (Zhongshan) and two Russian research stations (Progress I and Progress II) were established within approximately 3 km of each other on eastern Broknes[3].

Study Area

A major feature of the climate of the Larsemann Hills is the existence of persistent, strong katabatic winds that blow from the northeast in summer days. Daytime air temperatures from December to February frequently may exceed 4ÚC, with the mean monthly temperature a little above 0ÚC[4]. Mean monthly winter temperatures are between –15ÚC and –40ÚC. Pack ice is extensive inshore throughout summer and the fjords and bays are rarely ice-free. Precipitation occurs as snow and is unlikely to exceed 250 mm water equivalent annually[5]. Snow cover is generally deeper and more persistent on Stornes than Broknes, due to northeasterly prevailing winds and the perennial sea ice held in by the islands offshore from Stornes.

There are many regulatory authorities and regulations to protect the environment of Antarctica[6]. Few of them are given here:

- — Antarctic Treaty, 1959
- — Protocol on Environmental Protection to the Antarctica: Madrid Protocol, 1991
- — Antarctic Conservation Act, 1978

— Scientific Committee of Antarctic Research(SCAR)

— The Convention on the Conservation of Antarctic Seals and Whales,1972

— The Convention on Conservation of Antarctic Marine Living Resources,1980

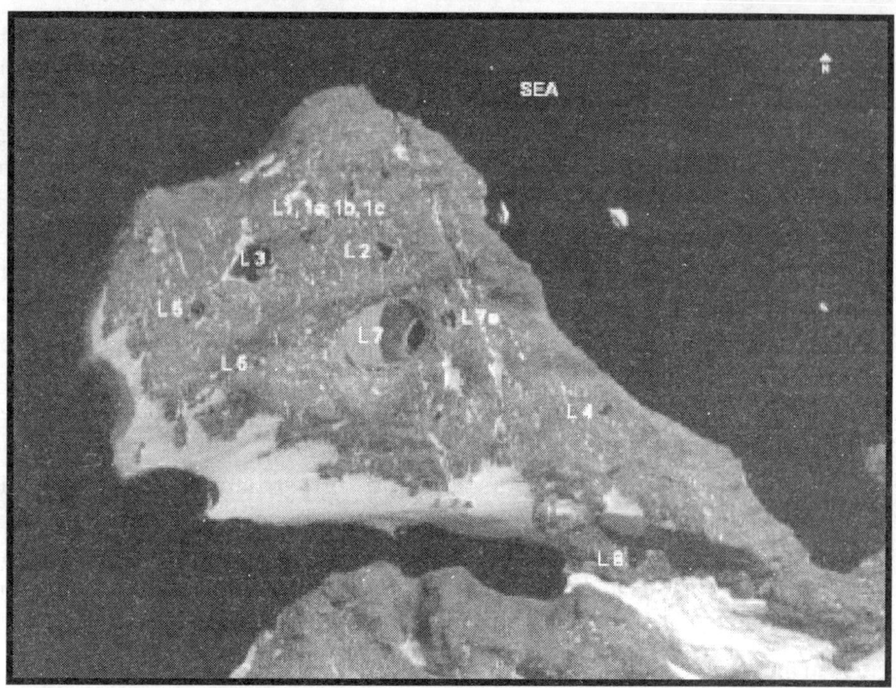

Fig. 11.1: Map showing the lakes (L) water sampling sites at the Larsemann Hills, Ingrid Christensen coast, east Antarctica

Environmental Research

A scientific study is being conducted in various island and peninsulas of Larsemann Hills. Ambient air quality monitoring was carried out to measure the pollution load in local environment. Water, soil, sediment samples were also collected from different locations. Dr. Pawan Kumar Bharti, scientist from Shriram Institute for Industrial Research, Delhi was the only environmentalist during the XXX expedition to Antarctica. These scientific tasks were also performed during the expedition:

— Ambient Air Quality

— Indoor Air Quality

— Lake and Sea water quality

— Soil quality

— Study of bed sediments

— Generator Stack monitoring,
— Indoor Noise level,
— Ambient Noise level,
— Machinery Noise level,
— Drilling and Blasting Noise level
— Lichen patches and Moss community assessment
— Collection of Planktonic diversity and Benthos from Lake water.
— Fuel consumption and pollution load.
— Solid waste generation, handling, separation and disposal practices and % composition.
— Ash analysis
— Waste oil analysis

Air Quality characteristics

The study of air environment of Antarctica is very essential to measure the pollution status. The following main parameters were selected for study in Antarctica:

Table 11.1: List of Parameters Analysed for the Indoor and Ambient Air

Sl.No.	Ambient parameters	Indoor air parameters
1.	SPM	Temperature
2.	RSPM	Humidity
3.	SOx	SOx
4.	NOx	NOx
5.	CO	CO
6.	VOCs	VOCs
7.	Ozone	Carbon dioxide

Fig. 11.2. Ambient air quality monitoring using RDS in Antarctica

Water Environment

Water quality was assessed by analysing the all parameters described in specification (IS: 10500). Besides, physico-chemical parameters, metals, pesticide & radiation contamination and biological parameters were also analysed.

Fig. 11.3: Water sample collection from frozen water

Soil Environment

Soil and sediment samples were collected from different locations covering important aspects of physical and chemical properties of soil quality therein and by adopting established sampling procedures given in the IS 2720 specifications. Undisturbed soils and sediments samples representative of the area was collected by means of auger. Besides physico-chemical parameters mmany heavy metals and radiation contamination was also monitored.

Fig. 11.4: Soil and Sediment Samples inside the Ship

Noise Level

Noise level was also measured for 24 hours indoor and ambient conditions. Noise level monitoring was also completed during the construction activity, especially for various vehicles, earthmovers, excavator, piston bully, dozer, stone crusher, drilling and blasting.

Noise pollution emanating from operation of generator, snow vehicles, incinerator, helicopter etc shall have adverse impacts on the human beings, marine, life and also on Antarctic birds i.e, Skua and penguin in long run.

Table 11.5: Noise Level Standards

Area Code	Category of Area	Limits in dB(A) Leq	
		Day time	Night time
A	Industrial Area	75	70
B	Commercial Area	65	55
C	Residential Area	55	45
D	Silence Zone	50	40

Fig. 11.5: Scene of operational activities

Biodiversity

Ecosystem of Antarctica is not so complex. Few species of flora and fauna are present there permanently or in migratory period. Moss, Lichens, and few microbes are the dominant species, while Penguins, seals skua, snow petrel and few avian species may be studied for their behaviour, feeding habit and breeding.

Solid Waste

To support the continuing scientific research and, stay of scientist and logistic staff, generators run throughout the study period to supply power to the station site. ATF is used as fuel to run generators, Cranes, Piston bullies, snow scooters and boilers. The supporting activities like storage of food material, cooking of food, maintenance of generators, cranes, snow scooter, piston bullies, supply of drinking water, temperature regulation inside temporary shelters, waste disposal, etc. are regular phenomenon. These activities may pose a little extent impact surrounding environment, but environment regulations are to be strictly adhered to in Antarctica. All the solid waste is stored in a separate container and brought back to the real land.

There are few separate bins for degradable and non-degradable types of solid waste. After separating, waste was dumped into a container, which was inside the ship.

A

B

Fig. 11.6(A-B): Segregation and Storage of Solid Waste

Fuel and Oils

Fuel and other oil quantity were also measured for various earthmovers, machines, helicopters, ships, etc. Pollution load can be calculated by fuel combustion. A prediction for SOx and NOx & other gases can be made using a formula.

The internal combustion engine converts the chemical energy contained in the fuel into mechanical power. During the operation of the Maitri station, air emission produced from generator, incineration, snow vehicles etc were estimated. The exhaust gas discharged from the operation of snow vehicles, generator, incinerator etc contain several gases and suspended particulate matter. The fuel consumption along with estimated air exhaust gases emissions of all activities of the generator, incinerator and snow vehicles was measured. The estimation of air emission was done based on fuel consumption as per the guidelines: Emergency of Manual of Antarctica.

A B

Fig. 11.7(A-B): Handling and spillage of fuel

Environmental Impact Assessment

The environmental study is necessary for the construction of new scientific base in Antarctica. So, after completing these tasks, final report will be given to national institute. The main steps of EIA are:

- Site selection / identification
- Sampling and monitoring
- Analysis
- Observations
- Data interpretation
- Modeling and prediction
- Mitigation and recommendations
- EIS

These are the many methodologies adopted for environmental study in Antarctica. We have adopted a few of them and generally make a focus on these things:

- Action and Impacts
- Environmental components
- Basic parameters
- Simple Checklists
- Leopold Matrix, etc.

Conclusion

The environmental assessment studies carried out at Indian Scientific Base, located in Antarctica throws light on the status of air, water and soil quality, Noise level, oil spillage and waste generated. Furthermore, the environment assessment and monitoring work will be beneficial while predicting the long term impacts to Antarctica. The data will be the baseline and reference for the further study in future.

REFERENCE

1. http://www.esri.com/news/arcnews
2. Antarctica: Fact sheet, september 200, page-14, http://www.antarctica.ac.uk
3. http://www.eia.doc.gov/emeu/cabs antarrctica.html.
4. Draft Comprehensive Environmental Evaluation for the concept of upgrading the Norwegian Summer Station Troll in Dronning Maud Land, Antarctica to permanent station, 2004, Norwegian Polar Institute, Polar Environmental Centre, Tromsa, Norway.
5. Report of the Norwegian Antarctic Inspection under Article VII of the Antarctica Treaty and Article 14 of the Protocol on Environmental Protection to the Antarctica Treaty, January 2001.
6. Erich R, Gundlach; John J, Gallagher; John Hatcher & Tom Vinsor. Planning and Hazards Oil Spill Response in Antarctic's. International Oil Spill Conference 2000, 241-244.
7. Malik, D.S. and Bharti, P.K. (2010): Textile Pollution. *Daya Publishing House, Delhi*, pp: 383.
8. Sharma, B.; Bharti, P.K.; Pal, N.; Singh, R.K.; Niyogi, U.K. and Khandal, R.K. (2011): Waste management practices at Indian research station 'Maitri', East Antarctica, In: 'Proceedings of Brainstorming session on Polar sciences' published by Indian Meteorological Department, MoES, Govt. of India, pp: 67-76.
9. Bharti, P.K. (2011): Environmental monitoring and assessment during the construction of Indian Scientific Base (Bharti Station) in Antarctica, In: Climate Change and Biodiversity (Eds.- Khanna et al), Biotech Books, Delhi.
10. Bharti, P.K. (2011): Assessment of Lichen patches and Moss communities in the vicinity of Larsemann Hills, East Antarctica, In: Climate Change and Biodiversity (Eds.- Khanna et al), Biotech Books, Delhi.
11. Bharti, P.K. (2011): Environmental research in Antarctica, In: Climate Change and Biodiversity (Eds.- Khanna et al), Biotech Books, Delhi.
12. Bharti, P.K. (2012): Anthropogenic activities and global climate change, In: 'Climate change and agriculture (Eds.- Bharti, P.K. and Chauhan, A.)', Discovery publishing house, Delhi, pp: 326.

12

Trend Analysis for Health, Safety and Environmental Concerns on Construction Site Based Upon Daily Observation Reporting System

A Case Study

—KumarSatish Chandra, India
—Uma Maheshwar K., India
—D.K. Singh, India

Introduction

Today's working environment is heavily influenced by the use and development of innovative technology. This puts company safety management under increased pressure to accompany these dynamic processes and actively prevent industrial/ occupational diseases and accidents from occurring (SAP 05/04). In this changing industrial scenario, an forceful world-wide attempt is visible in improving quality in all functions of an organization (Schwamm, 1997), acknowledging that workplace safety and workers health is a decisive factor in an organizational effectiveness and for this several framework have been proposed (ICMR, 2003). Survival and prosperity decide the success of any business activity. Risk is inherent in all the tasks we undertake. So also, with the business activity, no one likes to meet adverse effects while taking some risks, particularly the non-speculative or pure risks. Such risks, which involve only loss, include (Nedumaran, 2004):-

- Physical harm to employees
- Property damage to the organization
- Physical harm or property damage to public
- Capital income loss
- Security loss etc.

The primary aim of safety management is to intervene in the causation process that leads to accidents and incidents (Booth and Lee, 1995).

Elements of HSE Management

Declaration of Project Health and Safety Policy

The project health and safety policy shows basic concept towards construction work to ensure health and safety of the project site, and takes into consideration special features of the work at the site, the health and safety policy, the health and safety target, and the health and safety plan set by the contractor.

Feedback Employees' Opinion in Health and Safety Measures

The Chief project manager should endeavor to incorporate both employees' and subcontractors' opinion in setting a project health and safety target, as well as in planning, implementation, and evaluation of the project health and safety plan.

Ensuring understanding about an Organization for the system

- The Chief project manager should fully inform employees related to the project, subcontractors, and people concerned about roles, responsibilities, and authority of all who are responsible for the system management at every level.
- The Chief project manager should clearly show by using organization chart etc., who are appointed as persons responsible for the system management at every level related to the project.

Documentation

The Chief project manager should clarify the following in writing and keep those documents following the procedure specified in contract condition on HSE.

- A project health and safety policy
- A project health and safety targets
- A project health and safety plan
- Risk/Hazard assessment and analysis

Evaluation of Subcontractors' Health and Safety Management Capabilities

The Chief project manager should evaluate the subcontractors' capabilities regarding health and safety management etc. in accordance with the procedure specified in contract condition on HSE to select better subcontractors and also to foster good ones in terms of safety and health. The Chief project manager should report the result to the contractor.

Records

The chief project manager should keep and store records of their HSE management implementation and operation, including the implementation and operation of project HSE plan, routine inspections and improvements etc., and keep all those records.

Investigation of Risks and/or Hazards and Determination of Countermeasures

- The chief project manager should investigate construction activity risks and/or hazards related to the project based upon the Contact Condition on HSE.
- The chief project manager should determine measures to be taken in order to reduce or eliminate the risks and /or hazards or health impairment related to the project.
- The chief project manager should determine measures to be taken that are required under the terms of safety and health laws and related regulations.

Adoption of Project Health and Safety Targets

- The chief project manager should adopt project health and safety targets, based on the project health and safety policy, taking the following into consideration. By doing so, the project site manager declare the goals to be achieved within the construction period or the limited period.
- The chief project manager should ensure that employees related to the project, subcontractors, and people concerned understand the goals.
- Result of investigation of risks and hazards
- Past records of achievement of project health and safety targets, and industrial accident data.

Formulation of a Project Health and Safety Plan

The chief project manager should formulate the project health and safety plans within the project period or the limited period, to achieve project health and safety targets based on the result of investigation of risks and/or hazards related to the project. The chief project manager should also ensure that employees related to the project, subcontractors, and people concerned are informed of such plans.

Implementation and Operation of a Project Health and Safety Plan

- The chief project manager should implement and operate appropriately and continuously the project health and safety plans following the procedures specified in contract condition on HSE.
- The chief project manager should inform employees related to the project, subcontractors, and people concerned about measures that are required for the appropriate and continuous implementation and operation of the project health and safety plans.

Measures for Emergency Situations

The chief project manager should make in advance project emergency risk assessments, and carry out the necessary measures to counter with emergency cases.

Investigating Causes of Industrial Accidents etc.

- When an accident occurs at the project site, the project accident Investigation team should investigate the causes of the accident, determine the problems, and make improvements.
- If the project health and safety plans have been set up for a certain period, the project site manager should reflect to the next project health and safety plans, the result of the investigation of the accident and its cause, determination of problems and improvements.

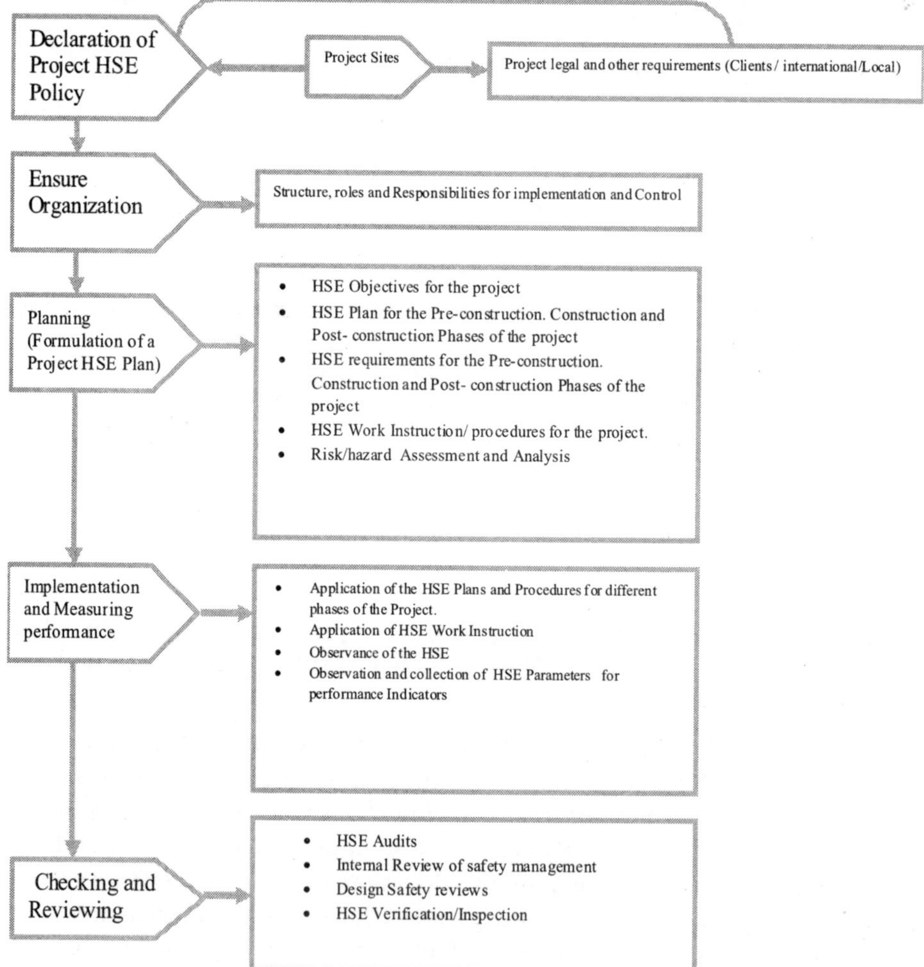

Fig. 12.1. HSE Management Arrangements (ICMR, 2003)

A healthy and safe workplace is important to the productivity, effectiveness and sustainability of any organization. Organizations that employ one or more person also have obligations under State laws to maintain a safe working environment. The Constitution of India contains specific provisions on occupational safety and health of workers, different component of HIS is shown in Fig. 1. Ministry of Labor and Employment functions as a technical arm of the Ministry in regard to matters concerned with safety, health and welfare of workers in factories. It assists the Central Government in formulation and review of policy and legislation on occupational safety and health in factories and ports; maintains a liaison with Factory Inspectorates of States and Union Territories in regard to the implementation and enforcement of provisions of the Factories Act, 1948; renders advice on technical matters; enforces the Dock Workers (Safety Health and Welfare) Act, 1986; undertakes research in industrial safety, occupational health, industrial hygiene and industrial psychology etc.; and provides training mainly in the field of industrial safety and health (OSH, 2004-2005). It is important to note that safety management system as a concept or as a matter of practice is not entirely new to the local construction industry, the major utility companies and large industrial undertakings. It has been a requirement for Airport Core Projects, Housing authority and Public works program contracts which record much better safety performance than the industry average (Education and Man Power Beureau, 1999).

Research Methodology

Unit of study

Study was conducted for diffract projects located in India:

- Power Projects (PP)
- Transmission and Distribution projects (T&D)
- Metro projects (MP)
- Building Projects (BP)
- Solar power projects (SPP)
- Roads and Airports (R&A)
- Water Supply projects (WSP)
- Industrial Projects (IP)

Method of Study

This study was a Quantitative research method that involves Daily HSE Observations revised from the sites mention above. It provides a systematic way of looking at instances or events, collecting data, analyzing information, and reporting the results (Flyvberj, 2006). Case study was found suitable for this study because an empirical in-depth understanding of aspects of safety management in construction industry, along with an exploration of the other relevant questions.

Data collection Techniques

The primary data was generated on sites using DOR (daily observation report) checklist (DOR-01) by site HSE Incharge. Generated DOR are sent to Head office on daily bases for compilation and analysis. DOR contained:

- Project Name
- Date of observation
- Location
- Issues (unsafe act/condition)
- Root cases
- Closing and Opening status
- Action taken by concerned to close the observation
- Departments (Issues related to)

Limitation of Study

One of the major limitations in the study emerged from the limited co-operation from the personals in the industry on certain aspects of the study and their hesitation to openly share all relevant information. This pertained particularly to the questions concerning safety management.

Objective

The overall aim of the present study was to examine the aspects of industrial safety management in relation to the construction industry that is being especially promoted in India. More specifically four objectives of study were identified:

(1) To identify the unsafe act and condition observed in construction industry.

(2) To achieve better understanding to the Construction safety process.

(3) To achieve better and safe work procedure and benchmarking of improvement criteria for HSE Management.

(4) To assess the instruction, rules procedures or documents to be written or received with a completion schedule.

Analysis and Interpretation of Data

As the data were compiled by concerned in head office, further segregation of data were carried out bases up on following criteria:

- Closed and Open Status
- Department concerned
- Observations Category (issues recorded on the sites)

Categorization of Issues (unsafe act/condition)

- Administration
- Emergency preparedness
- Housekeeping
- Working at Height

Table 12.1: Issus and Project-wise Description: Number of HSE Observation Recorded

Categorisation of unsafe acts / conditions W.R.T Activity	Project Name																					Total	% Contri-bution
	PP-01	PP-02	PP-03	PP-03	PP-04	SPP-01	PP-05	T&D-01	T&D-02	T&D-03	T&D-04	CP-01	CP-02	WSP-01	BP-01	BP-02	IP-01	IP-02	IP-03	RP-01	MP-01		
1	2	3	4	5	6	7	8	9	10	11	12	13	14	15	16	71	18	19	20	21	22	23	24
Access & Egress	15	18	30	13	26	4	3	0	0	0	1	1	1	33	0	0	2	10	0	0	0	157	9.35
Bar Bending and Cutting	0	6	12	2	3	0	0	0	0	0	0	0	0	3	0	4	0	5	0	0	0	35	2.08
Barrication/Edge Protection/Floor Openings	1	5	24	15	8	1	1	1	0	0	1	2	0	7	8	0	0	2	1	0	1	78	4.64
Behaviour Safety	0	0	3	0	0	0	0	0	1	0	1	0	0	1	0	0	1	0	0	0	0	7	0.42
Concreting	0	0	0	0	0	0	0	0	1	0	0	0	0	0	0	0	0	0	0	0	0	1	0.06
Electrical	8	10	71	22	28	6	3	7	0	0	1	3	1	37	10	9	12	1	9	0	2	240	14.29
Shutdown work of Electrical Line	0	0	0	0	0	0	0	9	0	1	0	0	0	0	0	0	0	0	0	0	0	10	0.60
Environmental Management	2	6	3	3	0	0	1	0	0	1	0	1	1	1	0	0	0	0	0	0	0	19	1.13
Lifting activity / Erection of Steel / structure	7	6	6	7	2	0	1	3	0	13	0	0	6	9	9	3	0	2	1	0	0	75	4.46
Shuttering & De shuttering	1	0	6	3	0	2	0	0	0	0	0	0	0	0	0	0	0	0	0	0	0	12	0.71
Equipment/Vehicle Safety	0	3	24	6	13	1	0	2	1	2	2	0	0	17	2	1	9	0	3	0	3	89	5.30
Excavation	1	3	2	8	31	0	0	0	0	0	0	0	0	3	1	0	0	1	1	0	0	51	3.04
Fall protection	5	6	3	2	2	1	0	6	0	0	0	0	0	1	0	1	0	0	0	0	0	27	1.61
Fire Safety	1	1	2	0	0	0	0	1	0	0	0	0	0	0	0	0	0	0	0	0	0	5	0.30
Gas Cutting/Welding	7	11	66	12	25	7	3	5	0	0	0	3	7	17	4	0	8	4	12	0	0	191	11.37

1	2	3	4	5	6	7	8	9	10	11	12	13	14	15	16	71	18	19	20	21	22	23	24
Health/Health Hazards	0	0	1	1	0	0	0	0	0	0	0	0	0	0	0	0	0	0	0	0	0	2	0.12
Housekeeping	5	5	36	11	19	18	1	1	0	3	0	2	3	7	5	2	16	6	1	0	0	141	8.39
HSE process violation	0	0	7	0	0	0	0	1	0	0	0	0	0	0	0	0	0	0	0	0	1	9	0.54
HR process Violation	2	13	12	22	0	0	0	5	0	1	3	3	0	5	1	2	2	5	2	0	1	79	4.70
Illumination	4	0	1	0	5	0	2	0	0	0	0	0	0	0	4	0	7	0	0	0	0	23	1.37
Sign Boards/Display Boards	1	0	0	0	0	0	0	0	0	0	0	0	0	4	0	0	0	0	0	0	1	6	0.36
Storage/Stacking of Material	5	6	27	5	17	1	2	0	1	0	0	3	2	4	1	1	11	0	0	0	0	86	5.12
material Handling and Shifting	0	0	4	2	2	1	1	7	0	2	0	0	0	4	2	0	0	0	1	0	0	26	1.55
Portable Power tool	0	0	4	1	2	0	0	0	0	0	0	0	0	0	0	2	0	0	0	0	0	9	0.54
PPE Violation	6	4	13	6	2	35	1	30	4	2	2	1	0	11	0	5	9	13	27	0	1	172	10.24
Working at Height	5	16	16	8	15	10	5	1	0	0	0	0	0	8	5	1	8	5	0	0	0	103	6.13
Simultaneous Activity	0	2	0	0	1	2	1	1	0	0	0	0	0	0	0	0	0	0	0	0	0	7	0.42
Working adjacent to Road/Traffic/Public	0	0	0	1	0	0	0	5	0	0	0	0	0	0	0	0	0	0	0	8	0	14	0.83
Miscellaneous	0	0	4	0	0	0	0	1	0	1	0	0	0	0	0	0	0	0	0	0	0	6	0.36
Total	**76**	**121**	**377**	**150**	**201**	**89**	**25**	**86**	**8**	**26**	**11**	**19**	**21**	**172**	**52**	**31**	**85**	**54**	**58**	**8**	**10**	**1680**	

- Lifting Operations and Gears
- Construction Machinery/Hand & Power Tools
- Vehicle/Construction Equipment Safety
- Electrical Safety
- Welding, Cutting and Grinding
- Excavations and Trenching
- Traffic Management
- Personal Protective Equipment
- Health & Hygiene
- Welfare Amenities
- Environmental Management
- Illumination and Ventilation
- Material Handling & Shifting

Statistical Tools Used

For Interpretation of observed data following statistical tools are used:

- Linear Regression Equation (Trend analysis)
- Histogram (Competition)
- Gap Analysis
- Problem Analysis using Pareto Chart

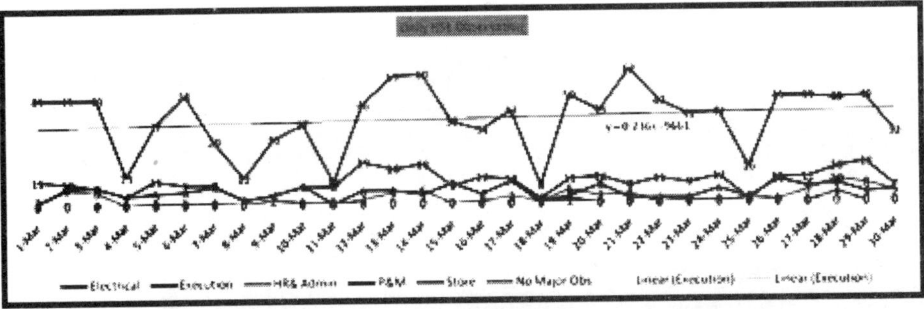

Graph: 12.1: Showing competitive daily trend between the departments and trend identified in inclined linear line

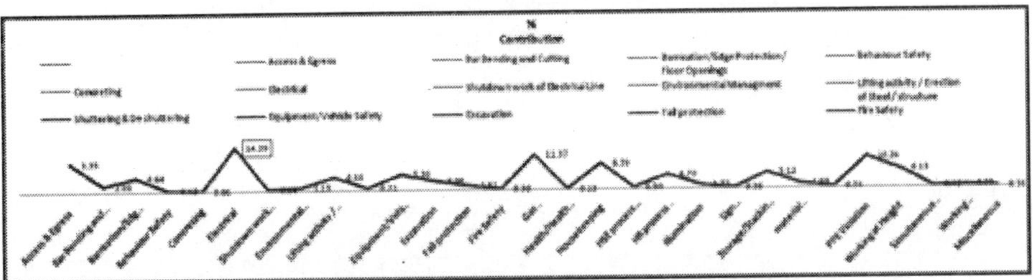

Graph: 12.2: Showing Percentage Contribution of HSE parameter for the monthly Observations identified in Projects

Table 12.2: Project-wise Description of Open and Closed Status

Name of the project	Total No. of Observations	Open	Closed	% Open
1.0 Power & Solar Project				
PP-01	77	74	3	96.10
PP-02	121	88	33	72.73
PP-03	375	66	309	17.60
PP-04	152	101	51	66.45
PP-05	207	70	137	33.82
PP-06	25	19	6	76.00
SPP-01	91	18	73	19.78
Total	1048	436	612	54.64
2.0 Water Project				
WSP-01	168	168	0	100.00
3.0 Industrial Project				
IP-01	95	55	40	57.89
IP-02	54	28	26	51.85
Total	149	83	66	54.87
4.0 Metro Project				
MP-01	10	9	1	90.00
T&D Projects				
T&D-01	116	50	65	43.10
T&D-02	21	2	19	9.52
T&D-03	26	1	25	3.85
T&D-04	11	8	3	72.73
Total	174	61	112	32.30
5.0 Building Project				
BP-01	46	33	13	71.74
BP-02	2	2	0	100.00
BP-03	31	20	11	64.52
Total	79	55	24	78.75
6.0 Chimney and Rihand Project				
CP-01	23	16	7	69.57
CP-02	26	20	5	76.92
IP-03	59	16	43	27.12
Total	108	52	55	57.87
G. Total	**1736**	**864**	**870**	**49.77**

Problem Analysis using Pareto Chart

When we look at a Pareto Chart, we can see **break points** in the heights of the bars which indicate the most important categories. This information is useful when you are establishing priorities. As you can see in the example we've just looked at, we can detect two big breaks in the heights of the bars when you categorize the data in a different way:

- The break point is between the 10th and 11th bars. The difference between these two bars is much more noticeable than the other differences.
- This shows the relative importance of the first two bars in relation to the others.

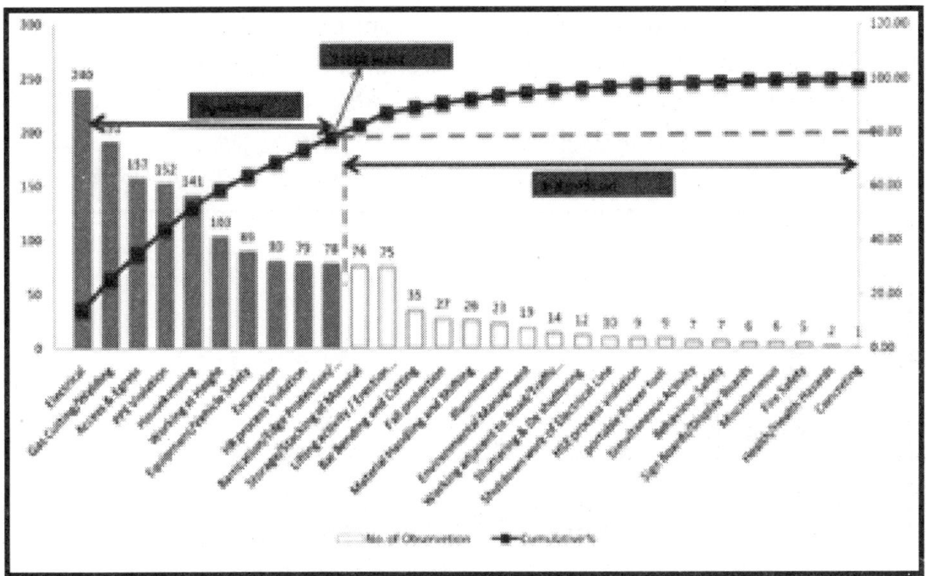

Graph: 12.3: Showing Pareto Trend Analysis for identifying the Major Contributing (or significant) issues

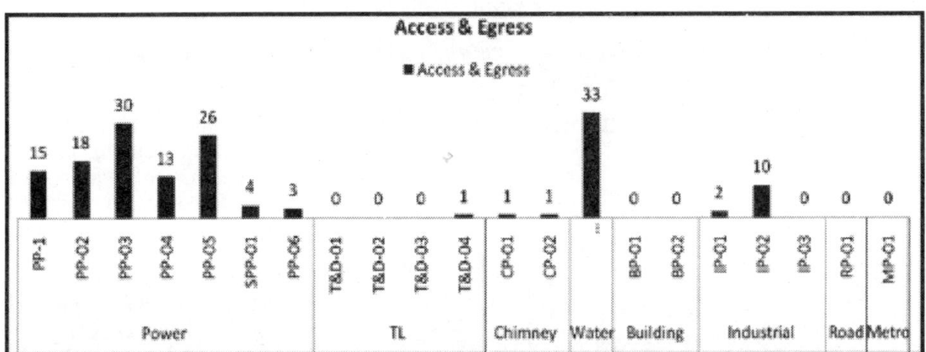

Graph: 12.4: Showing Trend Analysis for identified Major Contributing (or significant) issues (Access and Egress)

Issue	No. of observation	Open	Closed	Major Issues
Access & Egress	157	100	57	No proper access to work at height, scaffolding, etc.Ladder not provided, No proper access to work place, Access blocked due to material stacking / storage, No proper housekeeping in access

- The left hand side of the break point addressing significant (need more attention from management) issues and the right hand slowing insignificant (need less attention from management).
- Attacking the problems to the left of the break point will have the greatest payoff. In fact, if we solve these problems, we will have dealt with 81.7 percent of the deficiencies.
- Therefore, this is where we should concentrate our initial efforts.

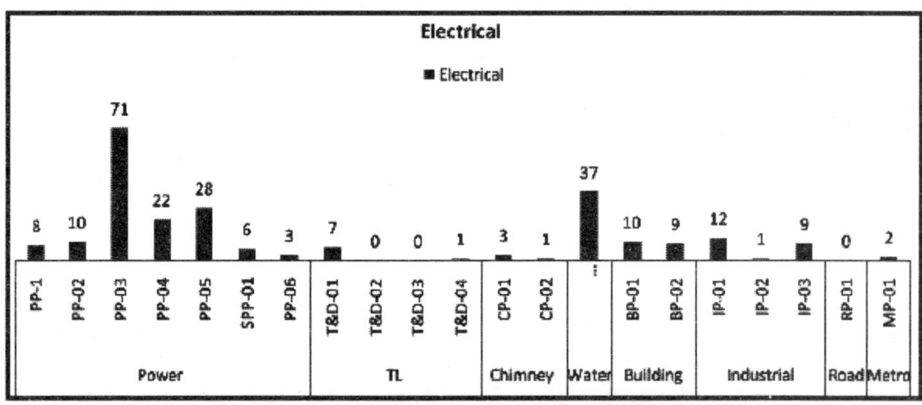

Graph 12.5: Showing Trend Analysis for identified Major Contributing (or significant) issues (Electrical)

Issue	No. of observation	Open	Closed	Major Issues
Electrical	240	115	135	Using equipment without plug tops, Cable routing, cables running through water logged area, Non provision of proper distribution boards, Non provision of ELCB's, Emergency switches not working in bar bending machines, etc.Non earthing of electrical (DG Sets), cutting & bending equipment, etc

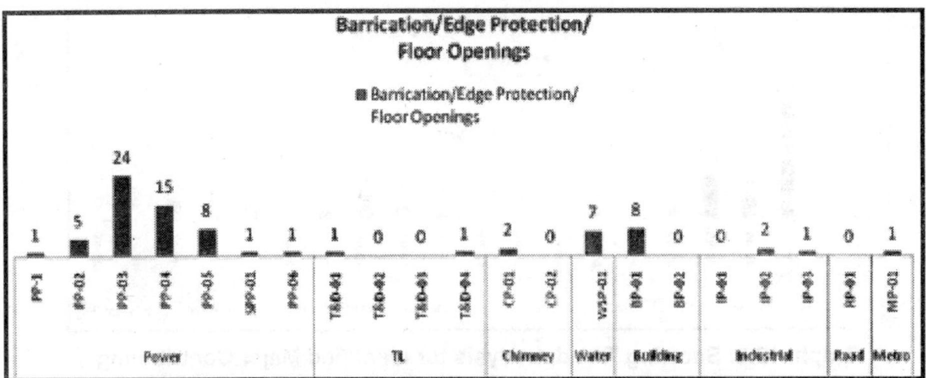

Graph 12.6: Showing Trend Analysis for identified Major Contributing (or significant) issues (Barrication/ Floor/Edge protection)

Issue	No. of observation	Open	Closed	Major Issues
Barrication/Edge Protection/Floor Openings	78	43	35	Access to excavations, Step cutting / slope, Barrication, Backfilling, Road work issues, Edge protection's for grid slabs to prevent fall of material

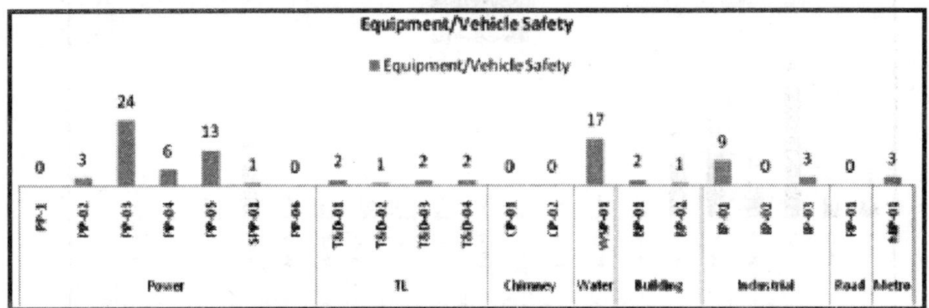

Graph: 12.7: Showing Trend Analysis for identified Major Contributing (or significant) issues (Equipment/ Vehicle)

Issue	No. of observation	Open	Closed	Major Issues
Equipment / Vehicle Safety	89	57	32	Reverse horns for the vehicles, Equipment maintenance, Test certificates for lifting Equipment, Unauthorized personnel operating the equipments, Non availability of banks man / helpers for equipments, Guarding of rotating Parts

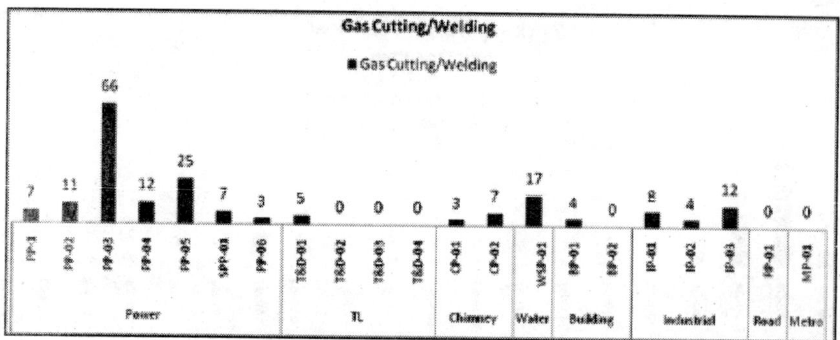

Graph: 12.8: Showing Trend Analysis for identified Major Contributing (or significant) issues (Gas Cutting/ Welding)

Issue	No. of observation	Open	Closed	Major Issues
Welding , Gas Cutting and Grinding	181	71	110	Trolley not provided for Gas cutting set, Non provision of Flash Back Arrestors, Non earthing of welding machine, Not using of welding lugs and damage welding cables, etc

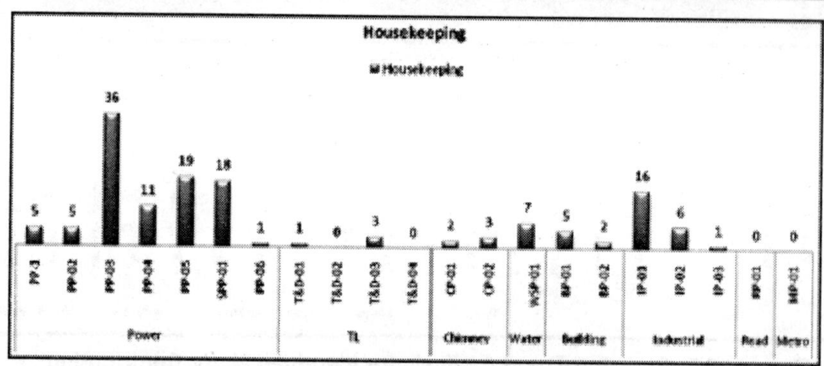

Graph: 12.9: Showing Trend Analysis for identified Major Contributing (or significant) issues (Housekeeping)

Issue	No. of observation	Open	Closed	Major Issues
Housekeeping	141	75	66	De shuttered material, Steel scrap near bar cutting machine, Empty cement bags in batching plant, Debris in the access not clearedPile debris not removed,Material stacked / stored adjacent to excavation edge, Area cleaning not don etc

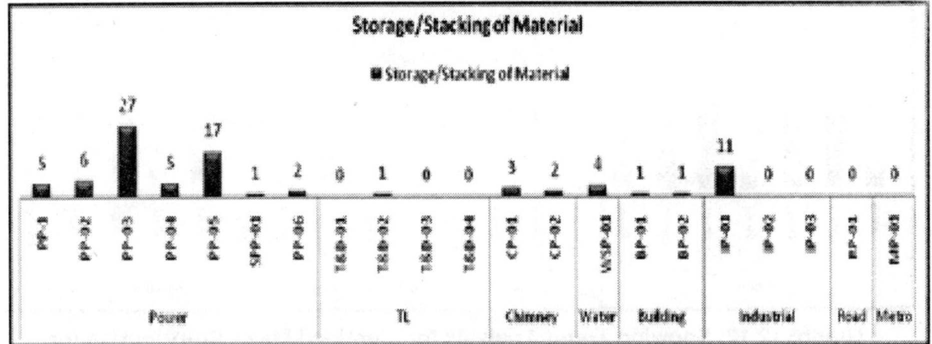

Graph: 12.10: Showing Trend Analysis for identified Major Contributing (or significant) issues (Storage/Stacking of Material)

Issue	No. of observation	Open	Closed	Major Issues
Storage/Stacking of Material	86	30	46	Using excavator for lowering pipes, Stacking of material (steel, shuttering, etc), Storage of gas cylinders, diesel, Using damaged web slings, Using fire buckets for carrying concrete, etc.

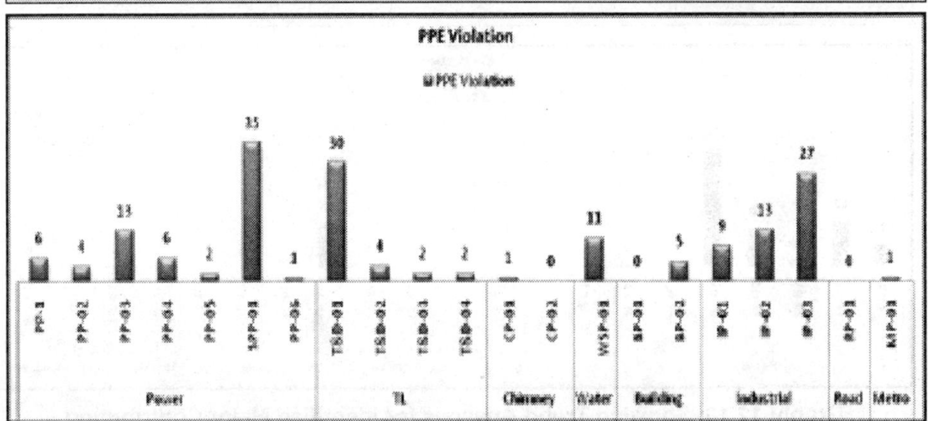

Graph: 12.11: Showing Trend Analysis for identified Major Contributing (or significant) issues (PPE Violation)

Issue	No. of observation	Open	Closed	Major Issues
PPE Violation	162	32	130	Personal protective equipment while working at height , Concreting Head Protection, Foot protection etc.

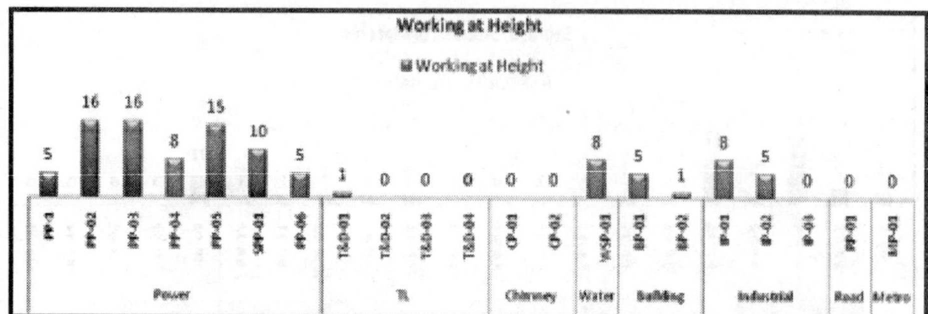

Graph: 12.12: Showing Trend Analysis for identified Major Contributing (or significant) issues (Working at Height)

Issue	No. of observation	Open	Closed	Major Issues
Working at Height	103	30	73	Non provision of working platform, Non provision of Edge protection for the people working at height, No proper erection of scaffolding, Persons working without fall protection / full body harness Non provision of lifeline rope, etc.

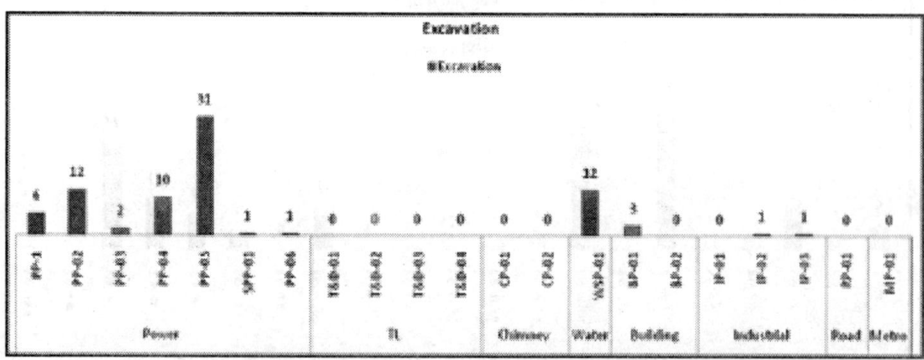

Graph: 12.13: Showing Trend Analysis for identified Major Contributing (or significant) issues (Excavation)

Issue	No. of observation	Open	Closed	Major Issues
Excavation	80	41	39	Shoring, storage of material on the edges of the excavation, etc.Access to excavations, Step cutting / slope , Backfilling, Road work issues.

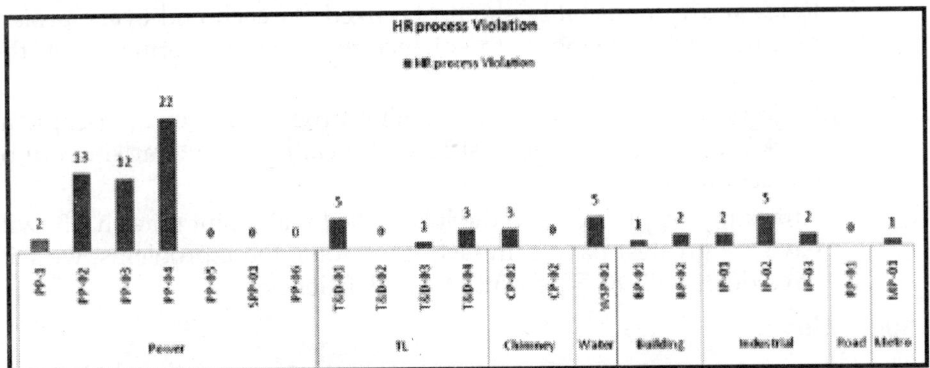

Graph: 1.14: Showing Trend Analysis for identified Major Contributing (or significant) issues(HR Process Violation)

Issue	No. of observation	Open	Closed	Major Issues
HR process Violation	79	40	39	First day Induction training, Medical Checkup for laboursChild Labours on sites.Enrolled with BOCWA

Finding and Suggestions

According to HSE, the most important written communications are the health and safety policy statements, organization documents showing the health and safety roles and responsibilities, the documented performance standards, the supporting organizational and risk control information and procedures and the significant findings from risk assessments. Health and safety documentation should follow the company's standards documentation procedures. For example, health and safety responsibilities should be presented in conjunction with the other responsibilities descriptions. Similarly, information on the required personal protective equipment should be integrated into the general work instructions.

Findings

(*a*) Electrical issues are more prominent in nature on construction sites.

(*b*) Need to review the safe working procedure and training for electrical execution on project sites.

(*c*) Trend analysis show the significant issues in following arrangement: **Electrical>Gas cutting and welding>Access and Egress>PPE Violation>Housekeeping> Working at height> Equipment/vehicle safety> Excavation> HR Processes violation.**

(*d*) These all contribution epoxy. 81.70% of the issues recorded form the sites.

(*e*) Projects have to develop some good safe work procedure for all above mention significant issues.

(*f*) Roles and responsibility should be fixed for each and every project executing team members to enhance the safety performance on the sites.

(*g*) Projects should keen to more training programme for the people at work place, to protect against risks to health or safety arising out of the activities.

(*h*) Attacking the problems to the left of the break point (Graph.1.3) will have the greatest payoff. In fact, if we solve these problems, we will have dealt with 81.7 percent of the deficiencies.

Suggestion

The company must communicate not only with the organization, but also to outside organizations and to the public. This includes information the authorities on accidents and illness and dangerous substances used at work. In some industrial branches, e.g. in the chemical industry, authorities also require information on emergency plans and risk assessments carried out in the company:

- To determine the conformity or non-conformity of the quality system elements with specified requirements.
- To determine the effectiveness of the implemented quality system in meeting the specified objectives.
- To provide the auditor with an opportunity to improve the quality systems.
- To ensure the regulatory requirements are met.

REFERENCES

Booth, R.T. and Lee, T.R., 1995. The role of human factors and safety culture in safety management. *Journal of Engineering Manufacture*, 209: 393-400.

Education and Man Poer Bureau, 1999. Information note on the proposed Factories and Industrial undertakings (Safety Management) Regulation.

Flyvberj, B., 2006. 'Five misunderstandings about Case Study Research'. *Qualitative Inquiry*, 12(2): 216-245.

ICMR, 2003. A national priority on occupational health and safety management system. *ICMR Bulletin*, 33: 11-12.

IFC, 2003. Environmental Guidelines for Occupational Health and Safety. pp: 1-14.

Nedumaran, B., 2004. *Modern concept of accident prevention.* Industrial safety and risk management. pp: 3.

OSH, 2004-05. *Chapter 14.* Occupational Health and Safety Annual Report.

Roberge, B., Deadman, E., Legris, M., Ménard, L. and Baril, M., 2004. Manuel d'hygiène du travail. Du diagnostic à la maîtrise des facteurs de risque, Edited by Modulo-Griffon. pp: 738.

SAP. Integrated Industrial Hygiene and Safety with SAP Environment, Health and Safety. SAP Solution in detail 50 073 668 (05/04)

Schwamm, H., 1997. World trade needs world-wide standards. *ISO Bulletin.*

http://www.tifac.org.in/index.php?option=com_content&view=article&id=690&Itemid=205, 2010

Index